D0396375

Kennedy and the Berlin Wall

Kennedy and the Berlin Wall

W.R. Smyser

ROWMAN & LITTLEFIELD PUBLISHERS, INC.
Lanham • Boulder • New York • Toronto • Plymouth, UK

ROWMAN & LITTLEFIELD PUBLISHERS, INC.

Published in the United States of America
by Rowman & Littlefield Publishers, Inc.
A wholly owned subsidiary of The Rowman & Littlefield Publishing Group, Inc.
4501 Forbes Boulevard, Suite 200, Lanham, Maryland 20706
www.rowmanlittlefield.com

Estover Road
Plymouth PL6 7PY
United Kingdom

British Library Cataloguing in Publication Information Available

Library of Congress Cataloging-in-Publication Data

The hardback edition of this book was previously cataloged by the Library of Congress
as follows:

Smyser, W. R., 1931–
    Kennedy and the Berlin Wall : "a hell of a lot better than a war" / W.R. Smyser.
        p. cm.
    Includes bibliographical references and index.
    1. Kennedy, John F. (John Fitzgerald), 1917–1963. 2. United States—Foreign
relations—Soviet Union. 3. Soviet Union—Foreign relations—United States.
4. United States—Foreign relations—Germany (West) 5. Germany (West)—Foreign
relations—United States. 6. Khrushchev, Nikita Sergeevich, 1894–1971. 7. Berlin
Wall, Berlin, Germany, 1961–1989. 8. Berlin (Germany)—International status.
I. Title.
E841.S57 2009
973.922092—dc22   2009006354

ISBN 978-0-7425-6090-1 (cloth : alk. paper)
ISBN 978-0-7425-6091-8 (pbk. : alk. paper)
ISBN 978-0-7425-9978-9 (electronic)

Printed in the United States of America

♾ ™ The paper used in this publication meets the minimum requirements of
American National Standard for Information Sciences—Permanence of Paper
for Printed Library Materials, ANSI/NISO Z39.48-1992.

For Cameron, with thanks

Contents

Preface

Ever since I served in the U.S. Mission in Berlin during the 1960–1963 Berlin Wall crisis, I have wanted to write this book about President John F. Kennedy and the Berlin Wall. But I have waited until I could get answers to my own questions about what really happened in Moscow, Washington, Vienna, and elsewhere.

I knew and could remember quite clearly what happened on the ground in Berlin. I was the last person to drive into East Berlin across Potsdamer Platz before the Wall went up and one of the last to drive through the Brandenburg Gate. I then served General Lucius D. Clay while he was Kennedy's personal representative in Berlin. I later returned to Berlin often, especially during the months before and the days after the Wall came down.

We now know much more than I or anybody else could possibly have known at the time. Many Soviet and East German documents came open after the fall of those regimes. The John F. Kennedy Library and the State Department have declassified tens of thousands of pertinent U.S. documents. Officials on all sides have published memoirs. For example, we can now tell much more clearly:

Why Nikita Khrushchev launched his Berlin ultimatum
Why he combined his Berlin and Cuban threats

How Kennedy hoped to negotiate about Berlin
How Kennedy grew during the crisis
How Henry Kissinger advised Kennedy to handle Berlin
How Kennedy's and Khrushchev's allies complicated and even stymied
their policies
How General Lucius Clay advised Kennedy, and what Kennedy's staff
thought of Clay
How Kennedy had to worry about more than a Soviet threat
Why Kennedy really made his dramatic *"Ich bin ein Berliner"* speech in
June 1963
That Kennedy ended the Cuban standoff as he had ended one in
Berlin
How Clay thought Kennedy might have avoided the Cuban crisis

Newly declassified documents at the Kennedy Library have been especially valuable. They show Kennedy's leadership style in more detail
than has been known to date, and they also reveal more about Kennedy
through the Berlin prism than one can learn from almost any other
source. Those documents also reflect Clay's and Kissinger's thinking as
well as the attitudes of Kennedy's advisers and staff. Those documents
and new biographies also show the views of such other Western leaders
as West German chancellor Konrad Adenauer, French president Charles
de Gaulle, and British prime minister Harold Macmillan. They show how
those leaders tried to pull Kennedy in different directions, for the Berlin
crisis cannot be fully understood as only a Washington-Moscow show.

By the time of his visit to Berlin, Kennedy worried more about his
allies than about Khrushchev. Khrushchev himself had to pay more
attention to East European attitudes than we knew at the time. Khrushchev's thoughts about Kennedy and Berlin before and after the summit
in Vienna have become clearer through his own writings, through Sergei
Khrushchev's thoughtful biography of his father, and through the work
of Western experts over the last five years. I have spoken to most of the
authors of those books to help flesh out a picture.

These materials enable us now to have a better idea of the Berlin Wall
crisis itself and of Kennedy's and Khrushchev's decisions. They make a
new book about the crisis necessary to help us understand the Cold War,
the Kennedy presidency, American as well as European history, and the

conduct of diplomacy under pressure. I have tried to pull all the new information into a single coherent picture in one volume. I have not tried to go into detail, concentrating instead on the essentials of what happened.

I began my research and writing on this book with a generous grant from the Woodrow Wilson International Center for Scholars. I completed it while at the Center for German and European Studies at Georgetown University. I also received a grant from the Kennedy Library in Boston to conduct research there. Talks with American, German, Russian, and other experts filled in the remaining gaps. I did some final editing while serving as the Henry A. Kissinger Scholar at the Library of Congress.

These sources have enabled me to combine the role of scholar with that of participant. At times I have written from my perspective at the U.S. Mission in Berlin and as assistant to General Clay. At other times I have written on the basis of my research. Often I have written from a combination of both. My role in the crisis has helped me to give other sources their appropriate weight.

I want to express my appreciation to the many persons who helped my research or provided support. I owe a particular debt of gratitude to Lee Hamilton, the president and director of the Wilson Center, who generously invited me to work there on the manuscript for this book. I also want to thank Christian Ostermann of the Cold War International History Project at the Wilson Center; Samuel Wells, the director of European studies at the Wilson Center; and Janet Spikes, the principal librarian.

For my research on Kennedy himself and on the American side of the Berlin crisis, I thank Sharon Kelly, Helen Desnoyers and Steven Plotkin of the Kennedy Library; Ted Sorensen, Kennedy's counselor and speechwriter; Thomas Hughes, Kennedy's and Dean Rusk's director for intelligence and research; Michael Maccoby of the *Harvard Crimson*; Jean Edward Smith, General Clay's biographer; as well as Ernest Nagy, Arthur Day, and Lucian Heichler, who served with me in Berlin.

For sensitive intelligence information showing the links between the Cuban and Berlin crises, I thank John Mapother, who served in Berlin at the time. Gregory Cumming of the Nixon Library helped to confirm my recollections of Richard Nixon's visit to East Berlin. I also had valuable talks with Henry Kissinger, who served as a part-time consultant to Kennedy.

For the German view of the crisis, I thank Willy Brandt, Egon Bahr, Hans-Peter Schwarz, Horst Teltschik, Lothar Loewe, and Karl Kaiser, all of whom gave me insights into crucial and diverse elements of German thinking, as well as Hans Peter Mensing, who made Adenauer documents available. I also thank Heinz Weber, who helped Kennedy to prepare his 1963 Berlin speech and then interpreted it for the crowd, and who straightened out some misunderstood points on that speech. The late Robert Lochner offered valuable comments about Kennedy's frustrating efforts to speak German. All of them played different but important roles in my research and writing.

I thank Hope Harrison and Vladislav Zubok for the careful research they have conducted on Soviet and East German documents and for the advice they gave me. I thank Andreas Daum who did the definitive study on Kennedy's 1963 visit and speech in Berlin.

For my understanding of Khrushchev, I thank Alexander Akalovsky, who served as interpreter for Kennedy's summit with Khrushchev and who briefed me on unreported points regarding Khrushchev's language and behavior during the summit; Sergei Khrushchev, Nikita Khrushchev's son; and Sergo Mikoyan, the son of Anastas Mikoyan. All of them helped clarify some important points. These persons are responsible for such contributions as this volume can make to the study of the Kennedy presidency and of Berlin.

Much of the source material for this book came from personal conversations between 2006 and 2008. I have cited these conversations to the best of my memory. And, I am, of course, responsible for any flaws.

Introduction

The Berlin Wall crisis, which began in 1958 but reached its climax during the presidency of John F. Kennedy between 1961 and 1963, dominated that presidency more than any other single issue. One member of his White House staff wrote that Kennedy was "trapped" by Berlin, as it was on his mind from the beginning to the end of his time in office.

The Berlin crucible molded Kennedy in the process. Forcing him to learn and to mature, it tested him in countless ways. One could almost watch him evolve, becoming a very different president in 1963 from what he had been in 1961.

The crisis played itself out all over the world, not only in Berlin but in Washington, Moscow, Cuba, Paris, London, Bonn, Vienna, and beyond. With its center moving from place to place and often right back again, it shaped events everywhere and was in turn shaped by them.

The Berlin crisis represented the first time that any state tried to use the open threat of nuclear war to force its own solution to an international problem. Soviet Premier Nikita Khrushchev chose Berlin to test what his newly minted strategic weaponry would produce. The combination of military menace and diplomatic stalemate deepened the crisis.

Khrushchev may well have chosen the city as the best spot to break out of America's containment ring. He used it as a lever aimed at the foundations of U.S. foreign policy, not only at Berlin but at Germany, Europe, and beyond.

Kennedy's Vienna summit with Khrushchev showed how difficult Kennedy found it to meet the Soviet challenge. He had never endured such merciless intimidation. Nor, by his own admission, had he ever faced anyone like Khrushchev. Kennedy's advisers, despite their star reputations, often did not help him. They sometimes even misled him badly. He had to rely on his own instincts more and more over time.

The Berlin crisis, therefore, was not only about a city but also about a young, charismatic but inexperienced chief executive who was overestimated by some, underestimated by others, and who had to learn quickly and often painfully how to work with what seemed to be irrational partners as well as opponents.

Kennedy had to deal with players who were twenty to forty-five years older than he. One of them called him "a boy in short pants." They brought their own psychic baggage and their own conflicting ideas to the table. Even his friends, including Chancellor Konrad Adenauer of West Germany, President Charles de Gaulle of France, and Prime Minister Harold Macmillan of Great Britain, often followed separate policies. Kennedy had to learn how to deal with them as well as how to deal with Khrushchev.

Berlin thus posed more problems for Kennedy than did the 1962 Cuban missile crisis. Cuba was like a chess game, with two players concentrating mainly on each other and on their moves across a single board. Berlin was like a team game played on several boards at different levels with Kennedy and Khrushchev as captains but with many other players having important roles and conflicting ambitions. Kennedy learned the hard way, and only over time, that in that kind of game it could be fatal to ignore any other player or to dismiss anyone else's ideas as irrelevant. He might have been the most powerful, but he still needed to keep all the others in mind.

Longer than the Cuban crisis, which lasted only thirteen days and which it probably provoked, Berlin required Kennedy's often intense concentration for thirty-three months. And, as he saw himself, they were tied to each other in many ways.

The Berlin crisis produced some of the most dramatic moments in the Cold War. Checkpoint Charlie on Berlin's historic Friedrichstrasse shopping street was the only place where U.S. and Soviet tanks faced each other at point-blank range. Paul Nitze, Kennedy's assistant secretary of defense, once told me that he thought the Berlin crisis was more dangerous than the Cuba crisis. Each in its own way brought forth the contrast between two leaders whom fate had linked at the crucial moment when mutual annihilation had first become a real possibility.

Kennedy's June 1963 visit to West Berlin and his dramatic speech at the city hall were part of his battle to keep Germany from turning to France as well as for his containment strategy. Facing in both directions at once, he was finally able to put his own stamp on the crisis. The Berliners loved him, and still do. With that speech and its memorable phrase, Kennedy showed that he had after two years in office finally grasped the essentials of successful statecraft: the overarching importance of measured diplomacy; the brutal requirement for sufficient military power; last, but by no means least, the strategic value of public support at the point of conflict.

When the Berlin crisis ended, it had drawn the East-West dividing line across Europe along the Wall. That line was to hold for almost three decades. It might have been drawn along the Elbe River or along the English Channel, as some others wanted. Kennedy was able to prevent that and to leave the future of Europe open for others to decide at a later and a safer time.

Yet it was close: There were moments when Kennedy almost lost Berlin, Germany, and Europe. He confessed in public to his own exhaustion and uncertainty. At the end, he emerged successful, with the Berlin visit as the climax and the mark of his success. And the Berlin crisis showed his personality and evolving decision style better than anything else.

The Wall outlasted Kennedy as well as five other American presidents, but neither the East Berliners nor the West Berliners ever accepted it. Finally, twenty-eight years after it had been built, it crumbled in the face of their constant pressure and of new policies on both sides of the Wall. Kennedy had contributed to the new policies, linking in himself both the construction and the destruction of the Wall and with it the division and the unification of Germany and Europe.

Kennedy's life remains etched into the history of Berlin although he had certainly not intended or wanted that when he first took office. It also remains intimately tied to what came to be the city's most famous and most infamous twentieth-century structure.

CHAPTER ONE

"Ich bin ein Berliner"

On the morning of June 26, 1963, U.S. President John F. Kennedy was flying to West Berlin. He was planning to tour the city and to make several speeches, including an open-air address in front of the West Berlin city hall.

Kennedy was making his second trip to Europe. The first, almost exactly two years earlier, had concentrated on his summit with Soviet premier Nikita Khrushchev in Vienna. The future of Berlin had dominated that summit, with Khrushchev threatening to sign a "peace treaty" that would put an end to the American presence in the city.

Reacting to Khrushchev's threat, Kennedy had virtually become the American "desk officer" for Berlin. He spent more time thinking and worrying about Berlin than about any other single problem faced by his administration. His policies had not kept the entire city free, but they had at least helped West Berlin to survive.

As Kennedy flew toward Berlin, he wondered whether the draft of his city hall speech was quite right for the occasion. To get a local reaction, he turned to Major General James Polk, the American commandant in the city. Polk, as the U.S. member of the four-power occupation authority for Berlin that had been established after Germany's defeat in 1945, had flown to West Germany to meet the president in order to escort him formally to the city.

Kennedy handed the draft to Polk and asked: "You think this is any good?"[1]

Polk, who had made his career in the days when senior military officers still told presidents the truth, read the draft and immediately recognized that its conventional platitudes and boilerplate language would not impress the Berliners.

He told Kennedy: "This is terrible, Mr. President." Kennedy replied, "I agree." He began to think about how to improve the text.

Berlin had never been easy for Kennedy. He could probably still remember how Khrushchev had threatened him during their Vienna summit discussion about Berlin. Confident that Kennedy's failure at the Bay of Pigs in Cuba had shown—in Khrushchev's words—that Kennedy wore "short pants," the Russian had shouted, jumped up and down, closed his fists, slammed his hand on the table, and even warned that there would be war if Kennedy did not yield.[2] He had harangued the president in crude and aggressive terms that no Soviet leader had ever before used with an American president.

Khrushchev had been able to intimidate Kennedy, as the president privately admitted, but not as much as he had hoped. Kennedy had returned to Washington, deeply worried but not ready to yield on all points.

On this trip, Berlin and the world as a whole looked very different. The city was divided by the Berlin Wall, which Khrushchev had put up on August 13, 1961, after surrounding the city with armored divisions to deter Western intervention. Kennedy had decided to accept the Wall because he hoped it would lead to a Berlin settlement.

Kennedy had then faced a potential Soviet missile threat from Cuba which Khrushchev supported with an even larger troop deployment between Berlin and the West German border. The missiles in Cuba and the buildup in Germany could have undermined the American position in Berlin and across Europe as a whole. That time, however, Kennedy had beaten back the threat.

In some ways, therefore, Kennedy's decisions could be said to have made the situation in Berlin worse than during his first trip to Europe. In other ways, his decisions could be said to have made at least West Berlin more secure.

Kennedy had not been sure whether he should even come to Berlin. He did not know how the Berliners would receive him. He had sent his brother Robert in the spring of 1962 to scout the city. During that visit, the president's personal representative in Berlin, General Lucius Clay, had told Robert that the Berliners would give Kennedy a fantastic reception. He later said that to Kennedy himself.

Once Kennedy had decided to visit Berlin, he had not found it easy to plan for his speech at the city hall. He had wanted to praise the West Berliners and to assure them that the United States would continue to protect them. He had wanted to thank them for remaining steadfast in the face of the Wall and of Khrushchev's threats. He had wanted to recognize that they were in an exposed and difficult position. He had still wanted to give them some hope for the future. But beyond all that, he had been advised not to provoke Khrushchev, whom he regarded as impulsive and unpredictable.

Kennedy knew that President Charles de Gaulle of France had made a long tour of Germany in the fall of 1962 and had made speeches in excellent German. He had called the Germans *"Ein grosses Volk"* ("a great people") and had begun to convince many West Germans—especially West German Chancellor Konrad Adenauer—that West Germany should rely more on a close relationship with France than on its alliance with the United States.

Henry Kissinger, Kennedy's former White House consultant, had encouraged the president to visit Berlin even earlier. He had also warned the president that some of his policies risked precisely what had happened, turning Germany toward France and Europe away from America. Kennedy now needed to reverse that if he wanted to hold the Atlantic alliance together.

Kennedy wanted to match de Gaulle by saying a few paragraphs in German. But he could not manage long German sentences despite all the phonetic spellings that his coaches might write out for him. He could perhaps utter some carefully rehearsed words in German but not much more. He had practiced a few before leaving Washington but his drafts did not include any German text because his advisers and speechwriters were not ready to risk it.

The final draft, which had been put on his speaking cards, recalled the Berlin airlift of 1948–1949 that had saved West Berlin's freedom in the face of what the draft called "a cruel blockade." The draft denounced the "ugly, shameful wall." It also recognized that "today, life in Berlin is hard" and that "it is not easy to live under the shadow of harassment and threat."[3] But, the Wall would "sooner or later" come down, according to Kennedy's draft, and Berlin would again be the capital of a reunited Germany.

> The draft concluded with a pledge that "Berlin is not alone" and that "you are not merely the object of our admiration—you are our partners in a common purpose."

The draft thus restated America's commitment but went no further. Kennedy's assistant for national security, McGeorge Bundy, had vetted and approved it after making sure that nothing Kennedy said would seem like an affront to the Soviet premier.[4]

Once he got to West Berlin, Kennedy's visit turned into a triumphal procession. Three-quarters of all West Berlin residents lined his route. They cheered themselves hoarse when they saw him. They threw flowers into his car. Some even tried to shake his hand. His military aide had to wipe the confetti off the windshield so that the driver could see where he was going. Standing up in his limousine, Kennedy could be seen and greeted by all. It sometimes seemed as if the massive sea of people would engulf Kennedy's motorcade as it inched its way through the crowds with the help of a phalanx of policemen on motorcycles who worked valiantly to clear a path.

Kennedy also went to the Wall. Looking into East Berlin, he saw only armed East German police, except for a few brave women who were surreptitiously waving to him while trying to avoid the gaze of the East German officers. The scene showed him clearly what life was like in East Germany and East Berlin. He looked grim, obviously affected by what he had seen.

About half a million Berliners jammed the square in front of the city hall and the adjoining streets while waiting for Kennedy's speech. They had gathered there since before dawn, hoping to find a good spot to see and hear Kennedy in person.

Kennedy, a born politician and a brilliant orator, thought about his speech and about General Polk's comment during his tour of the city. As the Berliners screamed "Ken-ne-dy!" at the top of their lungs along his route, from Tegel airport to the Berlin Wall and back to the city hall, he knew that he could not say what he carried on his cards. It smacked too much of tired rhetoric and bureaucratic wordsmithing.

Kennedy frantically rewrote the draft in his head, trying to find the words that would respond and appeal to the tumultuous crowds lining his route and to those he would find at the city hall.[5] Kennedy even added two short sentences in German, writing them down phonetically in red ink on his cards and on separate sheets of paper with the help of two interpreters at the city hall.

One of those sentences, "*Ich bin ein Berliner,*" entered the pantheon of German and American folklore. Hearing it, the Berliners went wild. They would not stop cheering, especially when he repeated it a second time and thanked his German interpreter for pronouncing it more correctly than he had himself been able to do.

Years later, Kennedy's widow Jacqueline even used to complain, perhaps half in jest, that it seemed unfair that the most famous words that her husband had ever uttered should have been spoken in a foreign tongue.

Kennedy also told his audience that anybody who thought they could negotiate with the Communists should come to Berlin to learn how the Communists really acted. He said that in German as well: "*Lasst sie nach Berlin kommen.*"

Not everybody in Kennedy's audience liked the speech as much as the Berliners did. Bundy looked on uncomfortably. He did not approve of Kennedy's hortatory tone and especially disliked his warning against dealing with the Communists. He knew—as Kennedy did himself—that Kennedy would shortly be negotiating with Khrushchev about nuclear weapons tests and other topics. He was afraid that Khrushchev would react badly to Kennedy's remarks.

When Kennedy turned back from making the speech, Bundy told him, "You went a little far."[6] He urged Kennedy to change the text of a later speech to show that he was still ready to talk with Khrushchev no matter what he had said at the city hall. Kennedy agreed. But he still believed that he had said the right thing to the Berliners. And they certainly believed it.

Kennedy's speech, Polk's comments on the draft, and Bundy's reaction reflected the Cold War ambiguities that the president needed to master in order to solve the longest-lasting and often most dangerous confrontation of his presidency. Kennedy had recognized the unique character of the city and of its people, and they had recognized that he was on their side no matter what might have happened at the Wall.

For those of us who lived and served at the U.S. Mission in Berlin, Kennedy's visit became a defining moment. He said things that we had hoped he would say, speaking to the Berliners from the heart instead of from some distant peak obscured by the emasculating rhetoric of statesmanship. We also believed that Khrushchev would be more impressed than provoked.

Kennedy had traveled a long and often treacherous path to reach that day in Berlin on June 26, 1963. This book is about that path and about the men and women who traveled it with him or against him.

CHAPTER TWO

"A Bone in My Throat"

On November 10, 1958, Nikita Khrushchev, the chairman of the Council of Ministers and premier of the Soviet Union, said that the time had come for the United States, France, and Great Britain "to give up the remnants of the occupation regime in Berlin." Khrushchev told a Soviet-Polish "friendship rally" in Moscow that the three Western states had violated the Potsdam accords and had therefore forfeited their right to remain in Berlin.

The Potsdam accords, negotiated between U.S. President Harry Truman, British Prime Minister Winston Churchill, and Soviet Premier Joseph Stalin in June 1945, had set the rules governing the occupation of Germany and Berlin after the Western allies and the Soviet Union defeated Adolf Hitler's German Reich in World War II. The accords ratified the formal division of Germany into four occupation zones and divided the city-state of Berlin into four occupation sectors that had a separate status although they were in the middle of the Soviet occupation zone.

Khrushchev charged that the Western allies were abusing the special Berlin occupation regime to "lord it in West Berlin" and to conduct subversive activities against East Germany, which he called by its official name, the German Democratic Republic (GDR). "On top of all this," Khrushchev complained, "they have the right of unrestricted communication between Berlin and Western Germany through the air space and by the airways, highways and waterways of the German Democratic Republic, a state which they do not even want to recognize."[1]

It was high time, Khrushchev said, to solve this problem by signing a peace treaty between Moscow, Washington, London, and Paris that would formally put an end to World War II in Europe. Such a treaty would, in his words, "give up the remnants of the occupation regime in Berlin." If the Western states would not sign such a treaty, Khrushchev threatened to sign a separate treaty with the GDR. That treaty would put an end to the Western presence in Berlin as well as to all Western rights there. West Berlin would become a demilitarized "free city." The Western occupying states would have to negotiate with the GDR for any rights they wanted to keep, including the right to cross East German territory and airspace to get to West Berlin.

> Khrushchev described West Berlin as "a bone in my throat." He said the situation was "intolerable."[2]

When Wladyslaw Gomulka, the Polish leader, expressed some concern about the risks of challenging the West directly, Khrushchev assured him that war would not result over Berlin. "There will be tensions, of course," but he could handle them:

> Five years ago . . . we did not have the hydrogen bomb. Now, the balance of forces is different. Then, we could not reach the USA. The USA built its policies upon the bases surrounding us. Today . . . our missiles can hit them directly.[3]

Khrushchev said, "literally several bombs will suffice" for Great Britain, France, or West Germany. He told Gomulka that the threat against West Berlin was "only the beginning of the struggle" and that the West would be forced to recognize the GDR.[4] Of course, Khrushchev added, if any Western states were not prepared to accept the GDR as their sovereign partner and if they tried to use the access routes as before, "We shall regard this as an attack on the Soviet Union." He predicted, "We shall then rise to the defense of the German Democratic Republic."[5]

Less than three weeks after Khrushchev's speech, on November 27, 1958, Soviet foreign minister Andrei Gromyko followed up with diplomatic notes to London, Paris, and Washington to give formal notice of what Khrushchev planned to do. The notes added that the Soviet Union regarded the Potsdam accords as null and void and that the Western states needed to stop using West Berlin as "a springboard for intensive espionage, sabotage and other subversive activities against Socialist countries." Gromyko wrote that the Soviet Union would be ready to negotiate with the Western states about ending the special status of Berlin. If, however, those talks did not produce agreement within six months, the Soviet Union would sign the separate peace treaty with the GDR.[6]

Khrushchev claimed to have invented the term *free city* after many months of thought. He used it repeatedly with great pride of authorship. He once slapped his knee in pleasure at having invented the term, and had even written many pages of personal notes to give Soviet foreign ministry officials his detailed ideas about how the free city was to function.[7]

Unknown to the West, Khrushchev actually intended that six-month deadline as a concession. He had originally wanted to move against Berlin immediately, but Gromyko and other Soviet officials had persuaded him to give the West some time to react.[8]

Soviet Communist Party Presidium members had not given Khrushchev unanimous support for his threat against Berlin. One member, Anastas Mikoyan, who knew the Western world as none of the others did, had wondered whether it might be best not to issue such categorical demands. Khrushchev erupted in anger. For him, Germany was an emotional issue. He had fought in World War II against German forces in some of the bloodiest campaigns along the Ukrainian front. He did not want Germany ever again to threaten the Soviet Union. Having Berlin as a free city would help stabilize East Germany, a vital source of industrial and military imports to the Soviet Union. In 1958, Khrushchev had defeated some of his rivals for the leadership of the Soviet Communist Party by insisting on a firm policy toward Germany.[9]

Mikoyan withdrew his challenge but remained skeptical. His son later said that Khrushchev, who had no real education and had spent most of his life either as a coal miner, mine director, or Communist Party operative, did not understand the dangerous implications of what he was doing. He did not even realize that his six-month deadline would be seen as a threat and as an ultimatum. He was inexperienced in foreign affairs, impulsive, and unpredictable.[10]

In a more mischievous vein, Khrushchev himself later wrote in his memoirs, "To put it crudely, the American foot in Europe had a sore blister on it. That was West Berlin." And he could "step on the Americans' foot and make them feel the pain" at any time."[11]

Sputnik

Khrushchev had every reason to feel confident about his ultimatum's prospects. Everything that had happened in 1957 and 1958 had burnished his personal standing as well as the image of the Soviet Union. At home, Khrushchev had soundly beaten his opponents in the Soviet leadership by a decisive vote of the Soviet Communist Party Central Committee. And on October 4, 1957, the Soviet Union had launched Sputnik, the first space satellite, a pumpkin-sized aluminum sphere that circled the earth every eighty-eight minutes while emitting a "beep-beep" signal that radio hams in America and elsewhere could pick up on their sets. Only a month later, on November 3, the Soviet Union had launched Sputnik II (which the Americans called "Muttnik"), a heavier satellite that carried a live dog, Laika, into orbit, while the American space program literally sputtered on its launch pad.

Khrushchev knew, as did the West, that Sputnik itself did not matter as much as the missile and the guidance system that had placed it into orbit. For Sputnik showed that the Soviet military could build and aim intercontinental ballistic missiles (ICBMs), the new monster strike weapons that could destroy American and other Western targets with the hydrogen bombs that Moscow had successfully tested. Khrushchev told Soviet officials, "We must make a big noise about this . . . a big noise."[12]

For John F. Kennedy, then the junior senator from Massachusetts, Khrushchev's Sputnik became a charm. He and his advisers immediately recognized that Soviet missile and space achievements would give him his main theme, the "missile gap," for his planned 1960 campaign for president. More than any other single issue, it won him the presidency.

Problems in East Germany

Khrushchev did not make his threat against Berlin only because of his confidence in Soviet missiles. He also made it because East Germany wanted and needed support. Walter Ulbricht, the Communist dictator of the GDR, constantly complained to Khrushchev about the "intolerable" situation in West Berlin. He saw West Berlin as a center of subversion and propaganda against his regime.

Ulbricht had some reason to complain. The three Western powers had kept their occupation rights in Berlin, a sprawling metropolis of almost four million inhabitants, even after Stalin had proclaimed the GDR a sovereign state in 1949. Those Western rights included not only occupation authority over all of Berlin but access rights for the Western allies from West Germany and elsewhere to Berlin. Stalin had challenged those rights in mid-1948, imposing a blockade on all land and water transport to Berlin. But the allies had overcome the blockade with the Berlin airlift, which continued until the spring of 1949 and supplied all of West Berlin's most important needs. The airlift, along with a Western counter-blockade of industrial exports to the Soviet Union, had forced Stalin to reopen the access routes in mid-1949 and to agree to full and free Western access to the city.

Those access rights, much to Ulbricht's annoyance, cut right across East German territory on specially designated roads and rail lines as well as through East German air space. Allied military and civilian aircraft had to stay within three twenty-mile-wide air corridors over East Germany but could then maneuver for their landing at West Berlin airports anywhere within a circular Berlin air safety zone over East and West Berlin.

Ulbricht had to hear American, British, and French military and civilian aircraft fly over his own office in East Berlin without being able to control either the people or the goods that they brought in and out. He particularly resented that refugees from East Germany could fly from West Berlin to West Germany without being blocked either by Soviet or East German authorities. Ulbricht could not even control the Western flights because the four-power agreement gave that authority to an air traffic control center called the Berlin Air Safety Center (BASC) run by the three Western powers and the Soviet Union. He could hardly claim to govern a sovereign nation if he could not even regulate his own airspace.

Although journalists often wrote about Berlin as a divided city, Berlin actually remained united even under four-power occupation. Western diplomats could easily enter East Berlin just as Soviet diplomats could en-ter West Berlin. West Berlin radio stations could broadcast to East Berlin and East Germany, with the main station being RIAS, the American-sponsored radio station that broadcast in German and was highly popular throughout East Germany for its news and music programs. West Berlin had its own fully independent city government, headed by Governing Mayor Willy Brandt, even in the middle of East Germany.

Most important, and most annoying to Ulbricht, East Berliners and East Germans could cross to West Berlin to visit friends and relatives, to shop, or to take courses at West Berlin universities, with most of them crossing the sector border by subway or elevated train. About 50,000 East Berliners even had jobs in West Berlin. They went by the name of *Grenzgänger*, (border crossers), benefiting from high wages in the West and low costs in the East. Ulbricht found it hard to persuade East Berlin-ers to support his Stalinist regime when they could visit the West at any time for a breath of fresh air.

East Germans or East Berliners who wanted to leave the GDR and get away from Ulbricht's Communist Party, the Sozialistische Einheitspartei Deutschlands (SED), needed only to walk or to take a train into West Berlin. East German police could not stop everybody on the hundreds of streets and rail lines that ran across the sector borders. Refugees could then go to the well-known West Berlin refugee center at Marienfelde and ask for asylum. They could get a free ticket to West Germany on any civilian flight out of the city, whether with Pan American Airways, Brit-ish Airways, or Air France. Many trained engineers and doctors joined the throng, for West German companies accepted their degrees from East Germany. Ulbricht particularly resented having to watch as more and more East Germans voted with their feet. The total population loss for East Germany had been estimated at over 3.5 million since the found-ing of the GDR. He could not accept that kind of loss, and he wanted Khrushchev to put a stop to it.[13]

Ulbricht had expressed some skepticism to Khrushchev about the free city concept. He wanted total control over West Berlin and over the access routes right away. But Khrushchev told him that he had to take Western "unrealistic policy" into account and give the West time to change its thinking.[14] The Soviets had already in 1955 given Ulbricht the right to control German and West European civilian traffic on the roads between West Berlin and West Germany, but they had never given him control over allied military traffic on the Autobahn or over allied civil air traffic. Khrushchev wrote that only a peace treaty could stop refugee flight, although even that would take time.[15]

Ulbricht insisted that a peace treaty should force Western aircraft to land at Schönefeld, the East German airport just outside East Berlin, instead of at the West Berlin airports of Tempelhof and Tegel. Western passengers would then need an East German transit visa to go back and forth between Schönefeld and West Berlin.[16] No refugee or anybody Ulbricht disliked would get to Schönefeld for a flight to the West. That would, over time, stop the hemorrhage. Ulbricht told Khrushchev that they should begin "a determined line for the political and economic conquest of West Berlin." He wanted Khrushchev to expel American, British, and French forces from Berlin. That would give Ulbricht control over the entire city and would solve the "West Berlin problem."[17]

Berlin and "the borders of the GDR" remained constantly on Khrushchev's mind.[18] A firm believer in a glorious future for Communism, Khrushchev wanted to make the GDR "a show-window." He thought that with Communism, the Soviet Union and all its allies could attract refugees, not generate them.[19] Thus, with his speech of November 10, Khrushchev launched one of the boldest moves of his career. His threat to use force if the West did not act by May 27, 1959, produced the most urgent Berlin crisis since the blockade that Stalin had called off almost exactly ten years earlier.

President Eisenhower and His Allies

The American ambassador to West Germany, James B. Conant, in 1955 had called Berlin a "superdomino" in a letter to Secretary of State John Foster Dulles. He had written that any American weakness on Berlin would undermine the American and the entire Western position in Germany and Europe.[20]

U.S. president Dwight D. Eisenhower had approved a 1954 National Security Council document that called for "immediate and forceful action" to counter any Soviet harassment of allied rights in Berlin. Eisenhower had decided that he would use nuclear weapons if necessary because he saw no other way to defend an exposed position like West

Berlin.[21] But all that had been before the Soviet Union had detonated huge hydrogen bombs, tested long-range missiles, and sent *Sputnik* around the world. Eisenhower recognized that he could not dismiss Khrushchev's threats as sheer bluster and that the West would have to be ready to talk. But he would not yield under pressure for he knew that American military power was still ahead of Soviet.

Eisenhower replied publicly to Khrushchev on March 16, 1959, asserting that he did not accept the Communist notion that "promises are like pie crusts, meant to be broken."

> He said, "We stand ready to participate fully in every sincere effort at negotiation that will respect the existing rights," but "we will not retreat one inch from our duty."

He admitted that the situation in Berlin was abnormal, but that did not mean that he would be ready to change it as Khrushchev wanted.[22]

Harold Macmillan, the prime minister of Great Britain, worried that tough talk would lead to a final disaster. He feared—as Khrushchev had threatened—that a few hydrogen bombs could put an end to life in Great Britain. Macmillan summarized his thoughts about the risk of war over Berlin in a confidential memorandum for the record:

> It would not be easy to persuade the British people that it was their duty to go to war in defence of West Berlin. After all, in our lifetime, we have been dealt two nearly mortal blows by the Germans. People in this country will think it paradoxical, to use a mild term, to have to prepare for an even more horrible war in order to defend the liberties of people who have tried to destroy us twice in this century.[23]

Macmillan decided to go on what he called a "voyage of discovery" to Moscow in February 1959,[24] in hopes of learning what the Soviet leaders were thinking. Recalling the wartime days when Winston Churchill dealt on an equal basis with Joseph Stalin and U.S. president Franklin Roosevelt, he hoped for a wide-ranging discussion about Berlin and Germany:

> "If I can bring something useful back with me in the shape of some insight into their motives this might in fact be of some help to us all in settling our line."[25]

Macmillan was not deterred by Eisenhower's warnings about the risks inherent in that kind of self-invited voyage. And, to avoid arguments with de Gaulle and West German Chancellor Konrad Adenauer, he did not tell them of his plans until the very last moment. He did not ask for their approval, did not expect it, and did not get it.

> Khrushchev welcomed Macmillan by saying, "We are prepared for useful talks . . . for the benefit of our two countries and the cause of world peace." He encouraged Macmillan to travel around the Soviet Union.[26]

Although Macmillan wanted very much to negotiate and seemed ready to compromise, he also insisted that the West could not permit itself to be pushed out of Berlin. He stated in 1958, "We will under no circumstances withdraw our forces from Berlin or abandon the West Berliners whom we are pledged to support."[27] He looked for a diplomatic compromise but did not want to appear weak at home. In one meeting, Khrushchev threatened Macmillan with a third world war. He warned that international gatherings might become conversations between "dead people." Even when he seemed calm and reasonable at the beginning of a meeting he often—in Macmillan's words—"worked himself up into a state of considerable emotion."[28]

At the last moment, as Macmillan had already made his plans to leave, Khrushchev agreed to have Gromyko meet with the three Western foreign ministers in April 1959. Because he set no time limit for the meeting, Khrushchev effectively lifted the May 27, 1959, deadline for a Berlin peace treaty. This gave Macmillan a success to report when he returned to England.

Macmillan's claim of a diplomatic breakthrough did not ease de Gaulle's and Adenauer's anger about the Briton's solo venture to Moscow. De Gaulle contemptuously dismissed the trip as a domestic political ploy. Adenauer complained that Macmillan had no right to negotiate with Khrushchev about the future of Germany. He himself had sent word to Khrushchev that the Soviet proposals on Berlin were "one hundred percent unacceptable."[29]

On March 20, 1959, Macmillan briefed Eisenhower on his trip and told the president that the Soviets had the upper hand and that the best that could be done would be to salvage something by negotiation.[30] He said he was an old man and owed it as a duty to his people to make a fateful decision correctly. Macmillan told Eisenhower that eight bombs would destroy the British Isles. Visibly upset, he then broke off the meeting. Eisenhower worried that Macmillan had become highly emotional.[31]

Of all the European leaders, Macmillan most wanted Kennedy to become president of the United States in the 1960 election. He knew that Kennedy had studied in Britain, had many English friends, and was looking for new ideas. He worried that he might be too old to work with Kennedy, but he certainly wanted to try.

Charles de Gaulle, who had returned as president of France in mid-1958 after a dozen years of self-imposed retirement, could not really concentrate on Germany at first. The French people had elected him to extricate France honorably from North Africa, especially from Algeria. In the meantime, however, he was not about to yield on Berlin. De Gaulle told Macmillan:

> You do not wish to die over Berlin, but you may be sure that the Russians do not wish to die either. If they see us determined to maintain the status quo, why should they take the initiative in bringing about confrontation and chaos? Moreover, even if any complaisance on our part did not lead immediately to a general aggravation of the crisis, the final consequence might be the defection of Germany, who would go and seek in the East a future which she despaired of being guaranteed in the West.[32]

De Gaulle had told U.S. Secretary of State Christian Herter on April 28, 1959, "We must hold firm."[33] If the West did not support Adenauer, de Gaulle feared that Germany would turn to Moscow. He thus opposed recognition of East Germany.[34] He would not yield to Khrushchev on Berlin and particularly not on the future of Germany as a whole.

Nonetheless, de Gaulle invited the Soviet leader to Paris in March 1960, for talks that de Gaulle called "extremely relaxed and easy-going." De Gaulle used those talks to warn Khrushchev that Western powers would brook no disrespect to their troops. If Khrushchev's threats led to war over Berlin, de Gaulle said, "It will be entirely your fault," and added, "If you do not want war, do not take the road that leads to war." He urged Khrushchev to negotiate a real peace treaty with Germany because there would be no true peace "as long as this great people has to accept an unbearable national situation."[35]

Like Macmillan, de Gaulle regarded himself as one of World War II's "Big Four" that should decide the future of the world.[36] Khrushchev seemed to accept that. He never threatened de Gaulle as he had threatened Macmillan, and he told de Gaulle that he would even wait for a couple of years before concluding a peace treaty.[37]

Adenauer had the least to gain and the most to lose in any talks about Berlin. He had worked with Eisenhower, Dulles, and major West European leaders during most of the 1950s to tie West Germany, the German Federal Republic, into the North Atlantic Treaty Organization (NATO) and into the European Community (EC). He feared that any negotiations on Berlin would weaken the Western position in the city and would undermine West German political and popular support for the Western alliance that he had helped to create. This could lead to a government that would, indeed, turn to Moscow. The chancellor felt that Macmillan was "unreliable and anti-German."[38] He agreed with Dulles that Macmillan's visit to Moscow had been dangerous[39] and he welcomed de Gaulle's stiffer tone with the Soviet leader.

As de Gaulle suspected, the Soviets had indeed contacted Adenauer separately at the same time as Khrushchev issued his November 1958 ultimatum. Gromyko had told the West German ambassador in Moscow, Hans Kroll, that "the conclusion of a peace treaty could lead to the resolution of the entire German problem." Despite broad hints that Moscow might be ready to deal directly with Adenauer about German unification, Adenauer refused to open such talks.[40] He had always despised Chancellor Prince Otto von Bismarck's nineteenth-century *Schaukelpolitik* ("seesaw policy") between East and West, preferring to tie Germany firmly into a union of Western democracies.

Adenauer's attitude encouraged de Gaulle to build a solid tie to West Germany. He began by inviting Adenauer on September 14–15, 1958, to his private home in the small town of Colombey-les-Deux-Eglises. He explained this invitation, which represented a singular honor for Adenauer, by saying that he wanted to place the meeting in a "family framework."[41] Adenauer seized the occasion, telling de Gaulle that he wanted to establish "cordial cooperation" for French-German relations. He intended to work with de Gaulle to establish a lasting relationship and he saw many possibilities for the two nations to work together. Recognizing that he had little time left in office, he wanted to set that new relationship in concrete before he retired as chancellor.[42]

In their next meeting, held at the German town of Bad Kreuznach in November 1958 right after the Khrushchev ultimatum, de Gaulle used the chance to tell Adenauer that he would fully support Germany against the Soviet threat. He would not accept Soviet or East German control over Berlin, an assurance that Adenauer welcomed.

Adenauer wanted Richard Nixon to win the 1960 U.S. election. He knew Nixon and expected him to oppose Khrushchev's and Ulbricht's grab for Berlin firmly and successfully. He did not know Kennedy and did not fully trust a man who had not experienced the world as Adenauer had experienced it.[43]

Meeting after Meeting

The four-power conference of foreign ministers upon which Khrushchev and Macmillan had agreed met in Geneva between May 11 and August 5, 1959. The Western delegates offered to negotiate limits on Western forces in Berlin and on radio broadcasts to East German audiences, but they would not surrender their occupation rights or fully withdraw their troops. The conference ended in deadlock.[44] Nonetheless, Khrushchev told Ulbricht that the conference ended favorably for their nations and Ulbricht should be pleased with the results.[45] Khrushchev then said, "Now it is necessary to create a safety valve." When Ulbricht said that he still wanted formal de jure recognition, Khrushchev replied, "We don't think it is worth it now to push the West to the wall." He thought it would be a good idea to maintain some pressure for one or two years, perhaps until after Kennedy's election in 1960, and then consider a peace treaty with the two German governments or with one German government.[46] The delay did not please Ulbricht.

Looking ahead, Khrushchev saw good prospects because he thought that Communist economies would soon outproduce capitalist economies:

> In 1961 the GDR will start to surpass the FRG in standard of living. This will have a very great political significance. This will be a bomb for them. Therefore, our position is to gain time.[47]

Yet Ulbricht still worried because refugee numbers had begun climbing after Khrushchev's 1958 speech. He told Khrushchev that the GDR would need more Soviet aid. Khrushchev agreed to provide help but added that "these times are difficult."[48]

Camp David

Eisenhower, increasingly interested in talking with Khrushchev himself, invited the Soviet leader to come to the United States. Khrushchev accepted quickly and met with Eisenhower at the president's Camp David retreat in September 1959. The two men reached no conclusions regarding Berlin but their meetings led to a friendly atmosphere that the press hailed as "The Spirit of Camp David."

Macmillan complained privately about Eisenhower's "stupidity, naiveté and incompetence" for inviting Khrushchev. Nonetheless, he said that he would publicly give the meeting a "warm and hearty welcome as a follow-up to my visit to Moscow."[49] For his part, Khrushchev was thrilled to be the first Soviet leader to be formally invited to the United States. He thought the West had shown respect for the Soviet Union by inviting him. He told his son Sergei that he was impressed to receive a twenty-one-gun salute and that, most important of all, President Dwight Eisenhower had greeted him personally at the plane.[50] Khrushchev said that the meeting showed how useful it had been to "scare" Western governments.[51] He appreciated Eisenhower's gestures because he thought they showed Eisenhower's recognition of the new reality of Soviet power.

In a private meeting at the end of his visit to Camp David, Khrushchev decided to drop his deadline even further.

> He told Eisenhower that "the question of a time limit is not one of principle." Of course, he continued, "It is clear that some day a settlement will have to be reached," and that it should not take too long. But the formal deadline had passed and could wait longer.[52]
>
> When Khrushchev passed through East Berlin on his return to Moscow from Camp David, he told an impatient Ulbricht: "Do not hurry. The conditions are not ripe yet for a new scheme of things." Ulbricht, though disappointed, could do nothing.[53]

Although de Gaulle had not dropped his reservations about negotiating with the Soviets, he sensed an inevitable drift toward a summit about

Berlin and he decided that it should be in France. He invited Eisenhower, Khrushchev, and Macmillan to join him in Paris in May 1960. All accepted, but the formal summit never saw the light of day. Shortly before its planned opening on May 16, 1960, Soviet anti-aircraft batteries shot down an American U-2 reconnaissance aircraft. Khrushchev announced that the Soviets had captured the pilot, Francis Gary Powers, who had confessed that he was flying a spy plane.

The Soviet presidium had met before the summit and had agreed that Khrushchev should complain about the U-2 flight but that he should still try to use the summit to improve relations with the West and specifically with Eisenhower. But during Khrushchev's flight to Paris, Soviet Defense Minister Marshal Rodion Malinovsky had told Khrushchev that the U-2 overflight had been a gross insult to the Soviet Union and that he should insist on an immediate public apology by Eisenhower. Khrushchev did that, although it went against agreed Kremlin policy.[54] Eisenhower refused the apology, commenting that all states engaged in espionage and that the Soviet Union knew it. He would suspend all flights in future, but he would not apologize. De Gaulle supported Eisenhower's refusal to issue a formal apology, although Macmillan tried hard to find other ways to save the summit.[55]

Whatever Khrushchev's feelings about the U-2 mission, he may have been glad to have an excuse to leave Paris because he had come to realize that the Western leaders would not yield on Berlin. Eisenhower and de Gaulle would not give up Western rights in the city and even Macmillan would not pull out all British forces. The summit did help de Gaulle with Adenauer, who was not formally invited. De Gaulle had told the chancellor before the meeting that he would defend German interests against Macmillan and Khrushchev. Adenauer appreciated de Gaulle's promise and his support, noting that they were lucky that the summit had never met.[56]

The summit collapse faced Khrushchev with a real dilemma. Eighteen months after his six-month ultimatum, nothing had changed in Berlin. Under the terms of his ultimatum, he would now theoretically have to carry out his promise to sign a peace treaty with the GDR. But Khrushchev did not want a confrontation with the West before he was ready. Khrushchev thus had to calm down an impatient and angry Ulbricht during his return trip from Paris. Ulbricht demanded that Khrushchev finally sign the promised separate peace treaty with the GDR and begin the process of turning West Berlin into a free city. Khrushchev increasingly worried that Ulbricht would try to end all occupation rights, including Khrushchev's own.[57] Khrushchev told Ulbricht that he thought they would have a better chance with Kennedy than with Nixon, and that Ulbricht should not jeopardize that chance by provoking a crisis that might help Nixon win the election.

Refugees continued to pour out of East Germany into West Berlin and then on to West Germany. Khrushchev's Berlin crisis, intended to stop the refugee flow, was actually fomenting it as East Germans decided to leave while they still could. Khrushchev waited eagerly, and desperately, for Kennedy to become president and to negotiate quickly on Berlin.

CHAPTER THREE

"Let the Word Go Forth"

John F. Kennedy, the youngest man ever to be elected president of the United States, moved into the White House on January 20, 1961, having narrowly defeated Richard Nixon.

Kennedy had told his speechwriter Ted Sorensen that he wanted to give a very short inaugural address fully devoted to foreign affairs. As usual, he edited and polished the speech himself up until the last possible minute, wanting to get it just right.

> Kennedy said: "Let the word go forth . . . to friend and foe alike, that the torch has been passed to a new generation of Americans."[1]
> Referring to the Cold War, he warned that Americans would face a long "twilight struggle." To show the depth of his commitment, Kennedy assured the world that the United States was ready to "pay any price, bear any burden, meet any hardship, support any friend, oppose any foe to assure the survival and success of liberty." But, to avoid blatant belligerence, he added, "let us never negotiate out of fear, but let us never fear to negotiate."

As Kennedy spoke, he had a potential crisis over Berlin very much on his mind. In a private meeting on the day before the inauguration, President Eisenhower had warned Kennedy that Berlin headed his list of potential global trouble spots. Outgoing Secretary of State Christian Herter added that sooner or later the Communists would have to do something to stop the flood of refugees leaving East Germany. Nobody knew what they might do. Eisenhower had resisted Premier Nikita Khrushchev's threats, but the Soviet premier had obviously not spoken his last word on the subject. Kennedy had to expect trouble.[2]

Kennedy made a tough inaugural speech. He obviously believed that he faced a tough world. He had become the first American president who needed to reckon with the risk of mutual nuclear annihilation. Since the mid-1950s, after the Soviet Union had tested its first multi-megaton hydrogen bomb and its first intercontinental ballistic missile, a foreign military power could theoretically hit the American mainland with nuclear weapons just as the United States could hit them. This fundamentally changed the balance of power.

Kennedy worried about Nikita Khrushchev's threat to Berlin and about general Soviet policies. Whereas Eisenhower had often dismissed some of Khrushchev's more belligerent speeches as canned Communist rhetoric, Kennedy—who had not been reading them for as long—took them literally. He worried that some of the things that Khrushchev said might mean war.[3]

Kennedy knew by the time of his inauguration that the United States did not need to fear the missile gap on which he had based his campaign. American nuclear forces still had an awesome lead over Soviet forces. But an American president had to recognize that the precious American sanctuary had been lost. He also had to worry whether an irrational leader anywhere could provoke a nuclear war.

In addition, Kennedy had to reckon with allies who might want to go their own way. Macmillan, while hoping to be close to Kennedy, might offer the same kind of unwelcome advice that he had given Eisenhower. De Gaulle had already made it clear that his ideas would not always echo America's. Even Adenauer, who depended on U.S. power for the defense of his country, could not be counted on to be obedient.

Looking out over a messy world from which America could no longer withdraw, Kennedy concluded that he had to concentrate his time and energy on dealing with Moscow and especially with Khrushchev. He would need to think carefully about keeping his allies and Europe fully on his side, but at least they posed no potentially murderous missile threat.

The Best and the Brightest

To prepare for his work with Khrushchev, Kennedy surrounded himself with experts on the Soviet Union. He talked at length with the best-known American Kremlinologists, Charles ("Chip") Bohlen and George Kennan. The former Secretary of State John Foster Dulles had exiled both of them from the State Department during his tenure. They were now delighted to be called back to serve a new president and especially one they already knew personally. Kennedy also brought Llewellyn ("Tommy") Thompson, then the U.S. ambassador to the Soviet Union, back to Washington for briefings. The Soviet experts became his closest advisers.

Kennedy's first meeting on foreign policy, within days of his inauguration, dealt with Soviet-American relations. For his second meeting, also on the Soviet Union, he invited many experts from outside government to the White House. The meetings offered no definite conclusions about what he should do, but most of the experts agreed that he would need to compromise with Khrushchev on Berlin and Germany.

Kennedy also called on Averell Harriman, who had known Joseph Stalin and other Soviet leaders when he had served as ambassador to the Soviet Union during part of World War II. Khrushchev had told Harriman that the Soviets wanted to disarm and end the Cold War but that Berlin stood in the way.[4] Harriman therefore believed that the key to better relations with Moscow was to negotiate some kind of deal on Berlin.

Kennedy's senior team did not include any full-time senior expert on continental Western Europe, on Germany, or on Berlin. Even Foy Kohler, the assistant secretary of state for Europe, had made most of his career in Soviet, not West European, affairs.

McGeorge Bundy, Kennedy's assistant for national security, regarded himself as supremely rational. He believed firmly that every problem could be solved by the application of intellect, and was thus confident that Berlin as well as other issues would yield to precise analysis. He was heavily influenced by Kennan's thinking and by Macmillan's views, for he knew England better than continental Europe.[5]

Kennedy himself had never shown a particular interest in Germany and, as one member of his administration commented, he had no particular sympathy for the Germans. His attitude was one of "disinterest, and even antagonism." He took a strong dislike to the earnest and rather pedantic West German ambassador Wilhelm Grewe, whose habit of quoting from agreements made between Dulles and Adenauer annoyed Kennedy immensely.[6]

Secretary of State Dean Rusk wrote in his memoirs that Berlin had been as much of a bone in his throat as it had been in Khrushchev's.[7] He said, "When I go to bed at night, I try not to think about Berlin." He complained that the Berlin situation was irrational. He had no interest in the Berlin issue, which interfered with his desire for good relations with Khrushchev, and his main ambition was to deliver it to his successor as he found it.[8] He had visited Germany as a student during the Hitler years, which had left him with a distinctly negative impression. Once, when he landed in Berlin in 1962 and saw a group of Berliners waiting for him, he wondered openly how many of them had been "cheering Hitler" during the Nazi period.[9]

Rusk had served in Asia during World War II and had always found that part of the world the most congenial. He and the Asia experts in the Department of State and the U.S. Central Intelligence Agency (CIA) wanted to draw Kennedy away from concentration on Europe and more into Laos and Vietnam. They thought that the most important confrontation with Communism would take place there.[10]

Having been at Oxford during the 1930s, Rusk once said: "It's wonderful to deal with the British. It's like putting on an old shoe." His biographer, Thomas Schoenbaum, wrote that Rusk was "immediately at home" with British diplomats, launching into talks about his dealings with Lord Mountbatten in India during World War II. As for the French, Rusk wrote, "Talking with de Gaulle was like crawling up a mountainside on your knees, opening a little portal at the top, and waiting for the oracle to speak."[11] He could not stand de Gaulle's habit of beginning a meeting by leaning back and saying "*Je vous écoute*" ("I am listening to you") as if the American secretary of state were a schoolboy trying to pass an examination.[12]

Kennedy's and Rusk's British connections got an additional boost from an unofficial adviser, David Ormsby-Gore, the British ambassador in Washington, whom Kennedy had known from their days at school in England before World War II. When Harold Macmillan came to Washington as Kennedy's first top-level foreign visitor, Kennedy asked him

Kennedy meeting with Harold Macmillan in the kind of informal setting, without note-takers, that the Prime Minister much preferred. Courtesy of the John F. Kennedy Presidential Library

to send Ormsby-Gore as the British ambassador, which Macmillan was delighted to do.

A debonair man of flashing wit, charm, and erudition, infinitely better suited to the Kennedy White House than was Grewe, Ormsby-Gore often joined Kennedy family outings. Members of the Kennedy clan sometimes referred to him as their tutor.[13] Ormsby-Gore could, and did, keep Macmillan's pressure for compromise on Berlin constantly on Kennedy's mind. His informal presence at Kennedy gatherings enabled him to make private comments to Kennedy without leaving the written records that

Macmillan preferred to avoid. He was as close to Kennedy as members of the president's cabinet.[14]

None of Kennedy's inner circle had been directly involved in the creation of the West German state in 1949 or in the transatlantic bargain of the 1950s under which Adenauer had reluctantly agreed to establish a new German army in exchange for a firm American commitment to German unification. When the State Department desk for German affairs wrote about those agreements, Kennedy thought they were wasting his time with meaningless history. White House staffer Arthur Schlesinger, Jr. thought that a paper sent over by the State Department about Berlin and Germany was "like the kind of speech that Andrei Gromyko might make if he were on our side." Kennedy wanted fresh ideas, not old arguments.[15]

Kennedy had put together a team of "the best and the brightest," as old Washington hands and journalists soon began describing them. No president could have found a more intellectually distinguished group. But the members of the group saw the world primarily through a lens focused on Moscow. Kennedy thus faced three of the most sensitive issues in the Cold War, the future of Berlin, the position of Germany, and the relationship between the United States and Europe, without having any full-time experts on these issues within his inner circle.

Easily bored by formal meetings with prepared agendas, Kennedy liked small informal discussions. He ran them like Harvard seminars in which nobody had more weight or authority to speak than anybody else. He wanted to hear many different voices and many different views. He liked to hear debates and arguments because he wanted to know his full range of options. Anybody who had an idea could, and should, feel free to speak up. Then Kennedy could decide what to do.

Kennedy tended to make decisions after meeting separately or jointly with people he knew and trusted. He drew more inspiration and ideas from an unstructured format than from a formal meeting with papers and a fixed agenda. His staff learned to present ideas to him on the run from one appointment to another.[16]

Rusk thought it below his dignity as secretary of state to say anything in that kind of free-for-all, or to chase the president down the hall. He thought that he should give his advice to Kennedy when the two sat alone in the president's office, without having to defend that advice against persons who did not have his responsibility. He knew that several

Kennedy White House advisers were keeping careful notes for their memoirs and believed they would later make him sound like a fool whenever he disagreed with them.[17] Often Rusk never had the chance or the wish to voice his views.

In that setting, a kind of informal National Security Council structure grew. It centered on Bundy, on Secretary of Defense Robert McNamara, whose direct and logical presentations Kennedy admired, and on Kennedy's brother Robert. Robert Kennedy became the most important single adviser on foreign policy. He had no formal responsibility and no more experience in the field than his brother, but the president believed that Robert could evaluate the domestic implications of diplomatic decisions better than anybody else. The president also knew that, unlike most White House staffers, Robert would not leak every secret to his favorite journalist over a free lunch at the Rive Gauche restaurant. Because Robert could choose to speak up in meetings or to meet with his brother privately, he had powerful influence.

Robert Kennedy found a contact to a Soviet intelligence agent who went by the name of Georgi Bolshakov. Although he was purportedly at the Soviet Embassy in Washington as the editor of an English-language magazine called *Soviet Life*, Bolshakov reported directly to the Soviet defense ministry. The ministry presumably passed his messages to Khrushchev when asked. Robert Kennedy met with him every few weeks, either on benches in public parks, on long walks, or in Kennedy's office at the Department of Justice.

The Kennedy brothers welcomed that kind of direct line to Moscow even when they did not use it, and the Kremlin almost certainly liked having a contact to Kennedy through his brother. It was very much a family secret. But they used it to send—and occasionally receive—messages supposedly to and from Khrushchev. Because Robert Kennedy regarded the meetings as informal, he usually kept no detailed notes of what he or Bolshakov had said. He prepared no memos to be sent either to Rusk or to the U.S. embassy in Moscow.[18]

The president wanted his brother to make it clear to Khrushchev that he was fully committed to the American position in Berlin. That may well have been important, because the Soviet ambassador in Washington, Mikhail Menshikov, was sending the message that Kennedy would not fight for the city.[19]

Dealing with Khrushchev

Kennedy had seen how Eisenhower used a deliberately confusing style to deal with Khrushchev on Berlin. Eisenhower had mixed firm statements of principle and definite commitments regarding American interests in Berlin with warm personal gestures. Khrushchev had appreciated how Eisenhower, a senior statesman with high standing as a World War II ally of the Soviets, had treated him and the Soviet Union with respect. He had not forced the Berlin issue with Eisenhower.

Being twenty years younger than Khrushchev or Macmillan, twenty-five years younger than de Gaulle, and a full forty years younger than Adenauer, Kennedy could never play the senior statesman role. He thus knew that he could not duplicate the way Eisenhower dealt with Khrushchev. He recognized that a Berlin confrontation had only been postponed and that he would now have to face it. And he might have to run the risk of war over Berlin that others had only deferred.

On November 21, 1960, before Kennedy's inauguration, Menshikov told Harriman that Khrushchev would be prepared to meet with Kennedy when he became president in order to discuss major issues in Soviet-American relations. On December 15, Menshikov told Harrison Salisbury, a correspondent for the New York Times, that Khrushchev would like to meet with Kennedy early in 1961. Khrushchev sent similar messages through several other officials.

As another goodwill gesture, nine days after Kennedy's inauguration Khrushchev released two U.S. Air Force fliers whose RB-47 reconnaissance aircraft had strayed over the Soviet Union in July 1960, and who had been captured after it was shot down. Khrushchev had not wanted to release them before the American election because, as he later told Kennedy, that might have helped Nixon.[20]

Miscalculation and Escalation

Kennedy's advisers and the president himself had studied how World War I had started because of mutual miscalculation. Neither the Russian nor the German emperor had wanted war in 1914 but they blundered into a ghastly conflict because they had not sent clear signals about what might or might not provoke such a conflict. Once they had triggered their mobilization plans, neither could call a halt. Kennedy and his advisers did not want to repeat that.

Beyond the risk of miscalculation, Kennedy feared escalation. He envisioned the possibility that some minor squabble over the access rights of a convoy or even of a solitary truck along the Berlin Autobahn might escalate to a major war. He feared that both sides might use ever stronger words and more powerful weapons. If war had begun by miscalculation, it might become nuclear by escalation. Like the Russian and German emperors in 1914, Khrushchev and Kennedy might tumble into a suicidal conflict that neither wanted or expected and that could destroy both countries in the nuclear age.[21]

To avoid miscalculation, Kennedy wanted Khrushchev to know precisely what the United States would do and not do. He hoped for similar precision from Khrushchev. If he and Khrushchev used clear language, they could understand each other clearly. If they took only carefully measured steps, they would not risk miscalculation. They could then reach negotiated solutions. Having heard Eisenhower's warning about Berlin, Kennedy wanted to know precisely which U.S. interests were worth the risk of war and which were only marginal. The words "miscalculation" and "escalation" became the touchstones. Any acceptable policy had to avoid those twin risks.

Kennedy's experts on the Soviet Union believed that the best solution to the Berlin problem was to try to persuade Khrushchev that he could get what he wanted by negotiation. They thought it might be possible to find a compromise acceptable to all. The experts could not, however, agree on what to offer Khrushchev. They did not want to pull all American and other allied forces out of Berlin, but they thought that it might be possible to offer Khrushchev some other changes within Berlin itself, such as limits on Western forces or on Western broadcasts. Gromyko had dismissed those ideas in the foreign ministers' conference in 1959, but they might still offer some negotiating room.

If that did not work, the West could yield on issues regarding Germany as a whole. It could perhaps formally recognize the Oder-Neisse line as the eastern boundary of any united Germany. Adenauer had never accepted that line, which Stalin had imposed between East Germany and the former German territory annexed by Poland after World War II, but Khrushchev might welcome it. The West could perhaps also accept the Soviet proposal for formal recognition of the GDR.[22]

Kennedy did not trust his own bureaucracy to guide him through this maze of proposals. He therefore asked Dean Acheson, who had been Harry

Truman's secretary of state, to chair a special study on Berlin and to make recommendations. He thought that American public opinion would respect and support Acheson's views. After concluding his study Acheson told Kennedy, "It seems more than likely that the USSR will move toward a crisis on Berlin this year." He thought Khrushchev would want to test the new president and Berlin seemed the most obvious spot to do it.

Acheson wrote that "in making military and political judgments affecting Europe, a major—often *the* major—consideration, should be their effect on the German people and the German government."[23] But several Kennedy advisers thought that Kennedy should not accept that recommendation because it would give Adenauer a veto over American policy. They wanted greater freedom to look for compromise with Khrushchev.

When asked to brief Kennedy and the visiting Harold Macmillan, Acheson argued that Khrushchev had started the entire Berlin confrontation not because he wanted Berlin itself but because he wanted to humiliate the United States in Germany and Europe. America could, therefore, not concede in Berlin. If Khrushchev chose to challenge U.S. rights, especially on the access routes, the United States should use military force. There was really nothing to negotiate.

Macmillan reacted in horror. Having heard Khrushchev's threats and experienced Khrushchev's roller-coaster emotions, he argued strongly that Kennedy should look for compromise instead of confrontation. Neither he nor Kennedy's Soviet experts knew what Khrushchev would accept, but they thought that Kennedy should offer a range of concessions to see what would work.[24]

Some of Kennedy's advisers agreed with Acheson that Khrushchev might want to humiliate the United States. Others thought that Khrushchev might want to use a Berlin crisis to block West German plans to get nuclear weapons, or that he wanted to prove that he was a better Communist than the Chinese leader Mao Zedong.[25] Thompson told Kennedy that at some point Khrushchev would sign the threatened peace treaty with Ulbricht and force a crisis over Berlin.

Rusk thought that if Kennedy could sit down with Khrushchev, "maybe something worthwhile would come out of it—at least some closer meeting of minds on various questions."[26] Kennedy agreed, telling his aide Kenneth O'Donnell: "I have to show him that we can be just as tough as he is. I'll have to sit down with him, and let him see who he's dealing with."[27]

Neither he nor his advisers knew whether a meeting might lead to good relations or to the opposite, but Khrushchev's release of the RB-47 fliers suggested that the Russian wanted good relations with Kennedy. It was worth a try to find out.

In February, therefore, Kennedy sent a personal letter to Khrushchev proposing a meeting. But Khrushchev sat on the invitation. He had received intelligence of an impending American attack on Cuba and probably wanted to see the results before he met with the president. He had alerted Fidel Castro, the Cuban leader, and now he waited.[28] So did Castro.

The Bay of Pigs

Khrushchev's intelligence had been correct. On April 17, 1961, the United States landed a contingent of Cuban exiles at the Bay of Pigs on the southern shore of Cuba. The exiles had been trained in Guatemala by the CIA and landed in Cuba with covert U.S. naval assistance.

The CIA director of operations, Richard Bissell, had drafted the original plan for the landing during the Eisenhower administration. Allen Dulles, the CIA director and a brother of the late John Foster Dulles, had strongly supported it. Kennedy had let it proceed but canceled an American air strike that might have helped the operation to succeed. He also changed the place where the exiles were to land to an area for which the exiles had not trained.

The operation turned into a total disaster. The exiles knew little about the new landing site. They could not melt into the hills as originally planned because the hills were too far away. Castro's army and air force, warned in advance, killed many, captured the rest, and paraded them as evidence of American aggression and ineptitude.

The entire effort served as a sharp blow to Kennedy's and America's standing in the world. He had launched an operation that was not only illegal but embarrassingly ineffective. "Bay of Pigs" became a code word for incompetence. Kennedy was able to recover politically in the United States because the American people rallied around him in defeat, but his reputation abroad sank deeply.

Khrushchev and his son Sergei watched in sheer amazement as they heard reports that the American ships and aircraft patrolling the waters and the airspace off the Bay of Pigs did nothing to help the marooned exile fighters. They could not imagine how Kennedy could abandon a force that he had himself sent into battle.[29] Khrushchev told Sergei that the Bay of Pigs operation was a "birthday present" from Kennedy because it fell precisely on his own birthday. But then Khrushchev added: "I don't understand Kennedy. Perhaps he lacks determination . . . can he really be that indecisive?"

A tenacious scrapper who had fought his way up from his early days in coal mines and metallurgy foundries through World War II and through the Communist Party bureaucracy, Khrushchev simply could not understand how an American president could launch an attack, commit his and his nation's prestige, and then let it fail for lack of support when he could easily have won it by sending in U.S. forces. He and his son, sure that Fidel Castro would be ousted, reacted in sheer joy when the Cuban exiles surrendered and the effort collapsed. He observed that Castro had not been a Communist before but that Kennedy was certainly making him one.[30]

Having first been rather uncertain about how to handle Kennedy, Khrushchev after the Bay of Pigs felt supremely confident that he could intimidate the new president. Ambassador Menshikov's comment that Kennedy was an "inexperienced upstart" who would "drop a load in his pants" when faced with a real crisis certainly reinforced Khrushchev's readiness to confront the president. Khrushchev was now certain that Kennedy was weak and would yield to the kind of powerful pressure that Khrushchev would now plan to exert. From hoping for good relations by making positive gestures, Khrushchev decided that he should try more brutal means.[31] He contemptuously referred to Kennedy as a young man in short pants, without real experience in world affairs and "worse than Eisenhower."[32]

Khrushchev now wanted to meet with Kennedy sooner rather than later. He became anxious to test the president. He also felt that he and the Soviet Union had received another boost in their prestige when Yuri Gagarin had become the first man in space on April 12, 1961. He must have felt that his own position was stronger than before and Kennedy's was weaker. He thus replied in early May to the president's invitation and suggested a meeting in June, relatively early. As Kennedy had already planned a visit to Paris to meet with Charles de Gaulle, he added the summit with Khrushchev to the same trip. The two agreed on Vienna, the capital of neutral Austria, as the meeting place.

In preparation for the summit, Kennedy told his assistant Kenneth O'Donnell: "Getting involved in a fight between Communists and anti-Communists in Cuba or Laos was one thing. But this is the time to let [Khrushchev] know that a showdown between the United States and Russia would be entirely something else again."[33]

Kissinger's Advice

In his search for the best talent to help guide his diplomacy, Kennedy also lit upon the name of Henry Kissinger, then a professor at Harvard University. Kissinger had written *Nuclear Weapons and Foreign Policy*, a seminal work that analyzed how the new super-weapons would affect foreign policy and diplomacy. Kennedy wanted Kissinger's thinking on strategy. He also wanted Kissinger's ideas on Berlin and Germany because he recognized his staff's weaknesses in those areas.[34] But Kissinger could only spend one-quarter of his time at the White House because of his commitments to Harvard.

As Kennedy prepared for the visit by Prime Minister Macmillan, Kissinger had sent him a memorandum warning that Macmillan's proposed concessions on Berlin were seen as "extremely dangerous" by "all those concerned with the German question within our government."[35] He also feared that Macmillan's habit of making separate approaches to Soviet leaders would encourage Khrushchev to delay serious talks with other Western leaders—including Kennedy—because he might hope to get a better deal through London. Contradicting much of what Kennedy was hearing from his other advisers, Kissinger wrote that the West should not act as if it was "terrified of the next Soviet move." In Germany, he argued, "our position is strong." The United States had to make clear to Khrushchev that he should not press demands "that can be achieved only by war," and that the West would not yield on Berlin.

One month later, in a thirty-one-page memorandum for the president, Kissinger reiterated his position on Berlin diplomacy.[36] He wrote that the United States should negotiate "purposefully and boldly" and should choose its own ground on which to stand. Kennedy should ask for what he and the United States wanted instead of trying to guess what Khrushchev might accept. Kissinger wrote that Western proposals should "depend not on Soviet purposes but on our own." He wanted to stress proposals that reflected Western values and would make negotiations a positive, not a negative, element of Western strategy. The West should not only make a list of its Berlin activities that could be stopped or cut but also look for activities that could be expanded, like bringing more private institutions or university centers into Berlin.

Outlining his own philosophy of diplomacy, Kissinger suggested several ideas that he thought would reinforce the Western position and that would attract public support for Kennedy's diplomacy:

The right of self-determination for all Germans

The German right to unification

The right of Germany and its neighbors for guarantees against any forceful border changes.

Even if Khrushchev and Gromyko rejected Kennedy's proposals, the United States would at least have a propaganda advantage for having launched them. It would look not weak but strong.

Knowing the argument of the Soviet experts that Khrushchev would not accept a proposal for German unification by free elections, Kissinger wrote that "unacceptability has never deterred Soviet negotiators." So why should it stop Kennedy from proposing what he wanted?

Kissinger even recommended that Kennedy pay a brief visit to Berlin before his summit with Khrushchev. That would give the president a chance to show how much he valued American rights in Berlin. It would also make a profound public impression in Berlin, Germany, and Europe. But Kennedy did not accept that advice. The files do not show if Bundy ever even sent Kissinger's papers to the president, for they went so strongly against the advice Kennedy was receiving from others.

On June 26, after the Vienna summit, Kissinger returned to this same theme. He urged Kennedy and the White House to take the initiative to propose negotiations on Berlin instead of waiting for the Soviets. He again suggested that the White House should propose German unification by a popular vote. Even if that might not help find a solution for Berlin, he noted, "negotiations have other purposes." For one thing, Kissinger wrote, negotiations "serve as a forum for propagating one's own principles and proposals." For another, negotiations could keep "insoluble problems from reaching . . . open conflict." Last but not least, they might offer Khrushchev a way out if he decided not to fight.[37]

Kissinger tried one more time in August 1961. He argued directly against Thompson's insistence that any proposal to be made to the Soviets had to be negotiable.[38] Kissinger wrote: "One of the most frequently used words in the State Department is the adjective 'negotiable.' Proposals are considered meritorious or not on the basis of whether they meet this criterion." Kissinger argued, "If negotiability becomes an end in itself, it is inevitable that the framework of every conference will be established by the Communists." Under that principle, the limits to any Western proposal would be determined by what the United States thought Khrushchev might want to discuss. This, he insisted, would become self-defeating, like the fear of "unacceptability."

The United States should not give up the principle of self-determination for the German people, Kissinger believed. Kennedy should not agree to any deal that did not give Germans some chance to voice their preferences on their future. In this context, he argued, "It is not clear to me why [our] allies should not have a major voice in decisions affecting the future of their own country."

In making these proposals, Kissinger outlined a diplomatic philosophy totally at odds with the ideas offered by Kennedy's other advisers and especially by Kennedy's experts on the Soviet Union. He believed that Kennedy's diplomacy should primarily reinforce the Western alliance, whereas they wanted to use diplomacy to improve relations with Moscow and to fend off Khrushchev's threats. In the Kennedy White House, with its focus on the Soviet Union, Kissinger was the odd man out.

Kissinger's view also went directly against the notion that the occupying powers in Berlin should make decisions affecting the future of Berlin and Germany without including the Germans in those decisions. Whether or not he knew of Adenauer's wish to be included in allied consultations on Berlin, Kissinger was indirectly supporting the chancellor.

Kissinger did not prevail in the White House debates about the diplomatic strategy for Berlin and Germany. Kennedy had known such Soviet experts as Bohlen and Kennan far longer. Besides, Kennedy was genuinely worried that a failure to make a deal with Khrushchev could lead to war. Kissinger's primer on diplomacy did not change Kennedy's ideas on what he needed to do.

Although he had a good meeting with Kennedy after he had returned from a tour of Europe, Kissinger resigned as a White House consultant by October 1961. He did not believe that he was being heard.

Kissinger also feared that Kennedy's policy on Berlin risked a major rift with West Germany and a crisis in the Atlantic alliance that would be fatal to the American position in Europe. He believed that the Atlantic alliance was much more important for U.S. security than a deal with Khrushchev.[39]

In a memorandum to Arthur Schlesinger, Kissinger observed wryly: "I am in the position of a man sitting next to a driver heading for a precipice who is being asked to make sure that the gas tank is full and the oil pressure adequate."[40] He thought the White House was only using him as a kibitzer, shouting comments from the sidelines but not centrally involved in decisions. He did not value that kind of relationship, as much as he liked Kennedy himself as a person.[41]

My Assignment to Berlin

Khrushchev's ultimatum had raised Berlin to the forefront of international concern. The State Department, responding to that concern, assigned more diplomats to the U.S. Mission in the city. It included me among them, as I had just completed training in German affairs at Harvard and had learned German as well as studied the Berlin problem.

I was assigned to the part of the mission that kept an eye on the situation in East Berlin and East Germany. We thoroughly read *Neues Deutschland*, the official daily newspaper of Ulbricht's party, the Sozialistische Einheitspartei Deutschlands (SED). It served us as the best public source for his and other East German official statements. We also subscribed to regional and local East German newspapers, which aped the official party line but also gave local news that reflected conditions throughout the country better than national propaganda organs such as *Neues Deutschland* or East German radio and television. Reading between the lines, in an art form described as "Kremlinology" when practiced in Moscow, we tried to learn what was really happening in East Germany and what it might mean for U.S. policy. We could notice, for example, from comments in the local press about labor shortages in factories and farms, that refugee flight was a genuine problem for East German producers and administrators.

Under the terms of Berlin's occupation statute, we were free to go anywhere in East as well as West Berlin. I went to the east several times a month to learn what was happening. We could, however, not go to East Germany because the United States did not recognize the GDR regime.

East Berlin belied whatever Khrushchev might believe or say about the glorious future of Communism. It was drab, gray, and cheerless. The shops featured few of the consumer goods and foods that one could easily find in West Berlin. Many blocks of the old city center, having been carpet-bombed by the allies during World War II, still remained as empty lots. Most cars were official government or diplomatic vehicles.

East Berliners did not dare dress brightly because they would be accused of succumbing to Western influence by shopping in West Berlin. They could lose their jobs, their housing permits, or their student assignments if they were too "Western" or spoke out too freely. Given the lively pace and free atmosphere of West Berlin and West Germany, one could understand why the young would head for life in the West.

The U.S. Mission was tied into a number of civilian and military intelligence services, all of which tried to follow the situation in East Germany. We were in constant touch with them, formally and informally. We also consulted from time to time with the British and French missions. But no Western diplomatic mission or intelligence service had penetrated the inner workings of Ulbricht's SED. We had no sources at policy levels. We could tell what East German leaders were thinking and what might be worrying them by reading the press, but we could not foresee what they would do about it. We always felt very uncertain about making predictions.

On the other hand, West Berlin was an open book. We could tell what the people were thinking because they would tell us, sometimes louder and clearer than the Western allies might want to hear. Most of all, we realized that the West Berliners wanted things to remain as they were and that they would never wish West Berlin to become the "free city" that Khrushchev proposed. The West Berliners had no illusions about Walter Ulbricht, whose high-pitched voice with an indecipherable Saxon accent they could hear on East German radio and television any time they wanted to listen. They saw him as a dictator in the Nazi mold, not as murderous or as belligerent as Hitler but certainly as brutal toward his own people. They wanted none of that.

We also learned that the only thing the Berliners wanted to know was the attitude of the Americans. They knew that they lived at the epicenter of a potential world crisis. They expected only harassment from the Soviets and trouble from Ulbricht. From the British and French they expected little more than words of sympathy and perhaps a certain jealousy about how much better West Germany had prospered after the war. The Berliners believed that the Americans held the key to the future of the city. If the Americans wanted to keep West Berlin free from Soviet encroachment, they could do it. If not, the city would die, either slowly or quickly.

This gave all of us a deep sense of responsibility. We realized that the Berliners hung on every word we said, personally or officially and especially in a time of crisis. We learned that we had to pledge U.S. support to assure them that we would not leave them alone in the middle of the sea of Communism that surrounded them.

Americans living in Berlin, like the Berliners themselves, did not know quite what to make of Kennedy's election. We welcomed a new and attractive personality. But we wondered if he could be tough enough to lean against the constant pressure from Ulbricht and Khrushchev. We liked the inaugural address and its focus on foreign policy but, like many other Americans, were left to wonder what it might mean in practical terms.

Willy Brandt, governing mayor of Berlin, felt a direct kinship with Kennedy. Both were young, both wanted to try new ideas, and both had high ambitions. Brandt hoped that Kennedy would protect West Berlin by resisting Khrushchev's and Ulbricht's demands. From what we heard in Berlin, he also hoped that Kennedy might, over the long run, unfreeze and perhaps end the division of Germany. Brandt disliked Adenauer and thought that Adenauer's policies had led Germany into a dead end. Perhaps Kennedy could help to change that. Kennedy also liked Brandt, in part because he had heard that Brandt regarded Kennedy as the model for his own policies and politics.

Brandt was encouraged by his meeting with Kennedy on March 13, 1961, one month before Kennedy received Adenauer. Brandt told American officials in Berlin that he and Kennedy had enjoyed a good talk that had lasted about an hour and that Kennedy had shown a real interest in Berlin. According to Brandt, Kennedy had told Brandt that he was fully committed in Berlin. Brandt returned from the meeting very impressed by the president's attitude.[42]

Kennedy's failure at the Bay of Pigs shocked West Berliners deeply, but East German propaganda agencies gloried in it. They gloated that it showed American weakness and indecision, with obvious implications for Berlin. We were afraid that it would encourage Khrushchev and Ulbricht to try new and different forms of harassment, confident that the United States would do nothing.

Those of us who sat in Berlin also worried whether Kennedy would have the time to learn the full Berlin story, including its wider impact. But the White House and Washington as a whole dismissed those considerations as "localitis" or as the grumblings of the "Berlin Mafia."

Neither Brandt nor anyone else knew what to expect from Kennedy in the crisis that we could all see looming. We recognized that he was a brilliant speaker who always knew what to *say*. We were less certain that he might always know what to *do*. We were sure, however, that actions would matter more than words in dealing with Khrushchev and especially with Ulbricht. We feared that Kennedy would not have much time to get ready for what was to come.

CHAPTER FOUR

"Alas, Mr. Ambassador,
We Shall Die Together"

As Kennedy surveyed the Berlin situation before his summit with Khrush-chev, he might perhaps have hoped to find a solid phalanx of allies ready and willing to support a common policy. But he would have been badly mistaken. His allies were as divided around him in 1961 as they had been around Eisenhower in 1959. Moreover, because they saw him as young and inexperienced, they were either confident that they could guide him or worried that they might need to protect Berlin from his mistakes.

Kennedy and the Allies

Harold Macmillan

Harold Macmillan, prime minister of Great Britain, still thought that "something had been gained" by his visit to Moscow in February 1959. At least, he thought, he had started the foreign ministers talking, relaxed Nikita Khrushchev's ultimatum, and eased the immediate threat of war over Berlin. He thought that President Eisenhower had not given him the credit that he deserved for that. He hoped for better from Kennedy.

During World War I, Macmillan had fought in some of the bloodiest battles on the Western front in France. He remembered having ordered his troops to attack out of their trenches even as he knew that they would be killed, gassed, or maimed beyond recognition. He had seen many of the best men of his generation, some of them childhood friends, killed or lacerated for life. He had himself been wounded four times. He shuffled as he walked due to shrapnel that he carried in his body forty-five years after the war. Macmillan had also served during World War II, this time in British war cabinets under the leadership of Prime Minister Winston Churchill.

Having fought two long and costly wars against the Germans, Macmillan viscerally despised everything Teutonic even when he had to deal with the Germans as allies in NATO. He could also understand how other Britons might feel. He believed that nothing about Berlin was worth the kind of sacrifice that soldiers and civilians would have to make in a modern war.[1]

To Macmillan, only the Americans really counted as Great Britain's friends. He remembered when the two nations and their armies had fought side by side to defeat the Axis powers. He also remembered how Churchill and U.S. President Franklin D. Roosevelt had negotiated the future structure of the world with Soviet dictator Joseph Stalin at their summits at Teheran in 1943 and at Yalta in 1945.

It seemed entirely logical to Macmillan that he should now serve as tutor to the young president as other British leaders had guided other Americans. He thought that Great Britain should be the Athens to America's Rome. Charles de Gaulle and Konrad Adenauer, he believed, did not belong in the same league. He felt sure that they would accept him as their senior. The Berlin crisis seemed the ideal place to exercise his new responsibility.

Macmillan firmly believed what he had told Eisenhower in 1959, that the premises of the Western position in Berlin were fading away. The Soviets had the upper hand and the best the West could do was to try "to salvage something by negotiation."[2]

When Macmillan became the first Western head of government to meet with Kennedy, visiting Washington in early April 1961, he and his new foreign secretary, Lord Home, told Kennedy that allied rights in Berlin were "slightly tarnished." Home added that the right of conquest that lay at the foundation of Western occupation rights in Berlin was wearing thin. Macmillan and Home both argued that the West had to be flexible enough to strike a compromise with Khrushchev.[3] Macmillan also told Kennedy in their first meeting that Adenauer would not come up with new ideas because he was lacking in imagination. Kennedy replied that he agreed fully.[4]

Yet although Macmillan seemed ready to compromise, he insisted that the West could not permit itself to be pushed out of Berlin. The British position, as he had stated in a telegram to Washington in November 1958, remained: "We will under no circumstances withdraw our forces from Berlin or abandon the West Berliners whom we are pledged to support."[5] He was looking for a diplomatic compromise but did not want to surrender any British rights. Therefore, Macmillan said, "I would not much mind if [the negotiations] ended up with the recognition of the GDR government," presumably as a price worth paying for a Berlin settlement. On this and on other points, the compromises that Macmillan wanted to offer to Khrushchev would protect British rights by yielding major West German interests.[6]

Charles de Gaulle

Charles de Gaulle, the president of France, told Dean Rusk in August 1961, that the West did not need to negotiate about Berlin "just because Mr. Khrushchev has whistled."[7] De Gaulle had not been in office long when Khrushchev launched his ultimatum. He had retired from French politics shortly after World War II but the French people brought him back in June 1958, when the postwar Fourth Republic had collapsed in the face of a revolt by French settlers in Algeria. A referendum had then approved a new constitution that granted him real power.

De Gaulle did not even bother to look at the texts of Berlin negotiating proposals. He believed that the Soviet Union could not expel the Western allies from Berlin except by force, and he firmly believed that Khrushchev did not want war. Therefore, de Gaulle reasoned, the West did not need to make concessions on Berlin. Khrushchev would have to find a way to get off his high horse.

De Gaulle thought Macmillan risked pushing his wish to compromise on Germany "to the point of surrender." He felt that Macmillan lacked sympathy for Germany's grievances to the point where Khrushchev might decide the West was weak. That, de Gaulle thought, would risk war more than a firm stand against Khrushchev's Berlin demands.[8] Summarizing his concerns about the Western search for compromise, de Gaulle said: "If we accept the Russian *diktat*, the Western alliance is finished."[9]

When the Soviet ambassador warned de Gaulle that a Soviet nuclear bomb could destroy Paris, de Gaulle—who did not like to be threatened—dismissed him: "Alas, Mr. Ambassador, we shall die together. Good day, Mr. Ambassador."[10]

Above all else, de Gaulle wanted to cooperate with Adenauer to build a strong Europe. They agreed that Kennedy and the West had to offer firm resistance to Khrushchev's moves against Berlin. De Gaulle wanted to become Adenauer's protector, not only against Khrushchev, but also against the pressures for accommodation coming from London.[11] Europe had once been a real force in the world, de Gaulle insisted. It should become that again. He did not want Macmillan as his partner because he thought that London was too close to the American line. Thus, Adenauer represented the ideal partner for the creation of a new Europe. Nor did de Gaulle parrot Kennedy's line that Adenauer was an "old man," for he was himself close to seventy years of age.

Eisenhower, recalling de Gaulle's attitudes during and since World War II, had said that de Gaulle had "an obsession about the Anglo-Saxons" going back to his frustrating experience in London during the war.[12] De Gaulle had painful memories of the way Washington and London had not properly appreciated what he saw as the major French contribution to the war against Hitler. His sense of national and personal pride had suffered deeply under what he perceived as haughty and degrading treatment by both Churchill and Roosevelt.

De Gaulle's main enemies, therefore, were not the Germans or the Russians but the "Anglo-Saxons." He not only remembered past humiliations but thought that the Anglo-Saxons continued to subject him to their "hegemony" in NATO. If there were now to be negotiations about Berlin and Germany, France should be recognized as one of the victors of World War II and thus fully equal to Washington, Moscow, and London.

When Willy Brandt once suggested that de Gaulle might visit Berlin, de Gaulle pointed out that Berlin was under French occupation and that Brandt had no authority to invite the head of state of an occupying sovereign power. De Gaulle alone could invite himself.

Konrad Adenauer

Kennedy in October 1957 had written that the age of Adenauer was over. Adenauer was "a shadow of the past" and the United States should look beyond him to his successors. He wrote that "American policy has let itself be lashed too tightly to a single German government and party."[13] Ted Sorensen told an interviewer that Kennedy paid little attention to the German chancellor.[14]

Kennedy's attitude toward the chancellor had darkened further during the 1960 U.S. presidential campaign. The *Baltimore Sun* ran a headline: "NIXON MORE ACCEPTABLE TO GERMANS."[15] Adenauer had indeed shown a preference for Richard Nixon because he thought that Kennedy had much to learn. One of Adenauer's friends reported that Adenauer regarded the prospect of a Kennedy victory as "frightening."[16]

For his part, Kennedy thought that Adenauer's close policy coordination with Eisenhower and especially with John Foster Dulles had been "narrow, cautious, and in the literal sense reactionary." He thought that the chancellor too often relied on agreements that he had made with Kennedy's predecessors, agreements that Kennedy questioned because he had played no role in making them and wondered if they should even still apply.

Adenauer sent Kennedy the traditional congratulations on his inauguration and expressed the hope that they could meet soon. But the president pointedly delayed any meeting until well into the third month of his presidency, after he had met with Macmillan and Willy Brandt, to make Adenauer understand that he could no longer expect unquestioning American support.

Generating more anxiety in Bonn, Kennedy sent John J. McCloy, who had been U.S. high commissioner in Germany during the early 1950s and had long been a good friend of Adenauer's, to tell the chancellor that the Germans had to be ready for sacrifices in Western talks with Khrushchev. The chancellor would, among other things, need to accept the Oder-Neisse line as Germany's permanent eastern border. Coming from McCloy, Kennedy's message was intended to make Adenauer worry.[17] But Kennedy also sent Dean Acheson, whom Adenauer knew almost equally well, to deliver a more positive message. The former secretary of state told Adenauer that Kennedy would not pull U.S. forces out of Berlin and that he regarded Europe as a crucial area for American policy. Adenauer, much relieved, told Acheson that "a heavy load had been lifted" from his heart.[18]

Despite misgivings on both sides, Kennedy's first meeting with Adenauer went relatively well. Adenauer needed and wanted to get along

Kennedy in one of his guarded meetings with Konrad Adenauer, reflecting but trying to contain their differences over Berlin. Courtesy of the John F. Kennedy Presidential Library

with Kennedy. The president, for his part, was tactfully polite. But Kennedy did not agree to Adenauer's principal request, which was that Bonn should be included in the consultations on Berlin between France, Great Britain, and the United States. Kennedy listened but did not react, and he did not grant Adenauer's wish until early August 1961.[19]

Kennedy said after the meeting that he felt he had been "talking not only to a different generation but to a different era, a different world." He told Jacqueline Kennedy that Adenauer had hung on too long and was turning bitter. He particularly disliked what his assistant Ted Sorensen called "Adenauer's thirst for repetitious assurances of our love and honor," and he probably put Adenauer's wish to be included in allied meetings into that category.[20]

Brandt, always ready for a negative story about Adenauer, enjoyed reporting that Kennedy's adviser Arthur Schlesinger, Jr., had said the Germans were like a woman who always asked her husband "Do you love me?" and then "Do you *really* love me?"—and then would hire a private eye to tail the husband.[21]

Adenauer actually briefed de Gaulle rather favorably about his meeting with Kennedy. He said that he had found Kennedy energetic and noted that he grasped things quickly, but he added that Kennedy's planned meeting with Khrushchev would really be the test of Kennedy's mettle.[22]

Beyond the age gap of forty years, Kennedy and Adenauer came from vastly different backgrounds, with different experiences, different views of the world, and widely divergent ideas about what to do on Berlin. Kennedy led a global superpower. He had been born to privilege beyond imagination. He was used to getting his way. He wanted to make the definitive global deal with the Soviet Union. All that stood in the way, for him as well as Khrushchev, seemed to be Berlin and Germany, with all the risks about miscalculation and escalation. Somehow, he had to settle that problem and then make Adenauer accept whatever deal he could make with Khrushchev.

Adenauer led a shrunken land that had been defeated, disgraced, and divided. He had spent time in Nazi prisons and his wife had died in one. He needed a quiet period for Germany and the Germans to recover from fifty years of war, hyperinflation, depression, revolution, and expulsion from their eastern lands. He needed to be sure that others would protect

Germany and Berlin against the Soviets because Germany could not protect itself.

When the West German ambassador in Washington, Wilhelm Grewe, kept reminding Kennedy about the postwar arrangements that had given West Germany its sovereignty, Kennedy complained that Grewe got on his nerves. Kennedy had not studied those arrangements. His closest advisers, who had concentrated on Soviet affairs, could not brief him. Moreover, Kennedy felt all that material was old hat; he wanted to strike out in new directions.[23] For example, Kennedy could not understand why Adenauer did not send German troops to Berlin to help the allies. According to Grewe, Kennedy "was irritated by the fact that Bonn did not want some of its units to form the spearhead" of any Western probe against a Soviet blockade of Berlin. Because the Western allies had always refused to let any West German forces go into or near Berlin, Adenauer simply could not grasp what Kennedy wanted.[24]

Because of West Germany's reliance on America, Adenauer suffered a major shock over the Bay of Pigs disaster. His intelligence chief, General Gerhard Wessel, said: "It was a catastrophe that the world's number-one power could do a thing like this. . . . Our feeling of trust in American leadership [fell] to a very low level."[25]

Looking at the impending summit in Vienna, Adenauer feared that Khrushchev would try to bully and humiliate Kennedy in Vienna as Khrushchev had tried to do with Adenauer himself when the chancellor had gone to Moscow in 1955. After the Bay of Pigs, he was not sure if Kennedy could take the heat. If Kennedy could not, then Germany and Berlin might be lost, as might be the entire foundation of Adenauer's hopes for a democratic and free Germany.

Dean Rusk in turn questioned the German commitment. During a NATO foreign ministers' meeting in early May 1961, Rusk asked whether the Berliners would really be ready to endure another blockade only for the sake of their freedom.[26]

Kennedy also abandoned the demand for Germany unification that had been a part of U.S. policy since the 1940s. He believed that he had more important and urgent matters to settle with Khrushchev. But Kennedy's view created immense domestic problems for Adenauer. Although the chancellor knew that early unification was unlikely, he needed allied support for it to protect himself against German right-wing charges that he had chosen an alliance with America instead of a deal with Moscow that might have brought unification. He told this to Kennedy, but the president did not really understand it.[27]

Kennedy's efforts for a common Western policy thus foundered on the separate histories of his allies and also on their different approaches to Berlin. Moreover, Macmillan and Adenauer increasingly disliked each other. The chancellor had first hoped to work with Macmillan as a fellow conservative. He had supported Macmillan's interest in having Great Britain join the European Community, but he resented Macmillan's 1959 trip to Moscow and Macmillan's efforts to negotiate with Khrushchev above Germany's head. Macmillan's relations with Adenauer never recovered.

David Bruce, U.S. ambassador in Bonn, warned Kennedy not to underestimate the depth of the chancellor's "settled suspicion" of British policy.[28] Adenauer feared that Macmillan wanted a "new Potsdam," negotiating about Germany with Moscow without consulting senior Germans. Only de Gaulle seemed to understand the chancellor's foreign policy and his domestic needs.[29]

Macmillan, de Gaulle, and Adenauer had been seared by their experiences during the violent three decades in Europe between 1914 and 1945. War, death, and ruin, personal and national tragedy had defined their lives. They shared an intensity of feeling about the past that those who wanted to approach problems rationally could not readily understand. All of Kennedy's allies carried heavy psychic baggage. Though they may not have shown it on the surface, it affected all their policies and behavior. Kennedy was to find it difficult to deal with these attitudes or even to understand them. He had not gone in the same way through the same wars or the same terrors. He could not intuitively grasp how they thought and how they would act.

As these ideas and debates flowed around him and through his office, Kennedy at first had few fixed positions. He had not come into the White House with a lifetime of experience behind him. Every topic, including Germany and Berlin, needed to be examined freshly. He could not be labeled a "cold warrior" or an "appeaser." Instead, as far as the Western alliance was concerned, he could best be called a "judge," one who would like to hear all the arguments, weigh them, and then decide what to do.

Khrushchev and His Allies

After Kennedy's election victory, Khrushchev invited Walter Ulbricht to meet in Moscow on November 30, 1960, to decide their next steps.[30] To help set the agenda for their consultations, Ulbricht on November 22 sent Khrushchev an eleven-page letter complaining that West German intelligence agencies were using their offices in West Berlin to build up an illegal resistance movement in East Germany and to foster subversive measures against the GDR. He wrote that the status of West Berlin needed to change to protect East Germany against such maneuvers. The refugee flow reflected subversive Western activities. The GDR economy could not compete when its best-trained people could be lured away at any moment. Ulbricht asked for more Soviet aid.[31] He promised that he would avoid a major crisis in Berlin but warned that there might be "small conflicts."[32]

Khrushchev, who had by then already sent out feelers about meeting with Kennedy, told Ulbricht to wait for that meeting:

Now, if you want to liberate yourself, . . . you will aggravate the situation. But this is not favorable to us now, since we gave our word that we would not change the existing situation until the summit meeting of the heads of government. And if we change something now, this will look as if we are violating our word. Let us wait.[33]

Khrushchev warned Ulbricht, "We are not obligated to repeat your position." Noting Ulbricht's need for further aid, he added, "Do not thrust your hands in our pockets." To appease Ulbricht, he did offer a substantial increase in Soviet assistance. Ulbricht replied, "We cannot act the same way that we did in 1960." Khrushchev accepted the implied rebuke, but said, "We have not lost the two years [because] we have shaken up their position."[34]

Khrushchev and Ulbricht came away from their meeting in full accord that there had to be some solution on Berlin, but without a precise formula for what it should be. Khrushchev wanted Kennedy to accept a "free city." Ulbricht wanted to get control over West Berlin. He kept repeating to Khrushchev that West Berlin sat on the territory of the GDR.

Mikhail Pervukhin, the Soviet ambassador in East Berlin, wrote Khrushchev that he could not blame only the West Germans for refugee flight. He blamed the GDR's "heartless" attitude as well as shortages in commercial and food products. He warned Khrushchev that Ulbricht had become so impatient that he did not seem to understand that sealing the sector border in Berlin would complicate negotiations for a German peace treaty.[35]

Pervukhin pointed to one of the more worrisome aspects of the refugee exodus. East Germans had long fled Ulbricht's state because they wanted to get away from what was the last truly Stalinist state in Eastern Europe. With the powerful Staatssicherheitsdienst (state security service), also known as the Stasi, controlling all aspects of East German life and watching closely over all residents, nobody felt free or safe. People could be arrested at any time, or their lives and careers could be ruined by a chance remark or action. The young often left as soon as they had finished their basic education, or even before, Pervukhin complained, because they could not contemplate life in a Stalinist state. Often they left for a combination of reasons, political and economic, but Ulbricht's brutal policies led the list. The ambassador commented that East German "attempts to impede the exodus of the population to the West with . . . police measures for limited movement in Berlin have only led to the opposite results," making people want to leave while it was still possible.[36] Perhaps Ulbricht had even done that deliberately in order to force Khrushchev to close the border, although nobody could be sure of that.

As the time for Kennedy's inauguration drew closer, Ulbricht detailed the specific items that Khrushchev and Foreign Minister Andrei Gromyko should demand in their negotiations with the new president. In letter to Khrushchev, sent two days before Kennedy's inauguration, he listed the following institutions that should be terminated in West Berlin:[37]

- The entire occupation regime, including allied and other foreign troops, all foreign agencies, the Berlin Air Safety Center as well as the Allied Travel Office (which controlled documents for East German officials and others wanting to go to the West)
- All West German offices
- Radio stations broadcasting to the East German population (which included the principal American station, RIAS)
- The so-called Potsdam Missions, Western military offices set up after World War II whose personnel could travel around East

Germany to keep contact with Soviet forces (and which were matched by Soviet military missions in West Germany).

Most explosively, at the end of his list, Ulbricht reiterated his old demand for all Berlin air traffic across GDR territory to be controlled by GDR officials rather than by Soviet officers or Western allies. There were to be no more direct flights from West Berlin to West Germany; instead, all passengers from West Berlin flying in any direction were to travel through the East German airport at Schönefeld, just southeast of Berlin. Ulbricht also asked for a special meeting of the Warsaw Pact, the alliance of East European Communist states, to support his proposals. That would give his demands more authority.

Khrushchev replied on January 30, voicing understanding for Ulbricht's list but not accepting it. He did not then want to confront Kennedy with such a long and categorical set of demands in their very first meeting. Instead, Khrushchev reiterated to Ulbricht that he wanted to "resolve the issue of a peace treaty and the normalization of the situation in West Berlin on the basis of an understanding with the USA as well as with the other Western powers." But he added that "we will, as agreed, choose together with you the time" to carry out other ideas "if we do not succeed in coming to an understanding with Kennedy."[38]

Khrushchev also informed Ulbricht that he had received a message from Kennedy telling him that Kennedy regarded the improvement of Soviet-American relations as his most important task and that he fully understood Soviet concerns about "German revanchism."[39] Khrushchev saw that as a sign that Kennedy was ready to make concessions on Berlin.

On March 28, at the Moscow meeting of the Warsaw Pact that Ulbricht had wanted, the East German leader called West Berlin "a huge hole in the middle of our republic" that needed to be sealed. He wanted to close the sector border that ran through the middle of Berlin. Ulbricht said that he could not promise to meet his trade commitments to other Warsaw Pact states if he could not block the border with barriers of some kind, such as barbed wire. He asked the Warsaw Pact leaders to approve such a move.

Khrushchev told the meeting that he wanted to be more patient. He wanted to talk with Kennedy before signing a peace treaty on Germany or trying to change the situation in Berlin. He wanted to give Kennedy a chance to help solve the Berlin problem and did not want to take any unilateral steps, with all the military risks, until he was sure that he had tried to come to an agreement with the new president. He said that Ulbricht's proposal, while perhaps commendable, was premature.

The East Europeans agreed with Khrushchev. They described Ulbricht's proposal to seal off West Berlin as too provocative. It could lead to war. It would also, they argued, "cause serious harm to the reputation of the entire Communist movement" and sully the Warsaw Pact. The Hungarian and Romanian leaders Janos Kadar and Nicolas Ceaucescu opposed Ulbricht vehemently.

More important, the East Europeans worried that Ulbricht's steps might provoke a West German economic embargo that would jeopardize their economic growth. They worried more about the West German than about the American reaction. They reminded Ulbricht and Khrushchev that they needed trade with West Germany. Even Khrushchev himself told Ulbricht that they must think everything through because he worried that a Western economic blockade would force the Soviet Union to support East Germany even more.[40]

Khrushchev and the other Warsaw Pact leaders agreed that Ulbricht should wait until after Khrushchev's summit with Kennedy. In the meantime, Ulbricht could secretly "prepare everything for a future contingency."[41]

CHAPTER FIVE

"I Never Met a Man Like That"

As the time drew near, both Nikita Khrushchev and John F. Kennedy got ready for their summit meeting in Vienna on June 3 and 4.

For Khrushchev, a summit with an American president was nothing new. He had joined in a four-power summit with President Dwight Eisenhower at Geneva in 1955. He had met again with Eisenhower at Camp David in 1959. He had also briefly (and explosively) joined the abortive four-power summit in Paris.

Kennedy, however, faced his first summit with a Soviet leader. Having suffered a humiliating defeat at the Bay of Pigs, he wanted very much to have it go well. He needed to persuade an American public that was hostile toward Communism, skeptical about diplomacy, and not yet sure about him, that such summits could have useful results. And he had barely three weeks to prepare.

Ambassador Tommy Thompson's briefing cable before the summit informed Kennedy that Khrushchev wanted the meeting to be pleasant and that he would take positions that would "have the effect of improving the atmosphere and relations." Thompson thought Khrushchev would emphasize general and complete disarmament.[1]

The State Department briefing for Kennedy had a similarly optimistic tone. It did, however, urge Kennedy to tell Khrushchev that the Soviet Union and the United States should not confront each other with "intolerable choices" offering no other option than defeat or war. As for Berlin and Germany, the department warned that Khrushchev would want some commitment to resume negotiations on Berlin and would try for an early "interim" agreement. The State Department predicted that Khrushchev would take a flexibile position and that he would settle for a conference on Berlin toward the end of 1961. It advised the president to inform Khrushchev that neither the United States nor its allies "would accept the political defeat involved in the loss or the weakening of their existing position in Berlin."[2] Rusk added a short personal note advising Kennedy that the president should warn Khrushchev about "the risk of war by miscalculation."[3]

Kennedy consulted with various U.S. government experts and outsiders as well. He wanted to know what he would face. They all told him that they expected the summit to go well. The only sour note came from Georgi Bolshakov, Robert Kennedy's Soviet military intelligence contact.

Although Bolshakov said that Khrushchev wanted to have good relations with the United States, he warned that there were serious disagreements about Berlin. He told Robert that Khrushchev would sign a separate peace treaty with the GDR "with all the attendant consequences for West Berlin" if the United States would not agree to sign a peace treaty for all of Germany.[4] Bolshakov's message, which parroted Khrushchev's public line, was the clearest and even the only warning Kennedy received that Khrushchev would push hard on Berlin at the summit. It turned out to be more accurate than anything Kennedy heard from any American expert.

Robert Kennedy in turn warned Bolshakov that his brother felt strongly about Berlin. He said the president would fight for the basic Western and American position in Berlin. But Bolshakov complained that the Soviet ambassador in Washington, Mikhail Menshikov, was telling Khrushchev that Kennedy would yield. Because that was what Khrushchev wanted to hear, it probably influenced him more than Robert Kennedy's warnings.[5]

Kennedy read everything that he could get his hands on about Khrushchev. He studied his briefing papers intently and listened carefully to the supposed experts. He prepared himself more carefully than he had ever done for anything, including his campaign debate with Richard Nixon.

In Paris the night before the summit, Averell Harriman told the president that Khrushchev "will try to rattle you and frighten you but don't pay any attention to that. . . . Laugh about it, don't get into a fight. . . . Have some fun."[6]

On May 26, 1961, as he prepared to leave for Vienna, Khrushchev called a special session of the Communist Party Presidium to tell them of his plans for the summit. He told his colleagues that the Americans did not appear any more ready than before to change their position on Berlin and that he would have to force "the son of a bitch" Kennedy to do it. He planned to sign a peace treaty with East Germany in 1961. Although he would not encroach on West Berlin itself, he would support the GDR in forcing all Berlin air travel to go through the East German airport at Schönefeld. Khrushchev said that he would put as much pressure as possible on Kennedy and would not offer any compromise.

Kennedy's vacillation at the Bay of Pigs had convinced Khrushchev that a firm and unyielding position would carry the day. He concluded: "The risk that we are taking is justified; there is more than a 95 per cent probability that there will be no war."

Only Anastas Mikoyan, who had met with Eisenhower in 1959 and who understood the depth of the American commitment to Berlin, advised against such tactics. Mikoyan thought that any demands to change the regime in the air corridors might indeed risk war, although the chances of that remained slim. Mikoyan suggested that Khrushchev instead offer a constructive dialogue on Berlin, leading to an improvement in Soviet-American relations across the board. He thought this would lead to the peaceful coexistence that Khrushchev himself wanted. Angrily and excitedly, Khrushchev once more rejected Mikoyan's advice. He wanted to exploit the favorable situation after the Bay of Pigs right then and there. Mikoyan backed off.[7] This left Khrushchev with Presidium authority to press what he saw as his advantage.

One of Khrushchev's staff, Fjodor Burlaski, later told a Western newsman that Khrushchev had decided that Kennedy was "too young" and "too intellectual." Kennedy's failure in Cuba had convinced Khrushchev that he could act in Berlin without fear of an American reaction.[8]

When the American columnist Walter Lippmann at White House request used an interview with Khrushchev to suggest a five-year moratorium on Berlin, the Russian stared at him "as if he were insane."[9] Khrushchev wanted and needed faster movement. To make sure the president understood his sense of urgency, Khrushchev used a Moscow performance by some American skaters as an opportunity to call Ambassador Thompson over to his box and tell him sharply that he wanted to settle the Berlin problem before the end of 1961 on the basis of a peace treaty. He warned Thompson that U.S. forces in Berlin "might have to tighten their belts" after the peace treaty was signed. Khrushchev told Thompson to make it clear that he saw Berlin as the top issue on the Vienna agenda. Speaking roughly, to make sure that Kennedy realized how strongly he felt, Khrushchev told Thompson that the peace treaty meant the end of American rights in Berlin.

Inexplicably, Thompson still briefed the president that Khrushchev would not raise the Berlin dispute to the level of a crisis. His cable advised Kennedy that it was possible that Khrushchev would try to slide over Berlin "in sweetness and a light atmosphere." He conveyed none of Khrushchev's force and anger.[10] Kennedy's own ambassador was letting the president walk into a trap.

On his way to Vienna, Khrushchev took a leisurely trip through the western Soviet Union and through several East European states. In a meeting with Czech Communist officials at a resort near Bratislava, Khrushchev said that he planned to scare Kennedy and that he would prepare for unilateral steps to eliminate Western rights in Berlin. He was sure that Kennedy would not dare to counter. He had not previously considered taking such steps but now believed he could.[11]

Khrushchev told the Czechs that he would sign the peace treaty with the GDR before the end of 1961, although Ulbricht wanted it signed immediately. He would most probably sign it after the October 22 Communist Party Congress in Moscow. Then Western investment would flee Berlin and the West would be powerless. Khrushchev added that these changes would show West Germany and some other West European states that the Americans would not fight for their allies. Those states would reexamine their membership in NATO. He was obviously thinking in wider terms than Berlin itself, and especially of West Germany.[12]

Allied Advice

Harold Macmillan had rallied to the president's side after the Bay of Pigs, showing that he was "100 per cent loyal in support of a colleague in adversity."[13] Now, he offered advice on the summit in a message that his ambassador Sir Harold Caccia was instructed to deliver orally so as to leave no written record. But Sir Harold had a previous speaking engagement and therefore sent Macmillan's advice in a "private" top secret letter to McGeorge Bundy that he asked Bundy and the president to regard as spoken words.

Macmillan warned Kennedy to recognize that Khrushchev was likely to raise the Berlin issue. He urged Kennedy to be careful and not "at this stage to mention the ideas put forward by Mr. Acheson." Advising Kennedy to be careful in his choice of words so as not to provoke a Khrushchev tantrum, Macmillan told the president that he was "at least doubtful about the wisdom of being very strong with Khrushchev about sticking to the status quo." He wanted Kennedy to show some flexibility. He warned that a firm statement by the president might precipitate a crisis. Recognizing that Kennedy would of course have to be "completely firm about our rights and about our determination to defend them," Macmillan continued, he hoped "that Kennedy might use some rather vague phrase to the effect that any interference in our position would lead to 'a dangerous situation.'" He added that Britain had "found this to be the best formula ourselves in Moscow."[14] Having experienced Khrushchev in the raw, Macmillan believed that he should warn Kennedy of the shoals that the president's own "voyage of discovery" should avoid.

Macmillan's use of the "spoken" words for his message marked his style with Kennedy. He much preferred to meet or talk with the president in person, perhaps over a drink, rather than in a formal meeting with others around to take notes. He thought that private meetings gave him a chance to speak more frankly without being criticized for being soft. That was why he later appreciated having an ambassador in Washington who could talk with Kennedy privately and informally.[15]

The advice that Kennedy heard from Charles de Gaulle when they met in Paris on Kennedy's way to Vienna could not have been more different:

> Since there is no fighting and the Cold War is very expensive, peace may be on the way. But it can only be based on a general and prolonged relaxation of tension. Anything that upsets [the balance of power], and in particular the German situation, would plunge the world into serious danger. Therefore, when Khrushchev summons you to change the status

of Berlin, in other words to hand the city over to him, stand fast! [*tenez bon!*] That is the most useful service you can render to the whole world, Russia included.[16]

De Gaulle said that Khrushchev's frequent postponements of the peace treaty showed that he did not want war. De Gaulle advised Kennedy to tell Khrushchev that it was the Soviets, not the West, that were trying to force change. He insisted that the Western position in Berlin was not as weak as some people thought. Kennedy's job, as de Gaulle saw it, was "to make sure that Khrushchev believes you are a man who will fight."[17]

De Gaulle also told Kennedy to rely on himself and on his own instincts and not to trust his advisers. He had obviously begun to harbor doubts about Kennedy after the Bay of Pigs and he wanted to do everything possible to make Kennedy remain as obdurate as he expected Khrushchev to be.

Kennedy and Charles de Gaulle in Paris after de Gaulle told the president not to yield to Khrushchev over Berlin. Courtesy of the John F. Kennedy Presidential Library

Khrushchev needed to understand, de Gaulle observed, that there would be general war the first time he used force against the West in Berlin: "That is the last thing he wants." He added that the West could also retaliate economically, where the entire Soviet bloc was very vulnerable. When Kennedy asked about a possible Soviet blockade of Berlin, de Gaulle did not recommend a ground attack but a new airlift. If the Soviets were to shoot down a Western plane, which he doubted, there would be no ambiguity about who was responsible and about what would happen next.

If Kennedy wanted France to join in any serious talks about Berlin, de Gaulle would agree because he believed that France had to have a role in any current diplomacy. But he would never center his policy on negotiations. Nor, he made clear, would he give Kennedy the power to decide for the alliance or for France.

De Gaulle later wrote that he saw in Kennedy a continuation of what he regarded as the American attitude of superiority. He had earlier tried to interest Kennedy in forming a triumvirate with himself and Macmillan in which the three principal leaders of the West would coordinate their global policies, but Kennedy had begged off. Summarizing his relations with Kennedy after their meeting, de Gaulle observed: "Basically, what Kennedy offered me in every case was a share of his projects. What he heard from me in reply was that . . . whatever France did she did of her own accord."[18]

As Kennedy and Khrushchev headed for Vienna, each by a very different route and with very different intentions and expectations, they had no definite agenda. They knew that they would be talking about Berlin, Laos, and arms control, but they had not agreed on the order of those topics. Nor had their diplomatic staffs coordinated any schedule except that dictated by Kennedy's travel plans to and from Vienna. That meant that they would meet for only a day and a half. All that Kennedy and Khrushchev knew in preparation for their summit was that they would meet, that there were several topics that they would both be ready to discuss, and that they had only about nine to ten hours to discuss them (with at least half that time to be used for interpretation).

Kennedy clearly saw the summit as a first chance to get to know Khrushchev, to exchange ideas on general principles, and to lay some foundation for good relations and further negotiations on specific topics.

His briefings suggested that he should not rush to agree on any issue, except perhaps Laos, and certainly not Berlin.

Khrushchev wanted the opposite. As he told Thompson, he wanted to get a quick result on Berlin. He had waited two and a half years since November 1958 and he could wait no longer. He wanted Kennedy to understand that and to act accordingly. It is not known whether Khrushchev ever received Robert Kennedy's warning through Bolshakov that his brother would not yield on Berlin, but if he had received it he would presumably have expected to change Kennedy's mind.

Dean Rusk later wrote that he opposed the very idea of a summit meeting, and that Kennedy "wasn't prepared for the brutality of Khrushchev's presentation."[19] But there is no evidence that Rusk himself took any steps to prepare the president for a rough meeting or to fix with the Soviets an agreed agenda and timetable for the summit

Kennedy Offers to Divide the World

In their first meeting, on the late morning of June 3 after Kennedy had flown to Vienna from Paris, both Kennedy and Khrushchev began by stressing the importance of mutual understanding and good relations. But Khrushchev immediately added the condition that some questions would have to be resolved before good relations could follow. He obviously had Berlin in mind as one of the topics to be resolved.[20]

Kennedy opened the substantive part of the discussion by very general speculation: he wondered "how it would be possible for the two countries—allied with other countries, having different political and social systems, and competing with each other in different parts of the world—to find during his presidency ways and means of not permitting situations where the two countries would be committed to actions involving their security or endangering peace." He said that securing peace was the basic objective of the United States and that both sides had to recognize the needs of the other. Kennedy added his impression that the Soviet Union was "seeking to eliminate free systems in areas that are associated with us," and identified it as a matter of significant concern.

Drawing on the many seminars that he and his advisers had conducted about the risks of miscalculation as well as on Dean Rusk's memorandum before the summit, Kennedy told Khrushchev that if the

Kennedy talking with Nikita Khrushchev in Vienna during one of their less acrimonious moments. Courtesy of the John F. Kennedy Presidential Library

two countries should miscalculate, they would lose for a long time to come.

At this point, barely an hour into the meeting, Khrushchev, in Kennedy's words, "went berserk." Kennedy later described the scene to his friend and assistant Kenneth O'Donnell while relaxing in the American embassy's bathtub:

> He started yelling, "Miscalculation! Miscalculation! Miscalculation! All I ever hear from your people and your news correspondents and your friends in Europe and everyplace else is that damned word, miscalculation! You ought to take that word and bury it in cold storage and never use it again! I'm sick of it!" So I'm trying to remind myself, the next time I'm talking to Khrushchev, don't mention miscalculation.[21]

Khrushchev said that Kennedy was asking the Soviet Union "to sit like a schoolboy with his hands on his desk." He asserted: "The Soviet Union supports its ideas and holds them in high esteem. It cannot guarantee that these ideas will stop at its borders." He added that the USSR believed in defending its interests and that the Soviet Union was for change.

Khrushchev charged that the United States seemed to regard Soviet defense of its vital interests as "miscalculation." The Soviet Union did not want war, but it could not be intimidated by this kind of talk. Kennedy tried to explain, saying that miscalculation had in the past led to terrible suffering in Europe and that he wanted to avoid it. He wanted to use this meeting to introduce "precision in judgment" and to get a "clearer understanding of where we are going."

Khrushchev backed off, saying that the purpose of the meeting was to improve relations between their countries, not to worsen them. But he clearly did not read the lessons of history as the White House did. He would not permit what he regarded as the foreordained march of humanity toward Communism to be interrupted by any fear of "miscalculation."

After their morning session's rocky start, both men agreed that they would prefer to meet alone with only interpreters present during the afternoon. Thus, they had a long bilateral session for several hours. Rusk, Foreign Minister Andrei Gromyko and other American and Soviet officials met separately to discuss disarmament issues, a meeting that Gromyko regarded as so certain to be fruitless that he hoped they would have a lot of cognac to drink.

Despite Khrushchev's morning outburst about miscalculation, Kennedy still returned to this general theme in the afternoon session: "It is obvious that when systems are in transition we should be careful, particularly today when modern weapons are at hand." He wanted to introduce more caution on both sides. Kennedy added very specifically: "Whatever the result of the present competition—and no one can be sure what it will be—both sides should act in such a way as to prevent them from coming into direct contact and thus prejudicing the establishment of lasting peace." He reiterated his intent to aim for greater precision, so that the two countries "could survive this period of competition without endangering their national security."

Kennedy said: "We regard the present balance of power between the Sino-Soviet forces and the forces of the United States and Western Europe as being more or less in balance" (a remark that thrilled Khrushchev and the Soviet military when they read it but infuriated the U.S. Joint

Chiefs of Staff). Khrushchev said he agreed and that "both sides know very well that they have enough power to destroy each other." Kennedy welcomed Khrushchev's agreement, and said that both countries should try to preserve the balance of power or at least not try to change it by military action.

Citing Poland several times as an example of a place where he would not challenge the Soviet position, Kennedy said that he recognized that the Soviet Union might have "strategic problems" if a government in Poland associated itself closely with the West. He said: "We do not wish to act in a way that would deprive the Soviet Union of its ties to Eastern Europe," and that Khrushchev in turn should not try to deprive the United States of its ties to Western Europe.[22]

Khrushchev would not accept any such restriction: he asserted firmly that Communism would triumph. It would be a victory of ideas, not of military force. Even if Kennedy wanted to build a dam, the ideas would live on and spread. But the president could not place the responsibility for the development and spread of Communist ideas on the Soviet Union. If so, Khrushchev asserted, conflicts would inevitably follow. Khrushchev said that he believed in the certainty of Communist victory because Communism represented the march of history. Nobody could stop the spread of ideas, and those ideas would inevitably lead to a Communist world. Unlike Kennedy, he did not appear to fear the risks of confrontation.

Summarizing his philosophy on the following morning, Khrushchev said he could not under any circumstances accept the American "don't poke your nose" thesis: "The Soviet Union does not wish to divide the world" as Kennedy had suggested. Khrushchev thought that Kennedy was trying to block the spread of Marxist ideology and trying to stop the Soviet Union from helping the oppressed in their struggle for independence.

Having only recently begun to support the uprisings of African and Asian colonial peoples against the West, and being hailed as a liberator by some of those peoples, Khrushchev would not accept any limits on the expansion of Soviet influence and power. He must have thought that Kennedy was trying to persuade him to accept the American doctrine of containment of the Soviet Union. Actually, Kennedy was asking Khrushchev to restrain Soviet adventurism and to stop attacking U.S. positions in places like Berlin. He wanted both superpowers to remain in their own areas. But Khrushchev must have thought that Kennedy was trying to prevent him from acting anywhere in the world.

After those sharp exchanges, Khrushchev and Kennedy discussed Laos and arms control during the remainder of the afternoon session. They reached a basic understanding about Laos, with both saying they did not have a real interest in what happened there. They left arms control for further discussion and negotiation.

Berlin at the Summit

Berlin had been a subtext during the entire summit discussion about dividing the world. Although he had not specifically mentioned the city, Kennedy had clearly pointed to Berlin when he asked Khrushchev not to challenge existing American interests and positions. In return, Kennedy made clear that he would not challenge Soviet interests, including East Germany and East Berlin. Kennedy was telling Khrushchev indirectly that he would not care what happened in East Berlin if Khrushchev would lay off West Berlin. Khrushchev's reaction showed that he would not accept that kind of bargain.

Khrushchev must have felt immensely frustrated that they had not discussed Berlin during the first day. As they closed their afternoon meeting, he reminded Kennedy that Berlin was very much on his agenda. He said that the Soviet Union wanted to sign a peace treaty for Germany with the United States. That, he said, would improve relations.

> "But," he concluded, "if the United States refuses to sign a peace treaty, the Soviet Union will do so and nothing will stop it."

He obviously wanted Kennedy to understand his priorities for the next day's discussion.

The next morning, however, contrary to Khrushchev's wish to discuss Berlin, the two leaders talked again about Laos and arms control. Kennedy even added some further anodyne remarks about Laos after Khrushchev had again said he wanted to talk about Berlin. When they finally got to Berlin late that morning, Khrushchev had only a little over an hour to deal with the topic that had brought him to Vienna. He had no time to negotiate, only to threaten. And he needed to make his position very clear in a hurry.

Once the Berlin discussion began, therefore, Khrushchev's tone grew harsher, more intense, and more insistent. Sixteen years had passed since the end of the war, he said, and now Germany was again becoming armed. It was time to draw a line, end the state of war, and decide what was to happen with Germany. Khrushchev said he would like to reach an agreement with President Kennedy—he stressed "with you"—on this matter. If Kennedy refused, the Soviet Union would sign a separate peace treaty with the GDR within six months. All Western rights in Berlin would then cease. If Washington wanted to have access to Berlin or any rights there, it would have to negotiate them with the GDR. The only concession Khrushchev offered was for a six-month interim arrangement, but then the peace treaty would follow.

Reacting to Khrushchev's change of tone, Kennedy came back hard. Although he did not talk as brusquely as Khrushchev, he did make clear that he took Berlin seriously. He said that this matter was "of the greatest concern" to the United States:

"Here, we are not talking about Laos."

The United States could not accept an ultimatum.

Every president since World War II had made a commitment to Berlin, and if the United States did not maintain that commitment, Kennedy believed that all its pledges would be regarded as mere "scraps of paper." What was at stake, therefore, was not only Berlin but Western Europe. Kennedy would not expect Khrushchev to accept such a change in the balance of power and Khrushchev should not expect Kennedy to accept it.

Khrushchev raised the temperature further. He said that "no force in the world will prevent the USSR from signing a peace treaty" and that "the sovereignty of the GDR will be observed." In reply to a question from Kennedy, Khrushchev said that the treaty would end all Western access rights to Berlin. He added that he regarded all of Berlin—including West Berlin—as part of GDR territory. Any violation of GDR sovereignty would be regarded by the Soviet Union as "an act of open aggression . . . with all the consequences ensuing therefrom," according to Khrushchev, and "responsibility for violation of that sovereignty will be heavy." He said that the demarcation lines for East Germany should become formal borders, as should the borders of Czechoslovakia and Poland. Kennedy replied that he had not become president of the United States "to accept arrangements totally inimical to U.S. interests."

Khrushchev even argued that, if the United States wanted to start a war over Germany, it should begin sooner rather than later, when even more horrible weapons might have been developed. The American and Soviet delegations agreed not to record those remarks in the transcript because they sounded so ominous.[23] They must certainly have sounded that way to Kennedy. Khrushchev ended the session and the formal summit meeting by saying that a paper that presented the Soviet position had been prepared and would be given to the American delegation.

No time remained for discussion or negotiation. Khrushchev had staked out his most extreme position. Kennedy, unprepared, was put on the defensive. All White House preparatory talk about possible compromise had been useless, as had all the American briefings advising Kennedy that Khrushchev planned to pass over Berlin lightly.

At lunch, Kennedy reiterated his proposal to divide the world, stating that peace could only be reached if each power kept to its own area. Khrushchev, as before, rejected that out of hand.

> Kennedy then said that he wanted to have another meeting with Khrushchev in private. When told that it might delay his flight, he said, "I can't leave here without giving it one more try."[24]

The two leaders thus met again with only interpreters present.

In the private session, Kennedy said that he hoped that Khrushchev would not present him with a situation so closely tied to the U.S. national interest. He wanted to change the tone of the meeting, but Khrushchev was not about to shift his rhetorical style. Perhaps believing that Kennedy had asked for the extra private session because the president might find it easier to yield in private than in an open meeting with full delegations, the Soviet leader pressed even more intensely than in the morning. He said that the peace treaty would guarantee GDR rights and promised to defend the borders of the GDR if they were violated by any Western state.

The United States wanted to humiliate the Soviet Union, he claimed, and "this cannot be accepted." Kennedy replied, "Either Mr. Khrushchev does not believe that the United States is serious or the situation in the area is so unsatisfactory to the Soviet Union that it has to take this drastic action."

Kennedy warned Khrushchev that decisions had to be carefully considered and that there was a difference between signing a peace treaty and actually trying to challenge Western rights of access to Berlin. The former would not matter; the latter would. He said that he wanted to avoid the confrontation to which such a challenge would lead.

At this point, Khrushchev became furious and began shouting. He warned that if the president envisaged "any action that might have unhappy consequences," then "force would be met by force." He repeated that U.S. troops would have to withdraw from Berlin.

Khrushchev added: "I want peace: but if you want war, that is your problem." He said "It is not the USSR that threatens war; it is the U.S." He repeatedly warned of war.

When Kennedy, following de Gaulle's suggestion, said "It is you, not I, who wants to force a change," Khrushchev bristled, repeating: "It is not the USSR that threatens with war; it is the U.S." He said it was up to the United States to decide whether there would be war or peace: "The calamities of war will be shared equally." Khrushchev finished with the assertion, "The decision to sign a peace treaty is firm and irrevocable. The Soviet Union will sign it in December."

There are different versions of how Kennedy replied at that point to conclude the meeting. The long-accepted version has been that he said: "Then it will be a cold winter." The Kennedy Library record of the Vienna summit shows those as the last substantive words of the summit. Before Dean Rusk passed away, however, he told his biographer and his son that Kennedy had actually said: "Then there will be war, Mr. Chairman," before adding "It will be a cold winter." But that remark was not recorded by anybody else nor by either interpreter. It is not in the Soviet or East German transcript of the meeting. Nor did Khrushchev report it to his son Sergei in their discussions about the summit.

The American interpreter for the private talk, Alexander Akalovsky, does not recall any such remark and even insists that Kennedy did not say it. There is, therefore, reason to believe that Kennedy never said it. It was certainly not within his style for the summit, when he often appeared to speak more in sorrow than in anger, and when he avoided issuing the kinds of threats that Khrushchev uttered almost continuously.[25]

Khrushchev remained inflexible and harsh throughout most of the summit, except on Laos, although he tried to appear friendly at times. In the early part of the meeting, he even suggested that he would be glad to welcome Kennedy in Moscow. But that pleasant mood did not last long. It vanished totally during the summit discussion on Berlin. Perhaps, after the Bay of Pigs, Khrushchev did indeed think that he could intimidate or, as he liked to say, "scare" Kennedy.

To "scare" Kennedy, Khrushchev may well have put on a show, deliberately throwing the kind of tantrums that he had thrown in some of his private meetings with Macmillan (but not with Eisenhower or de Gaulle). An American journalist told a U. S. official that Khrushchev appeared to have succeeded, for the journalist thought that Kennedy looked "green" at the end of the summit.[26] Another American wrote that Kennedy appeared "dazed" by the "sheer animal energy" of Khrushchev's presentation.[27]

Akalovsky believed that Khrushchev's language and style reflected his upbringing. The premier spoke in a Ukrainian peasant dialect and with a peasant directness, roughly and sometimes boorishly. He did not use the sophisticated syntax or phrasing that educated Russians might use, that Kennedy used and that Kennedy had heard at his schools in England and the United States. Interpreters often had to soften Khrushchev's vocabulary, substituting a word that might have the same meaning but a somewhat less crude and aggressive tone. The official transcript reflects their language and their style, not Khrushchev's. Nor does it reflect Khrushchev's behavior, also designed to make an impression on Kennedy.

After the Summit

Kennedy had obviously not been properly prepared for what hit him. None of the materials in his briefing papers had given him any idea that Khrushchev might behave as he did. After the first session, Kennedy asked his advisers, "is it always like this?" and Thompson replied "par for the course." But Thompson himself had not written any warning that might have predicted the kind of attack Khrushchev mounted against the president. Nor, indeed, was it "par for the course" for Khrushchev's talks with most of the Western leaders he had met, such as Eisenhower or de Gaulle. He might have been rough with others on occasion but not as consistently as he was with Kennedy. The Soviet leader appeared to have reserved a special style of attack for the president, as Sukhodrev implied.

Nothing about Khrushchev's behavior surprised those who knew him well. Nina Khrushcheva, Khrushchev's wife, had told the wife of Ambassador Thompson that her husband was "either way up or way down."[28] But, for Kennedy, who had not been warned to expect this and who prided himself on careful and rational analysis, Khrushchev's behavior must have presented almost insurmountable problems. Kennedy would have to try to manage Khrushchev's moods as well as his substantive positions on some of the most intractable issues in Soviet-American relations. Kennedy must have worried how a man with that kind of impulsive temperament would handle nuclear weapons in a crisis.

In his comments after the summit, Khrushchev frequently continued to refer to Kennedy as a young man.[29] He apparently could not get over Kennedy's youth, as he had shown in his earlier "short pants" comment. During the summit, he often talked down to Kennedy as a Russian adult might talk to a youngster. It almost seemed at times as if he was trying to teach Kennedy a lesson, as he might have scolded an ill-mannered child in Russia. He used the kind of language that a Russian might use with a younger man who needed to be taught his manners.[30]

Khrushchev came away from Vienna firmly convinced that his tough presentation had intimidated Kennedy and that the president would retreat on Berlin to preserve peace.[31] Every Kennedy statement about the importance of avoiding conflict, which the president had intended as an expression of mutual interest in exercising restraint, reinforced Khrushchev's conviction that Kennedy would do almost anything to avoid nuclear war.[32]

Kennedy did not relish personal confrontation as Khrushchev did. That—combined with Kennedy's failure at The Bay of Pigs—may have given Khruschev the impression that Kennedy was not only young but weak.

American newsmen and commentators present in Vienna concluded—although they did not write it openly—that the summit had been a disaster for Kennedy. Kennedy himself made gloomy assessments to several journalists whom he had known for a long time. He told James Reston of the

New York Times that it had been the "roughest thing in my life" and that Khrushchev "just beat the hell out of" him.

> He added: "I've got a terrible problem; if he thinks I'm inexperienced and have no guts, until we remove those ideas we won't get anywhere with him. So we have to act."[33]

When Reston came out of the meeting with Kennedy, he said to O'Donnell, "He seems very gloomy." The following day, he wrote in the *New York Times* that Kennedy seemed shaken and angry. And when some American intellectuals tried to tell Bundy after his return to Washington that they thought Khrushchev wanted to defuse the Berlin issue, Bundy screamed: "Khrushchev is a pig! He's just a pig!" He was as badly shaken as Kennedy.[34]

As one member of Kennedy's team later commented, Kennedy had not only been stunned by Khrushchev's presentation but it had forced him to shift his priorities. He had not realized, and had certainly not been warned by his advisers, that Khrushchev would put such weight on Berlin. He now understood that he had to become fully focused on the German problem when he would much rather have had other priorities.[35]

Nonetheless, although Khrushchev may have bullied and pushed Kennedy around, Kennedy had stood his ground on Berlin by telling Khrushchev that he had not assumed the presidency "to accept arrangements totally inimical to U.S. interests." Kennedy had not dared to show any flexibility on Berlin because he feared it would give Khrushchev the impression that he would not defend the American commitment. He also recognized that after the Bay of Pigs he needed to make sure that Khrushchev did not misunderstand the importance that he attached to Berlin.

Although Kennedy believed and later told others that he had been "beaten up" by Khrushchev, his replies must have given Khrushchev more pause for thought than Kennedy himself probably realized at the time. Although Kennedy spoke with restraint, his comment that Khrushchev would not accept such a shift in the balance of power and "we cannot accept it either" made clear to Khrushchev that Kennedy was prepared to defend American rights.

Robert Kennedy later recalled Vienna as a decisive moment in his brother's political education: "Vienna was very revealing. This was the first time the president had ever really come across somebody with whom he couldn't exchange ideas in a meaningful way and feel there was some point to it." Robert concluded that it had been a shock to his brother.[36] It must also have had a mixed effect, worrying Kennedy but making him realize that he was now in a rough league in which he could not always play the gentleman.

Allied Reaction

On his flight to meet with Macmillan in England, Kennedy called O'Donnell into his cabin and talked more openly than he might have spoken to others whom he had not known as long or as well. He vented his frustration about the meeting, especially the part about Berlin. He also showed his uncertainty about what he should do next:

> God knows I'm not an isolationist, but it seems particularly stupid to risk killing a million Americans over an argument about access rights on an Autobahn in the Soviet zone of Germany, or because the Germans want Germany reunified. If I'm going to threaten Russia with a nuclear war, it will have to be for much bigger and more important reasons than that. Before I back Khrushchev against the wall and put him to a final test, the freedom of all Western Europe will have to be at stake.[37]

As they were about to land, Kennedy added: "If we're going to have to start a nuclear war, we'll have to fix things so it will be started by the President of the United States, and nobody else. Not by a trigger-happy sergeant on a truck convoy at a checkpoint in East Germany."[38] After meeting Khrushchev, Kennedy clearly worried more than ever about the risk of escalation.

When Macmillan met Kennedy at the London airport, the prime minister immediately recognized that the president, exhausted and suffering from a sore back, did not want any formal government consultations but would prefer a private talk. He invited Kennedy to his room for a chat and a drink of Scotch. There, Kennedy unloaded his disappointment over the summit to Macmillan. The prime minister wrote in his journal that Kennedy had been "much concerned and even surprised by the almost brutal frankness and confidence of the Soviet leader." The Russian appeared to be "on top of the world." He concluded that it must have been "like somebody meeting Napoleon at the height of his power."

Macmillan took advantage of their talk and of Kennedy's dejected mood to present his own ideas about what he saw as the underlying realities of Berlin. He warned about the risk of nuclear war over Berlin and pressed Kennedy to compromise with Moscow. He wrote that he had been glad to do this privately because he feared being called "yellow," or afraid. He did not want to give an opening to the French and Germans who "talk tough but have no intention of doing anything about Berlin."[39]

Kennedy's meeting with Macmillan relaxed the president and left him rather fond of the British prime minister.[40] But Macmillan was less charitable about Kennedy. He told his biographer that "tough, cynical and ruthless Khrushchev danced rings around the young man inexperienced in diplomacy."[41] By the end of June, Macmillan even wrote in his private journal, "I feel in my bones that President Kennedy is going to fail to produce any real leadership." He worried about a "drift to disaster over Berlin—a terrible diplomatic defeat or (out of sheer incompetence) a nuclear war."[42] His private judgment on Kennedy certainly seemed less generous than what he showed in public.

For his part, Kennedy also had his doubts about Macmillan. He questioned whether Macmillan and the British would be prepared to stand up to the Soviets. De Gaulle, while more imperious and harder to handle, seemed more ready to be firm on Berlin.[43] Kennedy's appraisal may have been reinforced by a letter from de Gaulle that took the opposite tack from Macmillan's. Fearing that Kennedy had been overawed by Khrushchev and had become convinced that the West needed to compromise on Berlin, the general wrote to Kennedy on July 6 that "only an attitude of firmness and solidarity adopted and affirmed in good time by America, Britain and France, will prevent unpleasant consequences."

Looking far ahead, De Gaulle wrote: "Only after a long period of international détente—which depends entirely on Moscow—can we enter into negotiations with Russia on the German problem as a whole."[44]

Getting Ready for a Showdown

Upon returning to Washington, Kennedy made a short nationally televised speech in which he described the Vienna summit as "a very sober two days." He also used the term *somber* to describe the mood. He made it clear that he and Khrushchev had differed sharply, and he did not try to hide his disappointment. To play down the threatening tone of the summit in order to avoid Republican criticism of his first diplomatic venture, Kennedy said—falsely—that "there was no discourtesy, no loss of temper, no threat or ultimatum by either side." He tried to make a virtue of the open "channels of communication" by telling his listeners "our views contrasted sharply but at least we knew better at the end where we both stood."[45]

As he reflected on the summit discussion regarding Berlin, Kennedy must have found it difficult to see a peaceful way out. Khrushchev had used the kind of threats of war that world leaders usually avoided even in the most difficult situations. Kennedy could blame some of Khrushchev's bluster on the Soviet leader's peasant crudeness, but he had to take Khrushchev at his word.

Kennedy told *Time* magazine correspondent Hugh Sidey, "I never met a man like that." He realized that the rational and precise style he wanted to bring to his policies would not work with the Soviet leader. Khrushchev was as tightly shaped and imprisoned by his history and his experiences as all the other principals Kennedy had met. In addition, Khrushchev believed firmly in Marxist-Leninist ideology.

Kennedy must also have wondered about the briefings he had been getting from his vaunted experts on the Soviet Union. None of them had warned him of what lay ahead at the summit or prepared him adequately for his confrontation with Khrushchev. They had not given him any points that he might make in reply. At the end, he literally had nothing left to say except "It will be a cold winter." Only de Gaulle, who had met with Khrushchev several times, had told him that he would face intense pressure; he had also warned Kennedy that no leader could ever really trust his advisers. But Kennedy understood this too late.

Kennedy must have found the summit not only somber but frustrating. He had wanted to establish good relations and had tried to do so on the basis of the status quo. He offered Khrushchev an agreement to divide the world between East and West, although he did not call it that. He would not challenge Soviet positions if Khrushchev did not challenge Western positions (including Berlin).

American experts on the Soviet Union thought privately that Kennedy might have gone too far by implicitly accepting the Communist system where it already prevailed—including some of the "captive na-tions" in Eastern Europe whose independence the U.S. government had supported since their conquest by the Soviet army in 1945. He certainly spoke very differently in a speech to 100,000 cheering Polish-Americans at the Buffalo city hall a year later when he said (in Polish) that "Poland is not yet lost."[46]

A Soviet diplomat, Georgy Kornienko, reading the transcript of the meeting, recognized that Kennedy had made a major concession by not challenging Soviet domination over Eastern Europe,[47] but Khrushchev had rejected that offer. He wanted more, and must have thought he could get it.

Kennedy told John Kenneth Galbraith, his ambassador to India and an old friend: "There are limits to the number of defeats I can defend in one twelve-month period. I've had the Bay of Pigs and pulling out of Laos. I can't accept a third."[48] He could not rationalize a retreat on Berlin to the American public. He thus faced a domestic political as well as a foreign policy dilemma. He had to hang tough, no matter what concessions his advisers might propose, if he wanted to avoid Republican jeers.

As Kennedy had said to Reston, "The son of a bitch has got to see me move." He must have faced the stark realization that he would have to confront Khrushchev again and at some place other than a summit. Talking would do no good. If Khrushchev would not agree to a peaceful division of the world, Kennedy would have to impose it, and Berlin might have to be the place.

Khrushchev, in contrast, was almost bubbly after the summit. He had spoken more brutally to Kennedy than he had ever spoken to any other American, even to the hated Richard Nixon. Never before had any So-viet leader so openly threatened an American president with war. Never again was one to do so. Yet Kennedy had neither replied in kind nor walked out.

Khrushchev said later that he could not help feeling sorry for Kennedy. He had not wanted to humiliate Kennedy but did want to convince the president that he was ready to go to war over Berlin. Khrushchev told his assistant for foreign policy, Oleg Troyanovsky, that Kennedy was "inexperienced, even immature." Other Soviet officials reported that Khrushchev had concluded that Kennedy was a "boy" and that he did not have the courage to stand up to a serious challenge. Kennedy had apparently not shaken the disparaging appraisal that Khrushchev had made before the summit. Bolshakov told an American friend that the Soviets were amazed that the president seemed "scared" and added: "When you have your hand up a girl's dress, you expect her to scream, but you don't expect her to be scared."[49]

Khrushchev's son Sergei wrote later, "Father decided to exert the utmost pressure" to get the Americans to accept Berlin as an independent free city. But Kennedy, as the premier admitted, "was not ready to reach an agreement under pressure." Thus, Khrushchev said: "We parted in a state of heightened tension" and in "a mood of gloom."[50]

Ten days after the summit, Khrushchev published the full text of the six-month ultimatum he had given to Kennedy at the end of the meeting. This shocked some of Kennedy's experts on the Soviet Union, who had expected that Khrushchev would keep the ultimatum secret to give time for quiet diplomacy. But Khrushchev now told the whole world, and especially the East and West Germans as well as the Berliners, that he intended to act before the end of the year.[51] Peaceful coexistence would have to wait its turn.

On June 15, Khrushchev made a speech giving his own evaluation of the summit. It was a very different one from Kennedy's. He did not speak of "sober" or "somber" talks, though he did say the meetings had been frank. He said that the meeting had been necessary because President Kennedy now understood "the great responsibility that lies with the governments of two such powerful states." With regard to Berlin, Khrushchev reiterated his uncompromising summit statements. He stressed the threat of modern thermonuclear war, and he added that any country that wanted to preserve ties with West Berlin, whether by road, by water, or by air, would have to make agreements with the GDR. To underline his threat, he appeared in his World War II lieutenant general uniform. He offered no hint that he might retreat or compromise.[52]

Privately, Khrushchev continued to express contempt for Kennedy. He told his aides that Kennedy had "wishy-washy" behavior. He added:

"I know for certain that Kennedy doesn't have a strong backbone, nor, generally speaking, does he have the courage to stand up to a serious challenge."[53]

Worries in Berlin

We Americans living and serving in Berlin, like the Berliners, found the results of the summit depressing. The coverage in major American papers showed that the summit had gone badly for the president. Although American reporters tried to protect Kennedy in their writings by making the summit seem less of a disaster than Kennedy himself felt, those journalists coming through Berlin privately gave us a much more brutal description of the meeting.

Ulbricht's reaction, which was even more ebullient than Khrushchev's, also worried us. He congratulated Khrushchev for his success at the summit. His official publication *Neues Deutschland* pronounced itself gleeful over the results and said that the summit clearly promised an early solution for what it termed the "West Berlin problem." We did not think that was good news.

We learned that Ulbricht had ordered a new police security unit to be established for East Berlin and that the East Berlin police brigades assigned to crowd control were being beefed up with units from other parts of the GDR. It certainly sounded ominous. So did refugee statistics, which began climbing exponentially after the summit. We felt that the summit had solved nothing and might have even worsened the situation. We also felt that the real test was now to come, and that it might come soon.

CHAPTER SIX

"This Is the Answer!"

If Berlin had been on Kennedy's mind before the summit, it now dominated most of his waking moments. He would sometimes doodle *Berlin* over and over again on the yellow pad that he kept on the cabinet table during White House meetings.[1] Berlin had become the most urgent and perhaps the most explosive item on his agenda. Even more than before, he saw the city mainly as an issue for his relations with Nikita Khrushchev.

Having now met Khrushchev and experienced his tantrums, Kennedy must have genuinely feared the risk of nuclear war. The Soviet leader had appeared irrational and perhaps unhinged at times. One could not be sure what he might do under pressure. Kennedy and the American people had to be ready for anything.

Ulbricht Prepares

Khrushchev sent Communist Party Presidium member Anastas Mikoyan to report to Walter Ulbricht right after the summit. Mikoyan told Ulbricht, "The GDR is the western outpost of the Socialist camp. Our Marxist-Leninist theory must prove itself here." He said that the Soviet Union and the entire Socialist camp would never let East Germany fail: "If socialism does not win in the GDR, then we have not won." This added to Ulbricht's confidence that the Berlin crisis was moving his way and that Khrushchev would support him fully.[2] Ulbricht, like Khrushchev, could probably remember Lenin's dictum that "whoever has Berlin, has Germany."[3] He must have sensed that history was moving irrevocably in his direction.

On June 15, Ulbricht predicted at one of his rare press conferences that the West Berlin problem would be solved within the year and that the Western states would then have to negotiate with him for access to West Berlin. He left no doubt that no more refugees would be able to flee after that.

When he was asked if the "free city" would mean that the GDR state boundary would be at the Brandenburg Gate between East and West Berlin, Ulbricht replied rather strangely: "Nobody has the intention of building a wall."[4] Ulbricht's statement has often been interpreted as a sign of duplicity, pretending that he would not build a wall when he was actually planning to build one. But it was actually the opposite.

Having read the Vienna transcript, Ulbricht could easily have concluded that he could finally expect the peace treaty and the free city of West Berlin to be in place soon, definitely by the end of 1961 and perhaps before. Khrushchev had announced that at the summit and Kennedy had not been able to back him down as Eisenhower had done. The year 1961 would not be 1960 all over again.

Ulbricht must have concluded that he would soon have full control over all Berlin road and air traffic. He would certainly make sure that the free city of West Berlin would not accept refugees. Even if it did, the refugees would not be allowed to move on to West Germany. Berlin would not need a wall through its middle because there would be no reason to flee from one side to the other.

If Western airlines did not agree to fly to the East German airport at Schönefeld, Ulbricht planned to float weather balloons into the Tempelhof and Tegel airport glide paths because major portions of those glide paths went over East Germany and East Berlin. That would stop military and civilian aircraft from landing in West Berlin and would force them to land at Schönefeld Airport.

Combined with East German control over the Autobahn routes into West Berlin, nobody could enter or leave West Berlin without passing under Ulbricht's surveillance. All of Berlin would become subject to Ulbricht's political direction.[5] He established planning staffs to restructure the organization for the entire city once the peace treaty was signed.[6] Ulbricht much preferred this solution over closing the sector border. He showed in his press conference that he expected control over both halves of the city without a physical barrier between them.

In the press conference, Ulbricht outlined his own vision for the future of West Berlin:

> The free city of West Berlin, after the conclusion of the peace treaty, will not be disturbed either by occupation forces or by agents' centers, or by radio stations of the organizers of the Cold War, or by other measures which might serve the preparation of war. That is to say, West Berlin must not be used . . . against the interests of the German Democratic Republic and the Socialist states. . . . West Berlin is truly to be a neutral city.[7]

East Germans and East Berliners who heard Ulbricht's press conference knew exactly what he meant. Things would change, and not for the better. They knew that they had better get out fast if they wanted to be able to get out at all.

Many West Berliners wondered whether Kennedy had been as tough as he had needed to be with Khrushchev. They told us in the U.S. Mission that Ulbricht's words showed his confidence that he could change the very character of West Berlin. They reinforced the inclination of their friends and relatives in East Berlin and East Germany to come to the West while it was still possible.

German observers who noticed the dramatic increase in the number of refugees began to describe it as "*Torschlusspanik*," a panicky race to get through the exits to the West before those exits closed forever. More than 100,000 East Germans had already fled during the first five months of 1961. More than 20,000 fled in June and, after the summit, more than 30,000 in July. By the beginning of August, the figure was to rise to over 1,500 a day and to 2,500 a day on weekends.

The aircraft flying through the air corridors from Berlin to West Germany were so full of refugees that extra flights had to be added to carry them. Khrushchev's and Ulbricht's threats were driving people out faster than ever. If Ulbricht was doing it intentionally in order to force Khrushchev's hand, he was certainly succeeding. But, whatever his motive, he could see the demoralizing effect of the refugee statistics on his own dedicated Communist cadres. He could even see some of them joining the exodus. He faced a real and urgent problem.

Around the end of June, therefore, Ulbricht invited Soviet ambassador Mikhail Pervukhin for an urgent and secret meeting in his private villa. He did not want the ambassador to be seen coming to his office. He told the ambassador that the flow of refugees had become intolerable and risked destabilizing the GDR, and he "declined all responsibility" for the effects of the continuing open border in Berlin.[8] Ulbricht told Pervukhin that refugee flight through West Berlin had stripped entire East German counties of doctors and qualified technicians. In some factories, workers did not know whether a full new shift would arrive the next morning or not. Many workers were beginning to get restless.

Trying to make sure that Pervukhin fully understood the urgency of his plea, Ulbricht warned that there might be an uprising against the GDR regime—as there had been in 1953—if the border was not closed soon. He had noticed the first signs of rebellion, although the police had kept things under control by immediately jailing any real or potential agitators. He added that East German and Soviet forces might have more trouble putting down any uprising because, unlike in 1953, West Germany now had its own army. The West Germans might intervene and there could be war.

Ulbricht asked Pervukhin to inform Khrushchev personally and urgently of the situation and to warn him that Ulbricht could not guarantee that he could keep things under control. West Berlin had to be sealed off from East Berlin and East Germany as soon as possible if the GDR was to survive. Refugee flight, which Ulbricht called "*Republikflucht*" ("flight from the republic") was now more urgent than anything else.

Pervukhin rushed a report to Khrushchev. Within a few days, he replied to Ulbricht that Khrushchev agreed tentatively with Ulbricht's wish to seal the border. But Khrushchev feared that such an action would be like a "declaration of bankruptcy" for Communism. He did not want to make that kind of decision entirely by himself, especially as he still believed in Communism.[9] He informed Ulbricht that he would convene another special session of the leaders of the Warsaw Pact at which Ulbricht would have to convince those leaders.

By mid-July, Ulbricht had sent Khrushchev the text of the speech he would plan to make to the Warsaw Pact leaders. It included a proposal for sealing all borders around West Berlin. Ulbricht knew that he could not count on automatic approval because at the end of March the same Warsaw Pact leaders had rejected his plea for sealing those borders.

Ulbricht wanted to get the Warsaw Pact also to approve his plan for a peace treaty, but Khrushchev told him that he would himself decide whether Ulbricht could use that part of his presentation. If he did, then the Warsaw Pact leaders would have to decide what Ulbricht could do.[10]

While waiting, Ulbricht gave his deputy Erich Honecker the responsibility for planning and managing the border closure. He also instructed the leaders of East German security services to begin quietly collecting the materials they would need to seal off West Berlin without, of course, disclosing their purpose. By July 24, they had already assembled enough barbed wire to block off fifty-four kilometers of the border, with the material for the other ninety-two kilometers soon to be stored at secret sites. They collected the barbed wire and concrete posts from construction sites, from other civilian engineering projects, and from Soviet as well as East German military and police bases all over East Germany. Working at night or at odd hours, they moved the equipment to military and police installations closer to East Berlin.

Ulbricht also sent Honecker to Moscow in mid-July to consult about "political, diplomatic and economic preparations for the conclusion of a peace treaty." But he must have been disappointed with the visit's results, because the Soviet officials with whom Honecker met still did not know how to solve the questions. Soviet officials, Honecker reported, "have no definite ideas about the kinds of problems they will face."

Khrushchev worried about the risk of a revolt in the GDR. The Soviet army had put down uprisings in East Berlin in 1953 and in Hungary in 1956 but neither Khrushchev nor the army wanted to have to do it again. Khrushchev also wanted to make sure that the Warsaw Pact would agree with whatever he planned to do. He was not yet ready to support all of Ulbricht's ideas.[11]

To convince Khrushchev that he should sign a peace treaty as well as seal the Berlin borders, Ulbricht on July 25 sent him a study of various postwar peace treaties, including those for Italy, Hungary, Bulgaria, Romania, Finland, and Japan, as well as a detailed plan for the border closure. He made absolutely clear that he wanted both. The Soviet leader would have to decide.[12]

Kennedy Prepares

John Ausland, a member of the Berlin Task Force that Dean Rusk had assembled at the State Department, used to say that Kennedy had become "*the* Berlin Desk Officer."[13] Kennedy had learned during the Bay of Pigs episode and at the summit that he could not trust the bureaucracy, so he decided that he could not delegate Berlin. He spent much of his time reading, talking, and thinking about it.

Kennedy demanded dozens of diplomatic and military reports, estimates, and studies, often on very short notice, as he tried to master every aspect of the Berlin problem. Offices all over Washington, whether in the State Department, the Defense Department, or the CIA, were busily preparing briefing papers. So was the U.S. Mission in Berlin, where we learned to our surprise that our reports were actually going to the president himself or at least to his office.

Kennedy's cabinet members who could not reach him complained: "He's imprisoned by Berlin; that's all he thinks about."[14] Berlin was now at the center of his international strategy and his domestic standing. Kennedy brought members of his cabinet and of his White House staff to Hyannisport on weekends to think and talk about Berlin. This led to wild culture clashes, with some of Kennedy's advisers swimming around his yacht, the *Marlin*, as they tossed ideas around while Rusk remained on board in his formal suit and tie.

The words *miscalculation* and *escalation* became central to every discussion. After the Bay of Pigs, Kennedy could not dare to lose Berlin. But neither did he want a world war. He wanted to know very precisely which American interests were worth the risk of war and which were not.[15]

On June 29, Acheson delivered a second report in response to Kennedy's request after Vienna. It framed the discussion and the options more systematically and more brutally than was possible at Kennedy's yachting seminars. And it forced the president to move away from discussion toward decision.[16]

Acheson listed three "essentials," the vital U.S. interests that Kennedy needed to protect, even at the risk of war:[17]

1. The allied presence and allied [American] troops in West Berlin
2. Allied surface and air access to West Berlin
3. The freedom and viability of West Berlin.

Acheson was not the first to cite those three essentials. The State Department had first listed them after Khrushchev's ultimatum, but he was the first to bring them directly and forcefully to Kennedy's attention.[18]

Acheson recommended that Kennedy declare a national emergency, send two or three more divisions to Germany, and mobilize massive reserve forces. He wrote that Khrushchev would not be impressed by half-measures. If Soviet or East German police tried to block access to Berlin, Acheson recommended that Kennedy launch an airlift and send a task force of two or three divisions along the Autobahn to the city. If Khrushchev blocked either of those, he would risk war.

Acheson held out no hope for negotiating with the Soviets. He described diplomacy with Moscow as trying to "argue with a river." He concluded, "You can channel it; you can dam it up. But you can't argue with it."[19]

Like de Gaulle, Acheson believed that there was nothing about Berlin for the West to negotiate with Khrushchev. He thought that Khrushchev wanted to humiliate the United States on Berlin in order to destroy the Western alliance. Thus, he wrote, more than Berlin was at stake, and Khrushchev would not make any meaningful offers. Nor would he be deterred lightly.

With Ambassador Thompson taking at face value Khrushchev's words that "the matter cannot go beyond the fall or winter of this year,"[20] and thus reporting that Khrushchev would almost certainly proceed with the peace treaty in 1961, Acheson was presenting Kennedy with some life-or-death choices.

Bundy thought Acheson's recommendations were too provocative. Henry Kissinger recommended against a national emergency declaration, writing that Khrushchev would be more impressed by a broad and continued improvement in American military readiness.[21] Kissinger also continued to believe that the West should not be afraid to negotiate, but on its own terms.

Kennedy did not fully agree with any of his advisers, whether Bundy, Kissinger, or Acheson. He decided that he had to take some steps to convince Khrushchev that he could raise the stakes as well as the Soviet leader could, but he apparently did not want to alarm the American public by declaring a national emergency.

At several National Security Council meetings, Kennedy tried to split the difference, accepting Acheson's basic approach but not all his recommendations. He approved Acheson's demand for more conventional forces so that he would not be forced to use nuclear weapons at an early stage of any crisis. But he clearly worried about the political implications of turning the United States into a garrison state.

Acheson did not make himself popular with Kennedy by going around Washington complaining that "this nation is without leadership" because the president did not immediately accept all his recommendations. Bundy asked him to temper his remarks, although without much success.[22] But Kennedy still wanted to take Acheson seriously because he was the only person trying to confront Khrushchev instead of looking for new ways to yield. Kennedy respected the Soviet experts and their recommendation to negotiate, but he did not want to hear only one side of any argument.

After three NSC meetings, Kennedy made up his mind, and he announced his decision in a speech on July 25. Ironically, the speech fell on the same day as Ulbricht's memorandum (then still secret) urging Khrushchev to act.[23] In his speech, Kennedy called West Berlin "the great testing place of Western courage and will." He reiterated the three essentials that Acheson had listed: allied (American) troops in West Berlin, access to West Berlin, and the freedom of West Berlin. He spoke in a firm and determined tone, making clear that the United States would vigorously resist any Soviet action against those essentials. A Soviet or East German effort to drive the allies out of West Berlin would be met by force.

But Kennedy tied American rights and American protection only to *West* Berlin, not to all of Berlin. He said nothing about allied occupation rights over Berlin as a whole. The United States, he implied, would not resist Soviet actions against any other element of the allied position outside West Berlin, such as freedom of movement across the entire city. Kennedy's job was to protect U.S. rights, not the flight of East German refugees.

In a remarkable shift from his upbeat inaugural rhetoric, Kennedy noted, "I could not realize, nor could any man realize who does not bear the burdens of this office, how heavy and constant would be those burdens." He asked for support and prayers from his listeners, appearing to show his own exhaustion with the Berlin problem even as he tried to find his way out. The speech must have confirmed Khrushchev's view that Kennedy was in over his head.[24]

Around that same time, Robert Kennedy was meeting almost daily with his Soviet intelligence contact, Georgi Bolshakov, trying to tell him that the president was ready to face war if Khrushchev tried to interfere with U.S. rights in Berlin. But Bolshakov continued to repeat that Mikhail Menshikov, the Soviet ambassador in Washington, was telling Khrushchev the opposite.[25]

When the Berliners and the Germans, East and West, listened to Kennedy's speech, they interpreted it as a sign that Kennedy might be ready to defend U.S. rights but would not object if Khrushchev stopped the refugee flow. Egon Bahr, Willy Brandt's closest assistant, said: "This is almost an invitation for the Soviets to do what they want with the Eastern sector."[26] Brandt later wrote, "We did not regard these formulations as wholly satisfactory."[27] He and Bahr said that Kennedy's comments meant the end of refugee flight.

Bundy later admitted it was likely that Kennedy's July 25 speech may have given "advance encouragement" to Khrushchev by assuring him that Kennedy would not object if Khrushchev blocked refugees. Bundy wrote that Kennedy knew—and accepted—that Khrushchev would need to do something to stem the refugee flow. Bundy even admitted that Kennedy's speech might well have made it "easier" for Khrushchev to close the border.

Contemplating his options, Kennedy told his adviser Walt Rostow that Khrushchev might build a wall to stop refugees: "And we won't be able to prevent it. I can hold the alliance together to defend West Berlin, but I cannot act to keep East Berlin open."[28] When he referred to the "alliance," Kennedy was recognizing that Macmillan wanted no commitments in East Berlin and that even de Gaulle did not state what he would do in any contingency. So he wanted to be precise as well as limited in his commitment, and he was both.

Kennedy wanted no Soviet miscalculation. American actions were designed "to make clear our determination and our ability to defend our rights at all costs, and to meet all levels of aggressor pressure with whatever levels of force are required." But Kennedy had gone further than he or his advisers may have realized. By limiting American obligations to West Berlin only, he was putting an end to the four-power status of the city. He was accepting in advance whatever division of the city Khrushchev or Ulbricht might be planning. He thus gave them what amounted to very explicit instructions.

Kennedy concluded with an effort to rally support:

> I hear it said that West Berlin is militarily untenable. And so was Bastogne. And so, in fact, was Stalingrad. Any dangerous spot is tenable if men—brave men—will make it so.

Kennedy also showed his determination by raising the U.S. defense budget, calling up thousands of reservists, and lengthening the duty period for reservists.

Yuri Andropov, the modernizing Soviet Communist leader who later supported Mikhail Gorbachev's rise to power, complained privately that Khrushchev had forced Kennedy into an arms race that the Soviet Union could not afford and could not win.[29]

East Germans read Kennedy's speech exactly as Bahr and Brandt had read it. They began fleeing in record numbers. We Americans who lived in Berlin also knew that Kennedy had given Ulbricht and Khrushchev the green light to block refugees. But we could not get any precise information about where, when, or how they would do it. We could only wait.

Five days after Kennedy's speech, on July 30, U.S. Senator J. William Fulbright, chairman of the U.S. Senate Foreign Relations Committee, said in an interview: "The truth of the matter is, I think, that the Russians have the power to close [the Berlin sector border] . . . without violating any treaty." He added, "I don't understand why the East Germans don't close their border because I think they have the right to do it at any time."[30] Bundy sent press coverage about the Fulbright interview to Kennedy with a comment about "the helpful impact of Senator Fulbright's remarks."[31] Bundy's comment suggested that the senator had coordinated his interview in advance with the White House. Indeed, a week later, Kennedy refused to distance himself from those remarks when he was asked about them during a press conference. Fulbright had obviously been speaking for the president.

Ulbricht reacted immediately. On the very next day, July 31, he cited Fulbright's statement to Khrushchev as a sign that the Soviets could close the air corridors between Berlin and West Germany in order to stop refugee flight. Khrushchev refused to do that. But he agreed with Ulbricht that something had to be done about the refugees, even if not in the air corridors.[32]

Accurately, if perhaps uncharitably, Rusk said that the Germans were "nervous as cats" and "biting their fingernails."[33]

Khrushchev Decides

Khrushchev appeared at a military parade and rally on June 21, a date of great significance because it marked the twentieth anniversary of Hitler's attack on the Soviet Union. He clearly wanted to show that he was ready for a fight.

A Soviet marshal told the rally that only Soviet troops were in Berlin by right of arms. Soviet forces had given the Western allies their occupation sectors after the end of the war. They therefore had a legitimate prior claim to the city as a whole. The Western allies had no claim of any kind.

Even before he had left Vienna, Khrushchev had told Austrian Chancellor Bruno Kreisky:

Kennedy still doesn't quite understand the times in which we live. He doesn't yet fully understand the realignment of forces, and he still lives by the policies of his predecessors—especially as far as the German question is concerned.[34]

Khrushchev would now show Kennedy the new reality. He instructed the Soviet Communist Party Central Committee to pass a resolution that the Vienna summit "demonstrated the wisdom of taking a hard line on the Berlin question." On July 8, in a speech to the graduates of the Soviet military academy, he announced a one-third increase in the Soviet defense budget.[35]

Khrushchev told his son Sergei that Kennedy must not be allowed "to step on our toes." Although Kennedy had been a "serious negotiating partner," Khrushchev said he had no intention of retreating "one iota." [36] One expert on the Soviet Union who later read all of Khrushchev's comments on Kennedy concluded that Khrushchev had developed "a mixture of scorn and impatience" toward the president.[37]

Calling Kennedy a "son of a bitch,"[38] Khrushchev criticized Kennedy's Vienna suggestion to divide the world between the United States and the Soviet Union as a "provocative proposal." Given Soviet support for liberation movements in Africa and Asia, he could not accept it. As his son reported, "he lost no time going on the offensive."

Khrushchev thought he had little choice:

> We parted in a state of heightened tension. I warned the president that if we did not meet with any understanding on the part of the United States on the question of concluding a peace treaty, we would decide this question unilaterally and sign a treaty with the German Democratic Republic and then change the legal norms of access by the Western powers to West Berlin. I exaggerated the situation in order to put the Americans in an untenable position and force them to admit that our proposals made good sense. Otherwise a conflict would occur.[39]

Rather frustrated, Khrushchev concluded: "In a word, we utilized all the means available to give our opponents the impression that if they did not behave sensibly and agree with us, then we would carry out what we had said." But he said that allied access to Berlin was the subject on which Kennedy "was least likely to come to an agreement."[40]

Khrushchev recognized that Kennedy "could not permit himself to be portrayed" as having given way under pressure.[41] As he said to his son, Kennedy was not ready to capitulate, no matter how beaten up he might feel. Khrushchev later admitted that he had been impressed by Kennedy's readiness to stake U.S. security on the future of Berlin.[42]

Thus, as he was getting ready for a battle with Kennedy, Khrushchev had his doubts. Pervukhin warned him that Ulbricht had become increasingly impatient and irresponsible. He also warned that the GDR would not be able to overcome the effects of the expected Western economic blockade after a peace treaty. Khrushchev would need to help economically and perhaps in other ways.[43]

Khrushchev did not want to risk the entire Soviet empire for the sake of Walter Ulbricht.[44] He also feared that a West German embargo against East Germany might force him to sell perhaps as many as 400 tons of gold in order to make up for the loss that West German trade represented to the GDR. He could not afford such a sum.[45]

Khrushchev worried whether or not he had read Kennedy correctly. More gravely, he increasingly wondered whether he could trust Ulbricht with control over the access routes and especially the air corridors, the authority that Ulbricht wanted most out of a peace treaty. Ulbricht could provoke a crisis whenever he wanted, whether it suited Khrushchev or not, and Khrushchev would be forced to support him or appear weak before the Chinese and others.[46]

De Gaulle's analysis was bearing fruit. As Ulbricht became more assertive, Khrushchev became more cautious. He faced three risks: a war that the Soviet Union could not win; a potentially enormous financial drain; and, perhaps most worrisome, the risk of yielding one of the most potentially explosive problems in Europe to a man whose judgment he increasingly questioned.

The climactic summer of 1961 kept rolling forward relentlessly. Every day increased the pressure for decision. Khrushchev was not sure how to finish what he had started. The ever-widening flood of East German refugees, now moving at a pace of over half a million a year, was setting the agenda. So was the level of rhetoric on both sides.

The ball was in Khrushchev's court. After July 25, he could read Kennedy's speech telling him what to do and what not to do. He could also read Ulbricht's memorandum, telling him to do everything.

The German problem—specifically the Berlin problem—preoccupied Khrushchev all the time just as it preoccupied Kennedy. The premier said that he "spent a great deal of time trying to think of a way out." Sergei recalled that his father had nightmares about it.[47]

As Khrushchev looked around for his way out, he found three clues to a solution. First was Ulbricht's message to Pervukhin that the refugee flow was the top priority. It might bring down the GDR regime. As Khrushchev himself wrote later, a peace treaty would not have closed the border as soon as necessary.[48] Second was Kennedy's July 25 speech, which clearly said that Khrushchev could do what he liked in East Berlin or between the two halves of the city. Third was an earlier West German warning that any decision to sign a peace treaty with the GDR might result in a West German trade embargo against all of Eastern Europe.

Kennedy's words read very much like the division of the world that he had proposed in Vienna, except that this time he proposed only the division of Berlin and Germany. Khrushchev had rejected the division of the world, but he could perhaps see some logic in Kennedy's proposal for dividing Berlin and Germany. After all, if Berlin and Germany were divided and the refugee flow were stopped, Khrushchev would at least preserve the GDR.

Even before the Warsaw Pact meeting, Khrushchev had already decided that he would need to divide Berlin. He had told Pervukhin to send him Berlin maps with the main streets and the separate occupation sectors clearly marked. Khrushchev also decided to see for himself. He wrote in his memoirs that he had gone to Berlin incognito and had toured the city with only the Soviet commandant for company in order to get a better idea of what could be done there.[49]

Meeting with Ulbricht, Khrushchev showed him the map of Berlin and told Ulbricht that he would agree to cut the city along the sector border.

Ulbricht reacted enthusiastically: "This is the answer!"

He had still not given up on his peace treaty, but he needed the border closure immediately and even desperately.[50]

Khrushchev and Ulbricht decided that they would seal the border during the early morning of August 13, a Sunday, when there would be little traffic and few workers going back and forth. Khrushchev joked that the number thirteen was considered unlucky in the West but "for us and for the whole socialist camp it would be a very lucky day indeed."[51]

Khrushchev and Ulbricht still needed to win over the Warsaw Pact members. At a secret session of the top leaders, Ulbricht presented a forty-three-page paper and made a fervent plea. To hit his listeners in their pocketbooks, Ulbricht warned that the GDR could not continue to export industrial goods to Eastern Europe if refugees continued to flee. He also asserted that Adenauer was sending spies through West Berlin into East Germany and Eastern Europe. Those were the main reasons, he argued, to seal the border, and to seal it urgently.[52] Citing Kennedy's July 25 speech and Fulbright's July 30 comments as proof that the Americans would not resist, Khrushchev supported Ulbricht, but Ulbricht also insisted that only a peace treaty could bring true security and stability to central Europe. Closing the border would represent nothing more than a first step. The entire problem of West Berlin needed to be solved, and it needed to be solved soon.

The Warsaw Pact leaders gave their consent to closing the sector borders around West Berlin. Most of them did so unhappily, for they complained that it would be a black eye for Communism. They had not liked it in March and they did not like it now, but they recognized that it had become necessary. Several still ascribed the entire refugee problem to Ulbricht's Stalinist style of leadership.

Polish leader Wladyslaw Gomulka, Antonin Novotny of Czechoslovakia, and Janos Kadar of Hungary made clear that they did not favor a peace treaty because it might cut off their trade with the West and particularly with West Germany. They all insisted that they could not help Ulbricht if his policies led to an economic crisis. Khrushchev was taken aback by their refusal to support a fellow Communist leader, but he could not change their minds.

Nor did the Warsaw Pact leaders agree to all the controls over the access routes that Ulbricht wanted to impose. They feared those might provoke a Western and especially a West German economic embargo that would damage their economies. They were much more worried about losing their trade with West Germany than about U.S. military measures, and they were furious at Ulbricht for having put them into such a bind.

The Warsaw Pact meeting showed the dividing line between Ulbricht and his allies. He wanted the Wall as the first step to a peace treaty and to his takeover of West Berlin, but the East Europeans wanted the Wall to make a peace treaty unnecessary.

Khrushchev then gave Ulbricht another clear instruction: no permanent barriers were to be built in Berlin until after it was obvious that the Western allies would not react to the barbed wire that Ubricht planned as a first step. He also told Ulbricht that the barbed wire was to be pulled back some 100 meters from the border if Western troops challenged the barriers. Khrushchev later stated that he had personally never favored sealing the border with anything more than barbed wire. The Wall that Ulbricht built, said Khrushchev, had been a "purely German invention."[53]

In addition, Khrushchev ordered Ulbricht not to go "one millimeter" beyond the border closure that the Warsaw Pact had agreed to support. Ulbricht would have to wait on the peace treaty until later, perhaps after the Soviet Communist Party congress in October.

Khrushchev and the Warsaw Pact leaders thus did not give Ulbricht what he wanted most, the authority to force Western air traffic to land at Schönefeld. Although Khrushchev felt certain that Kennedy would not object to the sector border closure, he feared Kennedy's potential reaction to any controls over air traffic. And, like the East Europeans, he could not afford a West German economic embargo.

If Khrushchev really wanted to enforce Ulbricht's wish for allied aircraft to divert to Schönefeld, he might have to threaten to have Soviet fighters shoot down a civilian jetliner and he might then even have to do it. He chose not to take that risk, although he did start to organize some military units to practice putting balloons into the glide paths for West Berlin airports.[54]

Khrushchev continued to have high hopes for Communism and for the superiority of the Communist system over capitalism. He thought that the GDR with closed borders would still become "a showcase of moral, political and material achievement" that would win the competition with West Germany and even bring back persons who had fled earlier. But he had to get from here to there.

By a bizarre coincidence, the American, British, French, and West German foreign ministers met in Paris from August 4 to 6, right after the Warsaw Pact meeting. One of the American delegates said that Kennedy wanted to move toward "negotiations leading to a new contractual agreement on the status of Berlin and access thereto." Another spoke about the possibility of exchanging some form of recognition of the GDR for "a further period of stability on Berlin."

The new British foreign minister, Lord Home, was fully ready to go along with Dean Rusk on any ideas for a diplomatic solution to the Berlin problem. But French Foreign Minister Maurice Couve de Murville, acting on de Gaulle's personal instructions, would not agree to any negotiations. He even refused to telephone de Gaulle when Rusk asked if he would at least try to urge de Gaulle to change his position. He said that one did not telephone the president of the republic.

The German, Heinrich von Brentano, took no firm stand. He did not want to be difficult because this was the first time he had been invited to join the Western group. The foreign ministers reached no conclusion.

The West German publisher Axel Springer had informed von Brentano and U.S. ambassador Walter Dowling at the end of July that he had received information about plans by Ulbricht to draw a "perfect curtain" across the center of Berlin.[55] There is no indication on the record that this was discussed by the foreign ministers at their August meeting.

The foreign ministers did agree, however, that any steps Ulbricht or Khrushchev might take to block the refugee flow, or any other steps they might take in East Berlin, would be defensive and would not be worth the risk of war. They and Khrushchev were speaking the same language, and reports of their discussions probably soon reached the Soviet leader.[56]

Watching and Waiting

In Berlin itself, Brandt and other Berlin officials felt utterly powerless. They all knew that *something* would happen, but they did not know what. They could see that refugees were fleeing East Germany at the fastest rate ever. The *"Torschlusspanik"* was operating at full force. They knew this would become intolerable, but did not know when or how Khrushchev and Ulbricht would try to stop it.

The Americans and their allies in West Berlin felt the same way. We met almost around the clock with each other, with intelligence officers, with West Berlin police officials, and with journalists or others who might be able to learn what was being decided in East Berlin. We called the intelligence meetings "prayer sessions" because we often felt that we needed divine guidance to know what might happen. We sifted for clues in East German and Soviet official statements and newspaper editorials.

We knew that thousands of East Berliners were spending their weekends with relatives and friends in West Berlin because they were afraid the border would soon be closed, but we had no reason to believe that they had any special insights. They were just scared that they might be trapped in East Berlin.

We speculated on what Ulbricht and Khrushchev might do. Because of all the Soviet talk about a peace treaty, we wondered if Khrushchev might sign such a treaty and try to block American access to West Berlin. That was what we feared the most because it might well mean war. We also recognized that Khrushchev and Ulbricht might try to seal all access to West Berlin, but we thought they might hesitate because it would take a major effort. They would have to close over 100 miles of borders around the city. We could see some evidence of construction material being moved around, but we could not tell if it would be used to build a border in or around Berlin or perhaps to seal the access routes. Anything seemed possible.

Like everyone else, we wondered, watched, and waited. But we knew that, whatever might happen, it would have to happen soon if the GDR was to survive.

Khrushchev and Ulbricht Get Ready

Even after Kennedy's speech, Khrushchev still had his doubts about sealing the borders around West Berlin. He feared an allied reaction. To make Western leaders hesitate, he did what he could to frighten them. During a speech on August 9, he cited "the orange groves of Italy" and "the olive trees of Greece" among the targets that would be hit during a European nuclear war.[57] Two days later, at a Romanian-Soviet "friendship" meeting in Moscow, he said that if the imperialists should unleash a war, hundreds of millions might be killed: "They will force us, in self-defense, to deal crushing blows not only against the territories of the principal countries but also against innocents."

Khrushchev told the British ambassador, Frank Roberts, that eight hydrogen bombs would destroy England. Roberts, showing fine British aplomb, replied that six might perhaps suffice. But he warned that British bombs would then destroy many of Khrushchev's cities.[58]

To show off Soviet missile power as an additional deterrent to the West, Khrushchev moved up a planned orbital flight of one of his astronauts, Gherman Titov, to take place on August 7 instead of the originally planned date in late August. That flight, in which Titov circled the globe seventeen times in twenty-five hours, was an even greater achievement than Gagarin's. It reinforced the message that Moscow not only had powerful missiles but had mastered the precision needed to launch them into multiple orbits and presumably at selected Western targets.

Khrushchev reinforced Soviet forces along the border with West Germany and around Berlin. He ordered several additional divisions of Soviet forces, including one armored division, into the immediate surroundings of Berlin. Khrushchev wanted Western intelligence to notice those units and to recognize that Moscow could react with deadly force to any Western military moves.[59] He wanted the allies to think twice before mounting any military reaction to the border closing or before supporting any revolt that might happen in East Germany. As for Berlin itself, Khrushchev planned to encircle the city with "an iron ring."[60] Soviet troops would make up that ring, and Ulbricht's police and army would act inside it.

To show that he would keep firm control over all of East Germany as well as over Ulbricht, Khrushchev called one of Russia's most notoriously tough-minded officers, Marshal Ivan Konev, out of retirement to assume command of Soviet forces in East Germany. Konev, whose gruff manner and stocky build had earned him the nickname "the Tank," had helped to conquer Berlin in 1945. He was known to despise all Germans.

Konev brought with him another Soviet general who, in Khrushchev's words announcing the appointment, had "experience in Hungary." This was the Soviet leader's way of letting everybody know that the Soviets would deal firmly with any East German uprising, as they had dealt with the Hungarian revolt in 1956. Nonetheless, Khrushchev told Konev privately: "Not one shot without permission from Moscow."[61]

To underline Khrushchev's warning further, Western military liaison officers were invited to the Soviet military headquarters near Berlin on August 10. Much to their surprise, Konev appeared. He said: "My name is Konev. You may have heard of me." Then he smiled. He told the Western officers that they could relax because "whatever is going to happen in the near future, your rights will not be touched."[62]

Konev's arrival showed that Moscow would take complete charge of whatever was to happen. Nothing that Khrushchev could have done would have told the Western allies more sharply that they were facing a determined Soviet effort under a commander who would do whatever was necessary to win and who would not tolerate dissent.

Konev did not spend time only with Westerners. He had come mainly to coordinate with Ulbricht and with East German military and police units. He went carefully over all the plans for East German as well as Soviet forces. He wanted to make sure that everything was ready and would be executed properly, and that everybody understood who was in charge.

Even so, Khrushchev remained nervous. He wanted to be informed regularly as the preparations advanced. Recognizing the danger of leaks, he and Ulbricht insisted that there should be no telephone calls or cables about the border closure. Everything was to be handled by handwritten letters and through instructions sent by courier. There was a crisis atmosphere in Khrushchev's immediate office and in the Soviet foreign and defense ministries until they could be sure that Kennedy would not react to the border closure.[63]

On the afternoon of August 12, having returned secretly from his "vacation" in Moscow, Pervukhin had a last meeting with Ulbricht to review their plans. Konev joined the meeting. Ulbricht told them that he would begin by stringing barbed wire along the border and then, if the allies did not act during the first few days, would put up a concrete wall. That would delay other East German construction plans but would be worth the effort. The three agreed that Ulbricht's militia and police would cut off all access to West Berlin and that the East German army would support them in the first instance if necessary. Soviet troops would act as a reserve force and would fight only if needed, but would be ready to help if there was any civil disturbance.[64]

Ulbricht told Pervukhin that he had invited all senior East German politicians to his house for a private dinner that evening. He would brief them for the first time about the operation to seal off West Berlin the following morning. He would then make sure that none of them left his house in case they might give the alarm to their friends or to people in the West. Or, perhaps to make sure they did not also flee.[65]

Commenting on his plans to imprison his own government on the night before the border closure, Ulbricht observed with a wry smile:

"*Sicher ist sicher*" ("Better safe than sorry").

Pervukhin, who understood perfectly, agreed.[66]

To make sure that the forces assigned to seal off West Berlin would carry out their orders, Ulbricht did not use militia, police, or border guards from East Berlin to string the barbed wire. Instead, he ordered special units sent up from Saxony. They would feel no loyalty to the Berliners and would not even know where they were or what exactly they were doing. Berliners later called the Saxons the "fifth occupying power."

Early on the night of August 12, Soviet military units in the Berlin area began to roll into alert positions around the city. As Konev had planned, allied forces could hear the rumble of the Russian tanks and armored cars. They would know that the Soviets were ready for anything.

To keep the entire operation secret, Ulbricht gave it a code name. That code name was "Rose."

CHAPTER SEVEN

❦

"The East Germans Have Done Us a Favor"

Early on Sunday morning, August 13, 1961, I received a call at home from the U.S. Mission duty officer in West Berlin. He told me that something was happening in East Berlin and asked me to take a look. I decided to drive into East Berlin. I took along Frank Trinka, a colleague from my office. We went in my car, a Mercedes 190-SL, because it had a convertible top and we could see more than in an official sedan.

Trapped

Dawn had broken early, as it does in August in northern Europe, and the sky was already half-light at three o'clock in the morning. We decided to go into East Berlin by the most direct route across Potsdamer Platz, a wide square that had never been rebuilt after the war. There we found some East German Volkspolizei ("people's police," known as Vopos) and Betriebskampfgruppen (factory militia) busily unrolling barbed wire across the square. They had just started their work and they had unrolled only one strand. They stopped us and said we could not pass.

I told the Vopos that we were Western allied occupation officials from the American Mission in West Berlin, as they could see by looking at our official license plates. We had the right to go anywhere in Berlin and we wanted to talk to a Soviet officer who would give us clearance. We wanted the barbed wire removed so we could get through. The police officer hesitated, but he evidently had orders not to interfere with the movement of Western allied officials. He ordered the one roll of barbed wire to be pulled aside so that we could enter East Berlin.

We then drove around East Berlin for about an hour, seeing a concentration of many East German police cars and trucks close to the center of the city around Alexanderplatz. We saw what might have been Soviet army cars in the distance as well as a few startled Berliners wondering what was going on at that hour. We saw a lot of activity along the sector border. Vopos were unloading concrete posts and rolls of barbed wire from military trucks and were setting up a barbed wire barrier along the border. They totally blocked access across any streets that went from East to West.

We went into the main railroad station in East Berlin, Bahnhof Friedrichstrasse, through which dozens of elevated trains and subways would normally roll into and out of West Berlin every hour, even at night. There we found scenes of utter chaos, bewilderment, and despair. So many people jammed the station that we had trouble getting in and then making our way up to the train platforms. Armed East German police were blocking the platforms, not letting any passengers get past them. Other police were ordering passengers to get out of any trains headed toward West Berlin. Many people, obviously East Berliners and East Germans, were sitting on suitcases or makeshift bundles. They were weeping uncontrollably.

We had no trouble figuring out what it all meant. Ulbricht had decided to solve his refugee problem by closing off access to West Berlin. Of all his options, as we had discussed them in the U.S. Mission for months, he had chosen this one. He needed to do *something*, and this was what he had done. We picked up a copy of Ulbricht's official decree. It listed thirteen crossing points that were still open to leave East Berlin, but only for West Berliners, West Germans, foreign civilians, and Western allied forces. It listed no crossing points for East Berliners or East Germans. The decree asserted that the measures would protect the "socialist achievements" of the German Democratic Republic against Western smugglers and agents but would not affect allied rights. The steps were allegedly taken in response to a Warsaw Pact request to establish order along the borders of West Berlin and to prevent "subversive activities."

Having learned what we needed to learn, we decided to return to West Berlin. We tried to go back across Potsdamer Platz but that was impossible. Even if the police had wanted to clear the way for us, it was much too late. There must have been at least ten rolls of barbed wire stretched across the square and across streets leading into and out of it. There was no sense trying to get them removed. Only a few Vopos, heavily armed, remained.

We decided to go out through the Brandenburg Gate. We found Pariser Platz, the East Berlin square facing the gate, jammed with East German police and military vehicles, armored cars, and a number of trucks with water cannon on top. We maneuvered through them to get to the gate itself. We saw no Soviet vehicles.

Once again, Vopos blocked our way at the sector border, and we repeated that we were allied officials who had the right to go anywhere in Berlin. We asked to see a Soviet officer. One policeman who had blocked us went into a small office at the gate and came out in a couple of minutes to tell us that we could proceed. We were told that we had been cleared by a member of the East German Communist Party Central Committee who was in charge at the gate.

Ulbricht had obviously decided not to provoke any problem with the allies at that point. He would not go one millimeter beyond what Khrushchev and the Warsaw Pact had instructed. Allied officials could leave East Berlin although ordinary East Germans could not.

Soviet forces had stayed well back, as Khrushchev and Konev had ordered, although their tanks and armored vehicles had surrounded Berlin on all sides during the night. Konev had apparently sent some observer teams into East Berlin to make sure that everything was going well and to be prepared to call for help if the population revolted or if there were any Western military moves. But we saw no Soviet forces taking any direct part in the operation to seal the borders.[1]

Returning to West Berlin, we drove to the U.S. Mission to make a report. That report and some early German news wire flashes alerted the State Department in Washington that Ulbricht was sealing the border between East and West Berlin. The report also went to senior officials of the three Western allied missions in Berlin as they got together that same morning to discuss what they should do about the East German border closure.

The Western officials quickly realized that they could not try to remove the barbed wire. They would have had to bring soldiers and tanks up to the sector border and they had no authority to do that. None of them thought they could get approval from their capitals for it. They did not even think that on a Sunday morning they could get approval from their capitals for a formal protest to the Soviet Embassy in East Berlin. Nonetheless, they did agree that they should issue a public protest to the press and they agreed on a brief statement asserting that the East German border closure was a violation of allied rights in Berlin. They thought they could issue that statement without clearing it with their home offices.

Washington and Hyannisport

By then, a few staff members of the German desk at the State Department had been called about the cables from Berlin. One, who had been woken up around two AM (eight AM Berlin time), decided to go back to sleep for a couple of hours before going to the department. Nobody had expected Ulbricht to move at this moment, although they all knew that he would have to act at some point.

American intelligence agencies, including the CIA, had warned in general terms that Ulbricht would try to stop refugees, but none expected the borders to be blocked on that day, at that time, and in that way.

West German intelligence agencies had done no better. Egon Bahr, Mayor Willy Brandt's closest adviser, noted with disgust that the German agencies had even written on Friday, August 11, that no particular developments were expected that weekend.[2]

Neither allied nor German contingency plans had concentrated on a border closure around Berlin because they worried mainly about Khrushchev's threat to sign a peace treaty and to block Western access to Berlin. U.S. State Department offices had made all kinds of preparations for a Soviet blockade on the Autobahn or in the air corridors, but none for any East German actions in Berlin itself. When John Ausland looked through the files for any agreed allied plans that he could use, he found the file for "Division of Berlin" empty.

President Kennedy found this episode so frustrating that he later called a member of the Berlin Task Force and asked: "Why, with all those contingency plans, do you never have one for what actually happens?"[3]

Even without a contingency plan, the officers of the German desk at the State Department believed that there should be a firm allied protest to the Soviets against Ulbricht's action and perhaps even some kind of military reaction such as troop patrols at the sector border. They wanted to show the Soviets, the Berliners, and others that the Americans would not passively accept the new rules, which violated allied rights even if they did not explicitly block allied access to East Berlin.

But Foy Kohler, the assistant secretary of state for European affairs, who was called at home about the news from Berlin, said: "The East Germans have done us a favor." He would not even come to the office. He told the desk officers to play it cool and that the State Department would make no rash statements.

Dean Rusk reacted the same way. He came to the department, as he did most Sunday mornings, to look over cables and press reports. But he believed that any Western reaction to the border closure would run the risk of escalation. He supported Kohler. In addition, Rusk gave strict instructions that no allied statement was to be made in Berlin, not even the public protest that the allied missions had coordinated. He later approved a tepid Washington statement explaining that Ulbricht's action was aimed at East, not West, Berliners. It said nothing about any violation of allied rights. Shortly after noon, he left the State Department to attend a Washington Senators baseball game.

He left red-faced officials at the U.S. Mission in Berlin to explain the mute American acceptance of Ulbricht's action to their British and French colleagues as well as to Brandt and to the Berliners.[4] Our allies were kind enough not to comment, but we knew what they were thinking. When the State Department German desk officers told us that Rusk had gone to a baseball game after hearing about the border closure, we hoped desperately that Brandt would not learn of it. If he did, he decided never to talk to us about it.

Kennedy also reacted with glacial calm. He was spending the weekend at Hyannisport. When his military aide, Major General Chester ("Ted") Clifton, called to tell him what was happening, he felt relieved because Khrushchev had solved his most urgent problem without trying to cut allied access or to violate allied rights as Kennedy saw them. Khrushchev had not done what Kennedy had feared but had followed the intent of the president's July 25 instructions. Kennedy asked: "Why would Khrushchev put up a wall if he really intended to seize West Berlin? There wouldn't be any need for a wall if he occupied the whole city. This is his way out of his predicament."[5]

Kennedy told his assistant Kenneth O'Donnell that the border closure was "not a very nice solution but a wall is a hell of a lot better than a war."[6] He recognized that Khrushchev had not carried out the threats that he had shouted in Vienna. By closing the border between East and West Berlin he had taken a minimal step compared to signing a peace treaty, making West Berlin a "demilitarized free city," or blocking access.

Kennedy was wrong to assume that Khrushchev had not violated Western rights. On July 7, 1945, the military governors of Germany, including U.S. general Lucius Clay and Soviet marshal Georgi Zhukov, had agreed on free and unrestricted movement between all the occupation sectors in Berlin. This had been confirmed in the 1949 four-power agreement that ended the Berlin blockade, but it had been largely forgotten. Kennedy could hardly be blamed for not knowing it, but the State Department experts on Berlin should have known it and told him, even if they believed he would choose to do nothing about it.[7]

Other Western political leaders were also on vacation. Prime Minister Harold Macmillan was playing golf and shooting grouse in Scotland. He reacted even more calmly than Kennedy. But he provoked fury in Germany and Berlin when he commented that the excitement about the closing of the Berlin sector border had been all got up by the press and that "nobody will do anything about it." He had to offer lengthy explanations to Chancellor Adenauer because many Germans thought his comment again showed his already obvious disdain for his German ally's fate.[8]

Charles de Gaulle said nothing. He did not challenge Kennedy's and Macmillan's decision. He must have felt that the Americans and especially Macmillan were playing into his hands by disappointing and angering the Germans and the Berliners. He instructed French forces in Berlin to do nothing more than the other allies were doing and to make no military moves except on instructions from Paris.[9]

Konrad Adenauer and Willy Brandt were fighting a bitter campaign against each other for the West German election coming up in September. Adenauer wondered whether he should go to Berlin, but decided against it because he feared that his presence might stir up riots and perhaps a revolt in East Berlin. Moreover, the American ambassador, Walter Dowling, urged him not to go.[10]

In West Berlin

Brandt and Bahr flew to Berlin hurriedly on Sunday morning from a campaign swing through West Germany. They wanted to react to the new barriers but could do nothing without allied support. They could not understand why the three allied commandants had not reacted at all to the barbed wire snaking through the center of what was officially an allied occupation city.

When Brandt met in the late morning with the Western allied commandants, they said, "Our respective capitals have been informed. Our governments will make the necessary decisions." Without instructions, they were paralyzed. They mainly wanted Brandt to keep things calm and to make sure that there was no attack by furious West Berliners against the new barriers. Brandt told the commandants they should at least send jeep patrols to the sector border to let the Berliners know that the allies were concerned and that the Berliners were not alone, but the commandants said that they had no authority for that. Brandt also asked for a vigorous protest to the Soviets and to all the Warsaw Pact states who had instructed Ulbricht to control the West Berlin borders, but the commandants again said they could not act without instructions.

Brandt said, "*Dann lacht der ganze Osten*" ("Then the whole East will laugh") when he realized that the West would do absolutely nothing. He had to restrain his temper throughout the whole meeting as the commandants vetoed every one of his suggestions. Bahr denounced the allied reaction as "*lasch*" (feeble).[11]

Brandt and Bahr found it particularly galling that the Western powers, which were always asserting their authority as occupiers in West Berlin against many actions that the West Berlin authorities wanted to take, so meekly accepted and followed the rules laid down by Ulbricht. They referred to the three Western commandants as "*Scheisser*."[12]

Brandt worried that West Berlin crowds might indeed strike out against the new border barriers. He feared that any incident could provoke popular riots in East Berlin and perhaps some shooting by East German police.

Brandt had good reason to worry. As the day advanced and as more and more Berliners on both sides of the border learned what had happened, their reaction turned ugly. More than three thousand West Berliners gathered opposite the Brandenburg Gate. Others went to Potsdamer Platz as well as to other points at the border. They shouted insults (such as *Schwein*) at the East German police. They began to throw bottles and stones at the Vopos. West Berlin police had to make major efforts to push the angry crowds back from the border.

When I tried to drive to the Brandenburg Gate for another look that afternoon, I was stopped by some friendly Berlin students. They warned me that the crowds were furious at the allies for their inaction and they might take it out on me or on my car (which had U.S. Mission license plates). I decided to heed their warning, but over the next few days and weeks I often walked or drove along the border to see for myself what was happening there.

The East German police also drove back crowds from their side of the border. They used armored cars and water cannon. Walter Ulbricht sent massive police contingents to disperse East Berlin workers who assembled east of the Brandenburg Gate. He feared any kind of public reaction that might embarrass him in Khrushchev's eyes and might make Khrushchev hesitate to go further. Also, like many officials in the West, he must have feared an East Berlin uprising.

Heavily guarded, Ulbricht visited East German Vopo units on Sunday afternoon to congratulate them for "defending the Republic." On Monday evening he ordered the Brandenburg Gate crossing permanently closed in order to avoid more demonstrations that might give Khrushchev the impression that Ulbricht had lost control.[13]

The Wall Itself

In the hours after the border closed, East Berliners who wanted to get to West Berlin realized that they would have to move fast. Some of them found open spots in the barbed wire and fled on August 13 or the following days. Others swam across those parts of the Teltow Canal and the Spree River that flow between East and West Berlin and which only a few East German police had yet been assigned to guard. Others fled or sneaked across the less heavily guarded stretches of the barbed wire bar-

East Berliners fleeing across Bernauer Strasse just before the East German police seal the windows to the West. Courtesy of Landesarchiv Berlin

riers or across the lakes or the wooded parts of the border that separates West Berlin from East Germany. One man was able to cling to the bottom of a railway car that went from East Berlin to West Berlin, leaping off as soon as the train stopped in the West.

A number of East Berliners managed to escape from apartment buildings on Bernauer Strasse where the street itself was in West Berlin although the apartments were in East Berlin. The East German police had confiscated what they thought were all the keys to the front doors of the buildings, but some residents had hidden extra keys and could unlock the doors to walk into West Berlin before the police had time to block the doors with bricks and barbed wire from the inside. Others could jump from windows into the waiting arms or fire nets of West Berliners.

Not all escape attempts ended happily. The East German police soon learned what was happening at the canals and lakes and began firing at swimmers trying to make their way to West Berlin. They killed several. One woman died trying to jump from a third-floor apartment on Bernauer Strasse when she missed the mattress that she had thrown to the street ahead of her. Others were shot as they tried to jump over the barbed wire.

In the days after August 13, escape became more and more difficult. The East German police sealed holes in their barriers. They devised long-handled mirrors that could show whether potential refugees were hiding under trains or cars. They bricked up all the doors and windows along Bernauer Strasse to prevent further escapes there into West Berlin. The West Berlin media learned not to write about miraculous escapes because the East German police would close any loopholes they read about in the press. By the end of the week, few East Berliners were finding ways to escape, although many kept trying. Nonetheless, by the end of August, over 45,000 new refugees had registered at Marienfelde during the month, either having found a way to escape or deciding to stay in West Berlin if they had been lucky enough to spend the night there on August 12/13.

By Wednesday, August 16, Ulbricht's central command staff concluded that the Western powers would not react. Ulbricht could begin building a solid barrier as Khrushchev permitted if the allies did not react to the barbed wire. He had wanted to do that from the beginning and the West had now given him his chance.[14]

Thus, East German construction teams on August 16 began to build a wall of concrete blocks along the sector borders and across most of the streets between East and West Berlin. They built the new concrete barrier—which soon became known in the press as the Berlin Wall—to a height of six to eight feet, enough to block an open view across the barrier within the center of the city. Ulbricht saw that as an important psychological way of separating East from West Berlin whether Khrushchev liked it or not, and to show the Berliners that he could do whatever he wished with no allied interference.

The new construction did not, however, put an end to efforts by East Berliners and East Germans to flee. The area around the Wall stayed alive, especially at night, with police, armored cars, searchlights, baying hounds, shots, occasional screams, and a general air of insecurity. Many Berliners on both sides simply refused to accept the new barrier.

West Berliners, although not trapped like the East Berliners, felt as if they had lost half their city. Even if they had not gone to East Berlin often or at all, they had seen the open border as a vital part of the spirit of their city. It had made West Berlin a spot where their East German brethren

Ulbricht's armed police making sure that the East German masons building the Wall do not flee to West Berlin. Courtesy of Landesarchiv Berlin

could breathe free, if only for a day or a weekend. West and East Germans had often met in West Berlin because it had been an easy place to talk, to have a drink or a meal, to see and celebrate newborn babies. That was now finished. The Berliners felt that the Western allies, who had occupied the city and kept it under their own sovereignty and control, had failed them. They had always expected Ulbricht to act mercilessly, but they could not understand why the allies had let the Wall be built without even a protest and without ever showing their faces along the border.

Brandt had to deal with this anger as he tried to calm the city. On Wednesday he called on the Berliners to assemble at the Schöneberg city hall, which had long served as the city hall for West Berlin. More than 300,000 came to hear him. He urged them reluctantly to accept the new situation, as the allies had asked, to avoid incidents that might provoke a military reaction or an uprising. He asked his listeners to take no direct action against the new barriers. But Brandt said that the allies should understand that "Berlin expects more than protests. Berlin expects political action." Brandt also told the crowd that he had written a letter to Kennedy because he thought that the president would help. In the letter, he had pleaded for some American action. He had written the letter because Kennedy had asked him during their White House meeting to contact him directly when he thought it important.

Brandt warned Kennedy that a "crisis of confidence" was rising in Berlin. He asked Kennedy to reinforce the Berlin garrison and to consider declaring West Berlin a three-power city. He also asked Kennedy to bring the Berlin problem before the United Nations.

Luckily for Brandt, the mayor did not know that Kennedy had said "Who does he think he is?" when he received the letter. Kennedy thought the letter presumptuous. His reply had a cool and distant tone, to make clear to Brandt that he could not expect to address Kennedy directly and certainly not to talk about it in public. But he did take some of Brandt's comments to heart.[15]

Bahr reacted with particular fury at a news story in the Berlin paper *Der Abend* that the allies had known in advance about Soviet and East German plans to close the sector border and had decided to do nothing about it. This story, probably planted by Ulbricht's agents, caused genuine rage in Berlin. Bahr called the U.S. press officer and screamed that there had to be an immediate allied denial or Brandt would send the next protest rally to the American headquarters. The allies did issue a firm denial forthwith.[16]

> East Berlin radio told the following joke of the day: "Did you hear that Brandt called the allies for help?" "Yes, I heard, but the allies didn't."[17]

Ulbricht must have enjoyed heaping ridicule on the allies.

> Bahr later observed, "On the 13th of August we grew up. It was a shame that it had to happen that way."[18] Brandt wrote that "in August 1961 a curtain was drawn aside to reveal an empty stage."[19]

Rusk still thought that the Wall represented a "propaganda victory" for the West because it showed that Ulbricht had to build barriers to stop his people from fleeing. He did not appear to realize that Berliners and many others would see the Wall as a defeat for the West. From Berlin we had to discourage the State Department from claiming a victory. Nevertheless Rusk also took a step toward negotiations. He sent a letter to George Kennan, the U.S. ambassador in Belgrade and an expert on the USSR whom Kennedy respected, to ask Kennan to get in touch with the Soviet ambassador in Belgrade and tell him, "The U.S. Government is sincerely anxious to find a peaceful solution to the Berlin crisis and realizes that this must be one that takes account of the interests of all the various parties involved." Rusk instructed Kennan to tell the Soviet ambassador that Kennan would be available for any kind of informal exploratory contacts that the Soviet government might wish, and that he was to report such contacts to Washington.

If the Soviet ambassador asked whether Kennan was acting on behalf of the United States or of the West in general, Kennan was to reply that no other Western government knew of such contacts and that, "in particular, it is not intended that the Germans shall have any knowledge of them."[20] There is no indication in State Department files of how the Soviet ambassador replied, if indeed he did.

The biggest and most popular German newspaper, *Bildzeitung*, had a banner headline on August 17 occupying the whole front page and proclaiming "DER WESTERN TUT NICHTS" ("The West Does Nothing"). Berlin papers also began attacking the allies sharply for their inaction. If the allies did not act soon, they would lose the confidence of the Berliners.

More seriously, Western inaction risked giving Khrushchev the wrong idea about Kennedy's readiness to defend American interests. One of the State Department's leading experts on the Soviet Union later concluded that Kennedy's failure to react quickly to the Wall encouraged Khrushchev to send missiles to Cuba a year later because he thought the president suffered from an "endemic weakness" and would not react quickly or at all to any Khrushchev challenge.[21]

Kennedy's failure to respond immediately and firmly to the Wall may indeed have reinforced Khrushchev's impression from the summit that he could intimidate Kennedy. Khrushchev had been very nervous about closing off the sector border but must have concluded, as Ulbricht told him, that the West had reacted less strongly than might have been expected. It could have reinforced his belief that Kennedy would accept almost anything to avoid nuclear war.

Kennedy's Friends Act

Marguerite Higgins, a veteran reporter for the *New York Herald Tribune* and a frequent visitor to Berlin, had been stupefied by Kennedy's mute acceptance of the new Berlin barriers. She had known Kennedy for years and she now contacted first his brother Robert and then the president himself at his home in Hyannisport. She said that the president had to act, and soon. Higgins called General Lucius Clay, who had been the U.S. military governor of Germany after World War II and who had saved West Berlin by overcoming the Soviet blockade of Berlin with the Berlin Airlift of 1948–1949. She asked Clay, who was as angry as she about the lack of American action, if he would be ready to go back to Berlin if Kennedy wanted him. He said yes.

Higgins then also called James O'Donnell, who had been a correspondent in Berlin during the late 1940s and who was working in the State Department undersecretary's office. He was as shocked as she and Clay at what had happened in Berlin and wanted a strong American reaction.

Clay called General Maxwell Taylor, Kennedy's military adviser who had also served in Berlin and Germany, to urge him to tell Kennedy that he could not just ignore what had happened. Clay repeated to Taylor that he would be ready to help in any capacity. Taylor reported Clay's call to Kennedy.[22]

Kennedy must have recognized that he could not dismiss what Clay said because Clay was not only a hero in Berlin but a prominent figure in American politics and in the Republican Party. He had played a key role in helping to persuade Dwight Eisenhower to run for president and had helped to direct the campaign. Any public criticism of Kennedy's policies by Clay would get attention across the country and inflict major damage on Kennedy and the Democratic Party.

Kennedy also learned that many American newspaper editorials used the word *appeasement* to describe his acceptance of the Wall. The editorials compared him with British Prime Minister Neville Chamberlain, who had accepted Adolf Hitler's partition and conquest of Czechoslovakia in 1938. Many Americans even sent the White House black umbrellas which Chamberlain had often carried, and which had become signs of weakness.

Richard Nixon, whom Kennedy had barely beaten in the 1960 presidential campaign, accused the president of "a Hamlet-like psychosis" of indecision.[23] Members of Congress, Democrats as well as Republicans, weighed in openly against Kennedy. Most Americans did not want Kennedy to "play it cool." They did not see the Wall as a step back by Khrushchev, as Kennedy did, but as a step forward. The White House staff could perhaps claim to know something about Moscow but was tone deaf to U.S. public opinion. Kennedy would pay a high domestic political price if he did not act. Having failed at the Bay of Pigs and having apparently not stood up to Khrushchev in Vienna, he could not afford any more signs of weakness or defeat.

Edward R. Murrow, a veteran radio and television reporter whom Kennedy admired deeply and whom he had appointed director of the U.S. Information Agency (USIA), had the greatest direct impact on Kennedy. Murrow happened to be in Berlin on August 13. When he learned of the new barriers, he went with RIAS radio director Robert Lochner to see for himself what was happening in East Berlin. Murrow said, "I wonder if the president realizes the seriousness of this situation."[24] When he returned from East Berlin, working deep into the night he wrote a cable telling Kennedy that the United States and the president himself faced a potential political and diplomatic disaster. He predicted a crisis of confidence that could wreck the allied position not only in Berlin but in Germany, Europe, and beyond.

Murrow warned Kennedy that Ulbricht's actions were aimed not only at East Germans but at the trust that West Berliners and West Germans had in America. He compared Ulbricht's takeover of East Berlin to Hitler's takeover of the Rhineland in 1935. It required some American action in response. Murrow concluded his cable by writing: "What is in danger of being destroyed here is that perishable quality called hope."[25]

Murrow's message forced Kennedy to see Berlin for the first time in his presidency not merely as a distant game to be coolly analyzed by his Soviet experts but as a human drama as well as a potentially lethal global and American political issue. Kennedy now recognized that he would pay a high price with the American electorate if he did nothing. He had to react to Ulbricht's barbed wire even if he did not dare to tear it down.

As Kennedy looked around for ideas, Marguerite Higgins continued to offer suggestions, including that Vice President Lyndon Johnson go to Berlin. She also built political fires in Washington, telling House Speaker Sam Rayburn and other members of Congress that something had to be done. When Kennedy showed her Brandt's letter and criticized it, she said: "I must tell you frankly. The suspicion is growing that you're going to sell out the West Berliners." That remark, coming from a respected correspondent, brought Kennedy up short.[26]

James O'Donnell went around Kohler and other senior officials of the State Department to ask the German desk directly what they recommended. He brought their ideas to Higgins and the White House. He also spoke with Lothar Loewe, a veteran German correspondent who was serving in Washington but who was in constant touch with Berlin and could tell O'Donnell what the Berliners were thinking.

Higgins and others recommended to Kennedy that General Clay be sent to Berlin as Kennedy's man in the city. Clay in turn recommended that a full U.S. Army battle group of 1,500 soldiers be sent to reinforce the U.S. Berlin garrison. That would not only boost Berlin morale but would make clear to Khrushchev that he was playing with fire.

Kennedy did not want to send only a senior Republican such as Clay to Berlin to pull his chestnuts out of the fire. He therefore decided that he would send Johnson. He asked Clay to join Johnson, which Clay agreed to do.

On Friday afternoon, August 18, after alerting Johnson and Clay to be ready to go to Berlin, Kennedy held a meeting to consult one final time with his advisers and then to announce what he would do. Clay's proposal for sending an additional battle group to Berlin met with stiff resistance from the Soviet experts on Kennedy's staff. Charles Bohlen told Kennedy that it might be provocative. This did not surprise Clay, for Bohlen had recommended pulling out of Berlin in 1948 because he regarded the city as untenable after the Soviets had launched their blockade.[27] General Lyman Lemnitzer, chairman of the Joint Chiefs of Staff, also opposed the idea, as did NATO commander General Lauris Norstad (though he was not at the meeting). Rusk took no position.

But Kennedy went ahead despite the opposition. Acting again on a Clay suggestion, he told the U.S. Army to arrange for the arrival of the battle group at a time when Johnson could meet the troops in Berlin. That would reinforce the political impact of Johnson's visit and of the battle group's arrival.[28]

Kennedy's decision to send the battle group as well as Johnson and Clay marked an important turning point in Kennedy's evolution as president, not only in his policy toward Berlin. For the first time, on an important and risky policy issue he had openly and directly overruled not only several senior military commanders but also Charles Bohlen, one of his top Soviet experts and one with a towering reputation.

Clay thought that Kennedy's decision showed that the president "was learning and growing in stature."[29] Kennedy's relations with his advisers were never again the same, although he did continue to listen to them and to follow their advice much of the time. Clay found then, as he was again to find later, that Kennedy would sometimes—but by no means always—support action on Berlin even when his Soviet experts and other advisers as well as senior State Department officials wanted him to do nothing.

Kennedy was starting to make his own decisions and to trust his own judgment. He was also probably beginning to realize that his policy on Berlin could have a sharp and potentially deadly political impact in the United States.

Johnson in Berlin

Johnson's and Clay's Berlin visit on August 19 and 20 drew large and enthusiastic crowds. Johnson drove around the city in campaign mode, leaning out of his car door to wave at the crowds lining the streets. He handed out fountain pens and other souvenirs to the astonished and delighted Berliners. His presence and a short speech that he made at the city hall had a dramatic public impact, especially when he quoted the Declaration of Independence to say that Americans pledged "our lives, our fortunes, and our sacred honor" for Berlin. Johnson's presence when the U.S. battle group reached the Autobahn entrance to West Berlin was particularly effective because it clearly showed that the Americans had the courage to act in Berlin despite their decision to accept the Wall. It underlined the U.S. commitment.

Kennedy and senior U.S. Army commanders wondered how the Soviets and East Germans would react to the battle group traveling across East German territory. Kennedy stayed in Washington for the weekend and asked General Clifton to check the progress of the battle group every twenty minutes. General Bruce Clarke, the commander of U.S. forces in Europe (USAREUR), moved his field headquarters to the West German entrance of the Autobahn in order to be able to react quickly to any possible trouble.

Kennedy's brother Robert later said that the president was nervous as the battle group crossed East German territory, and that he was relieved when the troops got through. His advisers had feared that the Soviets would try to block the route. Kennedy himself had not been sure what Khrushchev and Konev might do, and whether they might even try to attack the convoy.[30]

Khrushchev's son Sergei wrote later that Soviet defense minister Marshal Rodion Malinovsky told Premier Khrushchev that he should block the passage of the convoy on the Autobahn. But Khrushchev overruled him, issuing "an unequivocal order to let them pass, create all conditions necessary for free transit, and behave with special courtesy." Like Kennedy, Khrushchev followed reports of the convoy's movement "with trepidation," knowing that just one shot might provoke a crisis. He did not relax until the convoy had arrived in Berlin, when he could report to his son in great relief that all had gone well.[31]

Colonel Glover Johns, the commander of the battle group and a combat veteran, was instructed to cooperate with routine Soviet requests for information about the number of soldiers and trucks in his column but to proceed without complying if he believed those requests were intended as a form of harassment or blockage. He was also instructed to try to over-come "passive obstacles," such as concrete blocks, but to halt his column and defend it if confronted with superior force.[32]

As it turned out, and in accordance with Khrushchev's instructions, the American troops did not need to take any drastic action to get to Berlin. Although Soviet military officers delayed the convoy by demanding a full accounting of the number of vehicles and soldiers, Soviet combat forces remained well back of the route and never interfered with the battle group's passage to Berlin.

Khrushchev later wrote that the GDR was "unstable" and the Soviet Union had to act by building the Wall. But, he wrote, "We did not want a war, we only wanted to conduct a surgical operation. . . .We did not want to attack U.S. forces in Berlin."[33] Khrushchev understood from his Vienna meeting with Kennedy that the Americans would insist on their access rights, and he was not yet ready to challenge those rights. He did not want to risk a confrontation with Kennedy at a time when the American vice president was in Berlin.

From August 1961 until the end of the year, Soviet forces in and around Berlin and East Germany were in a state of heightened alert, presumably to cope with any West German or allied military reaction to the Wall and to suppress any possible revolt by the East German people. They even had specially reinforced deployments around Berlin from August until the end of October.[34]

Brandt welcomed the Johnson visit and the U.S. troops. They gave the Berliners a chance to cheer an allied action for the first time in a week. The slide in Berlin opinion stopped. Brandt also believed that Kennedy's action would make Khrushchev and Ulbricht think twice about any further steps. He appreciated Kennedy's decision to take the risk.

Macmillan sent three British armored cars and a few soldiers to Berlin by rail, but he did not commit the full unit by Autobahn that Kennedy had asked him to send. He thought that "militarily, this [was] nonsense."[35] Konrad Adenauer could not send West German troops because West Berlin was not legally part of West Germany. De Gaulle did not send any French soldiers. He said that the French army was too tied down in Algeria to help in Berlin. De Gaulle saw the Wall as a retreat by Khrushchev. He observed that the Wall "provided physical proof that the Kremlin has given up hope of frightening the Americans, the British and the French into allowing them to lay hands on the city."[36] He did nothing because he saw no reason to do anything.

None of this bothered the Berliners, who knew very well that American power mattered more than any other. As they cheered the U.S. battle group, they did not care who else might come along. They had come to trust the Americans ever since the Berlin blockade, and the battle group reaffirmed the American commitment more clearly than any other step could have done. All the Berliners I saw over the next several weeks told me how impressed they had been by Kennedy's decision.

Johnson's visit did not please Adenauer, however. The chancellor wanted to join the vice president and Clay in Berlin but Johnson refused to take him. Adenauer believed that he would have been able to show that Berlin was a legitimate German interest even if it was not officially part of West Germany. Adenauer suspected that Kennedy did not want to offend Khrushchev. It took him a long time to forgive the slight, which worsened the difficult relations that he was already beginning to have with Kennedy.[37]

Walter Ulbricht, immensely frustrated that the U.S. battle group could cross East German territory without asking his permission, ordered East German troops and police to seal off the Autobahn so that no East German civilians could approach the column to ask for asylum or to show support. Although there is no record of any message from Ulbricht to Khrushchev about the convoy, he would certainly have wanted Khrushchev to block it and he may even have asked Khrushchev to do so.

But Ulbricht still wanted the last word. On August 23, three days after the U.S. battle group had arrived in Berlin, he closed many of the remaining crossing points between East and West Berlin. He left only seven crossing points, one of which he designated for Western allied occupation forces and for all non-Germans who might want to enter or leave East Berlin. To show his power and to underline Western allied impotence, Ulbricht limited the traffic of the theoretically sovereign allies to that one entry point, forcing the British and French to detour through the center of West Berlin and to go through the U.S. sector if they wanted to enter East Berlin.

The checkpoint for foreigners, located where Friedrichstrasse crossed between East and West Berlin, soon became known as "Checkpoint Charlie" under a U.S. military coding system that labeled the two Autobahn checkpoints as "Checkpoint Alpha" and "Checkpoint Bravo." All international military and civilian traffic passed through there, although Soviet forces occasionally used other crossing points to get to the Soviet war memorial in the British sector.

In the same decree in which he limited the crossing points, Ulbricht announced that henceforth no person could come closer than 100 meters to the Wall on the West Berlin side. In effect, he began trying to extend his rule into West Berlin, threatening to have his police shoot any West Berliner or any occupation soldier who got too close.

That was too much even for the allied commandants. They did not want Ulbricht telling West Berliners what to do. They sent military cars and patrols right up to the Wall and to other barriers, threatening to fire back if they were fired upon. West Berlin politicians and the West Berlin press greeted the allied reaction with cheers, but they asked why the allies had waited so long and had not brought patrols right up to the barriers when they were first being built on August 13. They thought that the allied reaction ten days later, with the Wall already going up fast throughout the center of the city, was too little and too late.

Charles de Gaulle did not agree with the allied action, which he thought was pointless. He criticized the French commander in Berlin for having joined the other allied commanders and having sent French troops toward the sector border. De Gaulle wanted no military reaction to the sector barrier at all. He still wanted the Germans and the Berliners to be angry at the allies.

The Battle for West Berlin

With the Wall and the new U.S. troop contingent firmly in place, East and West got ready for the next phase of the Berlin crisis: the battle for West Berlin. Ulbricht wanted to win this next battle. The barbed wire had saved his regime by blocking the refugee flood. The Berlin Wall that he was steadily building would give him more time to consolidate his regime. His use of East German troops to help build and protect those barriers had shown that he now exercised full power over East Berlin, especially while the Western allies still prevented the West German army from appearing or recruiting in West Berlin.

But that did not really solve Ulbricht's Berlin problem. It would not give him what he really wanted, which was to put an end to what he called the "*Frontstadt*" ("frontier city") of West Berlin. Ulbricht clearly thought that he had been let down. He felt that his rule was threatened as long as West Berlin remained an island of the West in the middle of his German Democratic Republic. He wanted to destroy West Berlin not only as a haven for refugees but as a beacon to all alienated East Germans. He wanted and even needed to begin controlling what could and could not happen there.

Khrushchev remained wary. Although he had permitted Ulbricht to divide Berlin, he worried about what Ulbricht might do next and how the West might react. There had been a crisis atmosphere in the Soviet foreign ministry on August 13 until the Soviets could be sure that Ulbricht would not overstep his instructions and that Kennedy would not take firmer action.[38]

Khrushchev warned Ulbricht that "steps which could exacerbate the situation, especially in Berlin, should be avoided."[39] He thought that the Wall was the best answer to the immediate problem that Ulbricht had signaled to Pervukhin. Sergei Khrushchev remembered that his father thought that Ulbricht had gained more from the Wall—at least to solve his refugee problem—than he could have gained from a peace treaty.[40]

In a talk with Hans Kroll, the West German ambassador in Moscow, Khrushchev confided: "Ulbricht had pushed me for a long time and more vehemently in the last months. . . . The Wall was ordered by me due to Ulbricht's pressing wish." He called the Wall "this hateful thing" but said that he had no choice because he had to stop the refugee flow to save the GDR.[41] Khrushchev nonetheless expected the Wall to have a slow but powerful effect on the minds of the West Berliners. He sent a message urging Willy Brandt to shift toward a more accommodating policy because, if he did not, the West Berlin question would resolve itself by economic collapse and mass flight. He did not think that West Berlin could survive surrounded by the Wall.[42]

Almost thirty years later, Erich Honecker told a German court trying him for the deadly shootings along the Wall that continuation of refugee flight "would have meant the risk of a third world war." There would have been a revolt in East Germany and the Soviets would have intervened. The Wall, he insisted, had actually saved lives.[43] That may have been the argument that Ulbricht made to Khrushchev.

But that was in the distant future. For the moment, the Wall was the new dividing line. It was also the new starting line. Everyone now had to act in a totally new situation, with Ulbricht's workers adding ever more concrete blocks and mortar to the Wall and with people being shot in the middle of one of Europe's great cities.

Ulbricht still wanted to do more than keep the East Germans in. He wanted to get control over West Berlin, which he had hoped to win through Khrushchev's peace treaty. He would have been immensely amused to hear that an American assistant secretary of state thought he had been intending to do the Americans a favor.

Thus began the next phase of the battle for Berlin.

CHAPTER EIGHT

"I Am Not Afraid of Escalation"

General Lucius D. Clay arrived in Berlin on September 19, 1961, as the "Personal Representative" of President Kennedy in Berlin. He was returning to a city he last knew in 1949 as the U.S. military governor of Germany and as the hero who had broken the Soviet Berlin blockade with the airlift of 1948–1949.

Kennedy wrote in his appointment letter that Clay was to be the "senior American in that city" but would be "free of routine responsibility." There was to be "no change in the regular military chain of command or in the political responsibilities of Ambassador Walter Dowling as Chief of Mission."[1] With a marvel of bureaucratic jargon, Kennedy was giving Clay responsibility but no operational authority.

Kennedy wrote Clay that he wanted his "prompt personal counsel" in responding to "any sudden Soviet moves in the Berlin area" and wanted everybody in Berlin to look to him for advice as the "senior American in Berlin." But he did not authorize Clay to give orders. Theoretically, people would obey him because of his prestige and personal presence, but they would not need to do so.

"It was very interesting," Clay later told his biographer. Kennedy had first telephoned him and asked him to go to Berlin to be "fully and completely responsible for all decisions in Berlin." But when Clay had called on Kennedy two days later, Kennedy told him with some embarrassment that there had been objections to the terms of the appointment and he had changed the letter that he had intended to give to Clay by removing Clay's authority to give instructions.

> "Mr. President, I don't really care," Clay replied. "If I have access to you if I need it, I would expect to have your approval or disapproval. If it was a matter of serious import, I would get in touch with you." Kennedy agreed.[2]

General Lauris Norstad, the U.S. Air Force general who was both supreme NATO commander and American commander in Europe, and General Bruce Clarke, the commander of U.S. land forces in Europe, had opposed Clay's appointment strongly. Walter Dowling, the U.S. ambassador to Germany, had also opposed it because he feared it would detract from his own authority as the senior American in Germany. Most White House advisers and senior State Department officials had opposed it. Harold Macmillan, though less directly affected, had also expressed his own doubts about the appointment to Kennedy.[3]

McGeorge Bundy had warned Kennedy: "You want no risk of setting up another MacArthur-Truman affair."[4] He reminded Kennedy how General Douglas MacArthur, the U.S. commander in Korea, had pressed President Harry Truman to bomb China during the Korean war and had generated a major political storm for Truman when the president relieved him. Clay might well demand that Kennedy do things he did not want to do, and Kennedy might face political problems if he overruled him.

Bundy pointed out that many officials in the White House and the State Department were thinking of making major concessions to Khrushchev and Ulbricht (he listed recognizing the GDR, signing a non-aggression pact, and perhaps even having two separate peace treaties with East and West Germany). If Clay did not agree with those ideas, there might be trouble for the president.

Significantly, however, Bundy conceded, "Maybe you are tougher than the line of thought I have sketched." Having seen Kennedy overrule Charles Bohlen and the military to send 1,500 troops to Berlin, Bundy may have begun to wonder if Kennedy might indeed be "tougher" than his advisers.[5]

Kennedy decided to go ahead with Clay's appointment despite Bundy's warning and the opposition in the bureaucracy. He thought Clay's presence would boost Berlin morale. He probably also wanted to hear other voices than those he had been hearing at the White House and from the State Department for nine exasperating months. Clay had at least made proposals that had turned around the desperate situation after the Wall, helping Kennedy overcome a crisis of confidence in Berlin and in American opinion. Others had proposed little or nothing. Having begun to recognize that Berlin policy could be more politically controversial and sometimes more explosive than he had first realized, Kennedy must also have hoped that he would be better protected from partisan attacks on his Berlin policy by having a senior Republican on the scene. He decided to take a gamble on Clay.

Clay also took a gamble on Kennedy. He had no idea whether Kennedy and he would understand each other. But Clay felt that he had no real choice. Having spent a lifetime in the military, he had enormous reverence for the office of the president and for the concept of service. He had to do what a president asked him. He also thought that he might be useful in Berlin. He gave up his chairmanship of the Continental Can Company, sold his apartment in New York, and left for Berlin with his wife.

Several days before Clay's arrival in Berlin, Allan Lightner assigned me to serve as Clay's special assistant. Clay needed somebody who spoke German. He also needed somebody to tell him who was who in the Berlin bureaucracy and in the city itself, and to accompany him on his trips and meetings around the city and elsewhere. Lightner did not tell me of the opposition in Washington to Clay's appointment. I was glad to accept the assignment because I thought it would be interesting.

Some friends then told me three things about Clay in the two days before his arrival: "He is the smartest person I have ever known"; "he has a steel-trap mind"; and "he's the worst chain-smoker you'll ever see." All turned out to be true.

Governing Mayor Willy Brandt called on the West Berliners to line the streets to welcome an old friend. That they did, cheering him from the time he left Tegel airport until he got to the U.S. Mission in the southwestern corner of the city. Those cheers reflected the Berliners' hopes as well as their despair. Some of them told me that they hoped that Clay could save them from Walter Ulbricht, but they wondered whether he could perform yet another miracle.[6] Clay also wondered whether he could. But he knew that Kennedy and the Berliners were counting on him to try. Investment in West Berlin had plummeted in the weeks after August 13. Young people were leaving for West Germany, as Khrushchev had predicted to Brandt. Clay knew that he would have to act quickly to change that.[7]

Clay believed that Ulbricht wanted the Wall not only to encircle West Berlin but to neutralize it and ultimately to take it over. He had carefully followed Ulbricht's and Khrushchev's remarks about the demilitarized "free city." Contrary to Washington's thinking, he feared that the Wall had actually begun, not ended, the battle for Berlin, and that the real trials lay ahead.

As he later wrote to Kennedy, he expected Ulbricht and Khrushchev to keep up the pressure. If they could not block U.S. access or end the U.S. presence quickly and directly, they would try to do it over time and by attrition. Ulbricht would in particular try to undermine the American position because he knew very well that it was the key to West Berlin's freedom, prosperity, and independence from East Germany.

Ulbricht was indeed thinking along the lines that Clay feared. Although, as Sergei Khrushchev remembered, his father was delighted about the Wall and thought that it had gained more for the GDR than a peace treaty would have, Ulbricht felt that he had been let down.[8] On October 27, 1958, even before Khrushchev had issued his demand to make West Berlin a free city, Ulbricht had made a speech in which he had said that he wanted to neutralize West Berlin.[9]

As part of that policy, the GDR announced on August 23 that West Berliners would henceforth need visas to enter East Berlin. It then proposed to open two offices in West Berlin to issue those visas, a move that Brandt vetoed because he did not want the GDR to have an official presence in West Berlin. After that, West Berliners could no longer enter East Berlin except with special permission. Ulbricht had wanted to use the visa offices to show that West Berlin was the separate political entity that he wanted it to become, and Brandt would not accept that.

Ulbricht had written to Khrushchev after the Wall had gone up that "the West took fewer steps [against the Wall] than we might have expected." He added that the presence of Soviet and East German troops had intimidated the West on August 13.[10] Now, having solved his refugee problem, Ulbricht was going to convince the West Berliners that they had no future with the Western allies and that West Berlin would slide unstoppably into being a "neutral" and "free" city by Ulbricht's definition.

Clay looked around urgently for a chance to counter Ulbricht's pressures, and the first chance came shortly after his arrival. On September 21, the East German People's Police (Vopos) and Traffic Police (Trapos) began harassing Americans traveling along the Autobahn between Helmstedt and Berlin. They especially harassed U.S. soldiers who were not in uniform but in easily identifiable American-made cars licensed by U.S. military authorities. The East German police stopped the cars, made the Americans get out, threatened them, and refused to let them proceed, sometimes delaying them for hours on end. Other travelers, including Berliners, saw how the Vopos and the Trapos could order the "sovereign" Americans around. The soldiers themselves felt helpless and humiliated. American officials had no idea how to counter the Vopos.

Clay immediately advised the U.S. commander in Berlin, Major General Albert Watson, to order American radio-equipped "courtesy patrols" in military cars or jeeps to travel back and forth at regular intervals along the Autobahn every hour or two. The courtesy patrol drivers had orders to stop whenever they saw an incident involving an American car. They were to help the Americans and were to ask for Soviet officers, telling the East German police that they had no right to block American cars. If they needed help, they were to phone Military Police headquarters. The Soviets protested at the sudden increase in U.S. military cars and jeeps but they could not block them. Within a week, the "courtesy patrols" had stopped East German harassment. But Clay kept the patrols going, although less frequently, in order to make his point that the Russians should not have permitted the incidents in the first place.

Ulbricht, frustrated, urged the Soviets to stop the American courtesy patrols. After some weeks, the Soviets tried to slow down the patrols by making them go through extensive questioning as they passed through Soviet checkpoints at the entrances to the Autobahn. The U.S. Mission told the Soviets that the patrols would stop when East German harassment stopped.

Clay then replaced the courtesy vehicles with convoys of U.S. military vehicles that traveled back and forth at random hours several times a day. The Soviets could not stop those convoys without interfering with Berlin access, one of President Kennedy's essentials, and they did not dare to block them. The convoys served the same purpose as the patrols, making the American presence felt by everybody who lived or traveled along the Autobahn. They prevented any further harassment of American cars. Americans and other travelers loved them, as did the Berliners.

Macmillan objected to the convoys as provocative. Some U.S. military commanders also objected that the convoys did not serve normal military training functions. Neither British nor U.S. military commanders saw the purpose of these courtesy convoys as Clay saw them, but Kennedy supported Clay, refusing to stop the patrols even when asked to do so. The Soviets may even have welcomed the patrols because they felt uncomfortable about actions by any German—friend or foe—against any occupation power.

Noting the "Soviet retreat from their transfer of this control to the East German government," Clay wrote in a cable to Washington that the Soviets had gone back to patrolling the Autobahn themselves. He saw this as a sign that the Soviets did not want to risk having an incident between East German police and U.S. travelers.[11]

Clay also took some steps within Berlin itself. He arranged with Watson for American jeeps and patrol cars to drive slowly and steadily along or near the Wall and near other West Berlin borders in the American sector, continuing to reinforce the message that East German police could not carry out Ulbricht's threat—which he had never formally rescinded—to shoot anyone who came within 100 meters of the Wall on the Western side. Clay had the patrols show themselves openly and frequently along and near the Wall to make clear that the West Berliners had allied protection. He also wanted to show that Ulbricht's writ did not extend into West Berlin.

Moreover, if East German Vopos blocked or harassed any U.S. civilian or official vehicle in East Berlin, Clay instructed U.S. soldiers to delay a Soviet car in West Berlin. Soviet marshal Ivan Konev, wanting to control the situation in Berlin, told Ulbricht to stop the harassment of American cars. He had already told Ulbricht to stop Vopos from firing into West Berlin. He may even have privately agreed with Clay's wish to keep control over the East Germans.[12]

Clay told me that he did not regard the patrols on the Autobahn or in Berlin as major exercises in allied power. He thought they would simply show Berliners and Germans that we were still there and would help them if necessary. He wanted people to notice that we could and would react to Ulbricht's actions and declarations and that we would not take them lying down.

Even as this was going on, Clay's other immediate chance to act came over a tiny village called Steinstücken. That community had been assigned to Berlin when the administrative borders of the city were drawn in the nineteenth century, although it was about 100 meters away from the main body of West Berlin. It consisted of several hundred square meters of land with a few dozen houses and about 100 inhabitants, mainly farmers and their families, and was connected to West Berlin by a narrow road. An East German refugee who wanted to get to West Berlin had fled to safety in the little exclave when he found his way blocked by the barbed wire. Vopos had then surrounded Steinstücken and were threatening to enter it to bring out the refugee, although Steinstücken was part of U.S. occupation territory in Berlin.

General Clay asked General Watson to send a small contingent of U.S. troops to the exclave, but General Clarke told Watson not to send the troops and went to see Clay to tell him not to give orders to "my troops." General Norstad, afraid of escalation, backed Clarke.[13]

Clay feared that Kennedy could never live down the sheer humiliation of having East German police seize a refugee who had sought political protection on American territory. He thought that Norstad and Clarke were not serving the president's interest by using the fear of escalation to paralyze the entire U.S. government.

Stopped from launching a ground patrol, Clay ordered a helicopter for his personal use. He instructed the pilot to land at Steinstücken and asked me to go along. Having learned that there was no television set in Steinstücken, he brought one along to leave there.

"President Kennedy has sent me to Berlin to help you and to help all Berliners," Clay told the villagers. He remained in Steinstücken for about an hour, leaving them feeling that they would be protected. East German border guards trained their guns on the helicopter in a show of force, but they did not dare shoot at an American military craft. I certainly sensed no fear that they would do so, and neither did Clay.

"I am not afraid of escalation," Clay cabled Kennedy when he got back to his office and reported to the president on what he had done.[14] He

knew that Kennedy's White House advisers as well as U.S. military officers and the British would criticize his flight as provocative, so he wanted
to tell Kennedy directly what he had done. He then asked Watson to
begin regular helicopter flights to Steinstücken, showing the American
presence and also flying out refugees.

Kennedy understood what Clay had done and expressed his support,
although his advisers as well as Macmillan pilloried Clay. De Gaulle, as
usual, said nothing. John Ausland, a member of the State Department
Berlin Task Force, later wrote: "A problem that had vexed U.S. officials
was settled by a simple action, and one can only wonder why it had not
been taken before."[15]

After a rather grainy amateur photograph of Clay's Steinstücken visit
appeared in a Berlin paper under the headline "CLAY IN STEINSTÜCKEN,"
the Berliners reacted enthusiastically. They cheered Clay when he next
appeared in public as he and his wife did their Saturday shopping on the
Kurfürstendamm.

Berliners usually whispered "Das ist der Clay" whenever they saw him
in public, whether on the street, at the opera, or at a restaurant. Being
rather diffident, they would usually not approach him directly, but they
always loved to see him. It gave them reassurance. Clay thought that
was part of what Kennedy had sent him to do. Berliners began writing
to Clay, sometimes two dozen or more letters a week. He answered each
letter, usually with a very brief note, which they found absolutely fasci-
nating. One newspaper even wrote about it, commenting that the editors
had never heard of any senior German official doing that.

Clay wrote a long personal cable to Kennedy on October 18 summarizing his concern about "the trespassing of our rights which has taken place
in the last several months by East German forces while Soviet forces have
been far in the background." That permitted Ulbricht to look stronger
than the Americans while the Soviets avoided risk. Khrushchev was
content to let others do his dirty work.[16] Clay warned Kennedy that there
were times when one had to flush Khrushchev out of his bunker:

> We can lose Berlin if we are unwilling to take some risk in using force to
> bring about Soviet confrontation even if we withdraw immediately when
> confronted with superior force. We could easily be backed into war by fail-
> ing to make it clearly evident . . . that we have reached the danger point.

"Of course, we cannot solve the Berlin problem by using force in Berlin," Clay wrote, for Berlin was a political more than a military problem. But he noted that the risk of escalation "works both ways" and that the Soviets also had to hesitate before they decided to go up to another level. He thus warned Kennedy that it would sometimes be necessary to take some risk by using force to bring the Soviets out of hiding, but added that he would pull back after he had made his point.

Clay also pointed out that "the measures that you have taken to increase our military capabilities have been noted by the Russians and I have a feeling that they are being much more careful here than a few weeks ago." He added that he had noticed clear differences between East German and Soviet views on Berlin and that the United States could and should take advantage of that.

Clay warned the president that "prompt reaction is essential when an incident occurs which threatens a right." He added that the rescue of the refugees from Steinstücken as well as the military patrols on the Autobahn had reinforced the U.S. position in Berlin by showing that Ulbricht could not push the United States out of Berlin bit by bit. He added with some annoyance, "I cannot accept the recommendations I do make to be tossed lightly aside at higher headquarters in Europe." He said he would call Washington on a "major matter," but that the accumulation of many minor failures could build up to a major loss. Having gone to Berlin as requested by the president, he at least deserved to be heard and taken seriously.

Challenging Kennedy's advisers directly, Clay wrote "I can be of no real service if it is deemed wise to be extremely cautious in Berlin." He warned Kennedy that consistent U.S. failure to act would erode confidence so deeply that it would have been useless to send him to Berlin. Kennedy would be seen as personally responsible for any Western failure as long as he kept Clay in Berlin.

In concluding his cable, Clay made clear that he would not become another Douglas MacArthur:

> I did not come here to add to your problems and I am gladly expendable. I do want you to know that I would never permit myself to be made into a controversial figure in these critical times and that if you do decide, or if I find that I must report to you, that I serve no useful purpose here, I would

134 ━ Kennedy and the Berlin Wall

withdraw only in a manner which would meet with your approval and would not add to the problem here.

In an earlier message to Dean Rusk, Clay had written, "We are fighting a political battle here, not a war." He wrote that the allies could not win a war, but that they would not even need to fight one. They could win the political battle in Berlin, but only if they did not let their rights lapse one by one. Most important, they would have to consider the political impact of any action or inaction. Too many allied officials, Clay continued, had begun to accept harassment or to bend with it. They had permitted the slow but persistent erosion of rights and were ready to let it continue. Clay wanted to stop that. He added, perhaps as a political warning to Rusk and others, that Americans as well as Berliners would agree with him.

Clay wrote: "There is no longer time for either caution or timidity when our basic rights are threatened. . . . We must be bold without truculence, quietly and not ostentatiously determined, and completely sure of those rights to which we are committed." He concluded by telling Rusk, "This does require a change in thinking in the long channel which comes from you."[17] The files do not show any reply from Rusk.

Clay had drawn his own conclusions about Khrushchev's policies on Berlin. He did not expect Khrushchev to escalate as long as the Americans held firm. He thus believed that Americans need not fear Khrushchev's bluff. Like de Gaulle, Clay thought that Khrushchev did not want war. And he wanted to make Khrushchev clamp down on Ulbricht.

Clay wanted the Western allies to become unpredictable. Until Clay's arrival, Khrushchev could be certain that the allies would do no more than send a protest note some days or weeks after any Ulbricht harassment. Neither Khrushchev nor Ulbricht needed even to read the notes. But Khrushchev would keep Ulbricht under control if he was not sure how the allies would react, because Khrushchev feared escalation even more than Kennedy did.

Because Ulbricht wanted to make West Berliners feel insecure, Clay needed to make Khrushchev feel insecure. If Khrushchev believed that he could control the temperature of the Berlin crisis, he would keep it bubbling. If he feared it would boil over, he would turn down the heat. The allies had to act as if they might destabilize the situation around

Berlin as much as Ulbricht and perhaps more. Then Khrushchev would call a halt.

Clay believed that the West—and especially the United States—had to retaliate to any East German harassment by doing things that Khrushchev had not expected and would not like. He once told me: "We have to make them sorry when they harass us."

Having worked with the Russian military closely in Berlin during his years as U.S. military governor, Clay knew that they did not like to take pointless risks. He also knew that they regarded Ulbricht with absolute contempt. Kennedy's advisers, and especially his experts on the Soviet Union, disliked this kind of thinking. They told Kennedy that Khrushchev would not change his strategy or tactics no matter what the president did. They warned that Clay's actions would lead to a confrontation and that Kennedy would have to back down.[18] Clay regarded that kind of talk as self-defeating.

Documents released by the Soviet government after German unification have confirmed that Clay was correct. The documents record frequent complaints by the Soviet military about the behavior of East German guards. Marshal Konev told Ulbricht himself that "disorderly firing" by trigger-happy Vopos along the sector border might lead to "undesirable serious consequences." He said that he himself, not Ulbricht, would give orders along the sector borders. Soviet Defense Minister Marshal Rodion Malinovsky in mid-October wanted Khrushchev to warn Ulbricht not to take any further measures without consulting Moscow.

Soviet officials specifically said that Ulbricht should "halt such actions of the police and GDR authorities which create tensions not corresponding with the requirements of the moment." Khrushchev repeated some of those concerns in a letter to Erich Honecker, Ulbricht's closest adviser and later successor. But Ulbricht had his own plans.[19]

Checkpoint Charlie

Within days after Clay had sent his cable to Kennedy, Ulbricht gave Clay his most dramatic chance to show that escalation "works both ways." It began on Sunday evening, October 22, as Allan Lightner and his wife wanted to pass through Checkpoint Charlie to attend the opera in East Berlin.

The Soviet Communist Party (CPSU) Congress had begun meeting six days earlier in Moscow. On October 17, Khrushchev had given a key-note speech that sounded belligerent in its tone but that actually drew back from the brink over Berlin. Obviously noting the opposition of the East Europeans and the risk of Western retaliation, he did not mention the December 30 deadline that he had given Kennedy in Vienna for the German peace treaty. He said that "What counts most is not the particu-lar date but a business-like and honest settlement of the question."[20]

Ulbricht, also at the congress, had reacted angrily. Until Khrushchev's speech, he had still expected a peace treaty by the end of 1961. His notes on his meeting with Khrushchev on August 3 had even specified that some West Berlin border controls were to apply only until the conclusion of a peace treaty because he then hoped to control West Berlin as well.[21] In his own speech to the congress three days after Khrushchev's, he in-sisted that the peace treaty was "a task of the utmost urgency."[22]

Ulbricht wanted to make West Berliners as well as East Germans rec-ognize the impotence of the United States. He presumably thought that the best way to do that would be to spark an incident that would show that the allies would not react strongly to further action along the Berlin border. He thus decided to move on his own even before senior Soviet officials had returned to Berlin from the congress in Moscow.

East German police stopped Lightner as he tried to drive through Checkpoint Charlie. They asked for his identification documents. Light-ner, following long-standing practice, said that he was a member of the U.S. occupation authority, as shown by his U.S. Mission license plates. He refused to show identification and demanded to see a Soviet officer. Normally, after several minutes' delay, the East German guards would let U.S. officials pass (as they had let me pass at Potsdamer Platz on August 13). The Soviets had not authorized East German guards to stop allied personnel for long. On that evening, however, Ulbricht wanted an inci-dent. He wanted to show Khrushchev that he knew better how to deal with the Americans.

Soviet officials in Berlin had not been expecting any trouble. Ulbricht had not warned them. Marshal Konev was in Moscow attending the CPSU Congress. So was the senior Soviet political adviser in Berlin. His deputy hurried to the scene just as a squad of U.S. soldiers arrived. He pro-tested to U.S. political adviser Howard Trivers about the American show of force. Trivers asked the Soviet official what the East Germans would do if the car proceeded. The official said, "They have their orders." Clay and Watson then ordered the U.S. soldiers to escort the car through the checkpoint. The East German police drew back and let the soldiers and the car pass. Lightner drove in and out several times to make the point. Several more American cars went through that evening and were not blocked.[23] The Soviet official told an American officer that the incident had been a "mistake."[24]

Ulbricht decided to force Khrushchev to support him. On Monday morning, the GDR published a decree, obviously prepared in advance, stating that all foreigners except those dressed in allied military uniforms would have to show identification to the East German police. Khrushchev could no longer stand aside without making himself or his ally lose face. He ordered Konev to return to Berlin immediately to take control.

Kennedy's advisers criticized Clay's action as provocative. Kennedy himself commented that "we didn't send Lightner over there to go to the opera." But Clay cabled the president that he intended to meet the East German action firmly. He wrote that American officials had to keep showing themselves in East as well as West Berlin as a sign of the American presence. He reiterated what he had cabled to Kennedy on October 18, that failure to deal with the incident could have a sharply negative effect in West Berlin.

Clay next launched a probe. On the morning of October 25, the U.S. Mission sent a car to Checkpoint Charlie with two soldiers dressed in civilian clothes. They were, as expected, stopped by East German guards. When Trivers again appeared to insist on a Soviet officer, the new Soviet political adviser himself came to the checkpoint to tell Trivers that the American drivers had to follow East German regulations. Khrushchev had decided to support Ulbricht.

Clay mounted a bigger show of force, bringing ten tanks to a short distance from the checkpoint. Once the tanks were there, a squad of U.S. soldiers escorted the American car in and out of the checkpoint again. The Soviet political adviser walked around the American tanks and told Trivers: "We have tanks too."

The arrival of U.S. tanks, some equipped with bulldozer blades, alarmed the Soviet military. Konev realized that the tanks could easily enter East Berlin and could go straight through East Berlin's Mitte district, which at that point forms a salient only about ten blocks wide toward the Brandenburg Gate. The tanks would isolate all major East German ministry buildings as well as the Soviet Embassy from the main body of East Berlin.

Konev must have felt that the Soviets had better block the American tanks themselves because he could not predict what Ulbricht would do in an already tense situation. To make sure that nothing went wrong, Konev assigned a Soviet officer to take control of the checkpoint and over the East German guards. Konev acted very carefully. He brought thirty Soviet tanks to a bombed-out empty lot in East Berlin, but never more tanks than the Americans had in all of Berlin. He obviously wanted to make clear that the Soviet tank deployment remained strictly defensive.

The Soviets did not want it known that those were Soviet tanks, for they were in the capital of the supposedly sovereign GDR. They covered their insignia with mud. But U.S. officials monitoring their radios heard them speak Russian, not German. Some American newsmen, including Daniel Schorr of CBS News, even went up to the tanks to speak to the crews in Russian.

Clay welcomed the arrival of the Soviet tanks because they showed that Konev and Khrushchev were finally taking control in East Berlin, but he wanted to bring the tanks further into the open, as he had written Kennedy he would do. Clay therefore had an American car repeat the test. Once again, the East German police blocked the car. Once again, the U.S. military escorted it through the checkpoint. Once again, the East German guards had to draw back. The American tanks again moved forward, but this time they moved up further, right up to the dividing line between East and West Berlin. In response, the Soviet tanks rumbled up to the checkpoint on their side of the line.

From late afternoon through the evening, with searchlights glaring on all sides, the Soviet and American tanks faced each other directly. The tank confrontation generated dramatic photo coverage. It was the only time during the Cold War that American and Soviet armor confronted each other directly at point-blank range.

Clay immediately issued a press release saying that: "The fiction of an East German stoppage is now destroyed."[25] The presence of the Soviet tanks proved that the GDR was a puppet regime. Clay relaxed because he knew Konev would not start anything. So did other Americans in Berlin as well as the Berliners. However, alarmist press reports published

Unmarked Soviet tanks matching the American tanks at Checkpoint Charlie. Courtesy of Landesarchiv Berlin

in Washington and elsewhere gave the impression that there might be war over a checkpoint.

Macmillan called Clay a "senile embittered ass" engaged in "foolish posturing" that was dangerously provocative. He, as well as Kennedy's advisers, urged the president to call off the confrontation by ordering the U.S. tanks to withdraw. But Kennedy told them he wanted to talk to Clay before deciding anything.[26]

To show his staff that he felt fully in control of the situation, Kennedy leaned back in his chair, put his feet on his desk, and called Clay at the operations center in Berlin. When Clay said, "Hello, Mr. President," the center fell dead silent. Kennedy asked Clay about the situation. Clay told him that the Soviets had been matching the American task force tank for tank, and that this showed that the Soviets wanted no trouble, for they could easily have brought up much more armor than the Americans had. They wanted only to hold the line.

Clay added that the Soviet tank deployment showed that Khrushchev did not trust Ulbricht and wanted to take over when the risks grew too high. He said that the Soviets had moved in "because they are afraid it will get out of hand. . . . What we've done is to prove that the Russians are still in charge."

Kennedy said, "Well, that's all right. Don't lose your nerves."

Clay replied: "Mr. President, we're not worried about losing our nerves over here. What we're worried about is whether people in Washington are losing theirs."

Kennedy, who had received Clay's October 18 cable and understood exactly what Clay was doing, replied "I've got a lot of people here that have, but I haven't."[27]

Once again defying his advisers' recommendation, Kennedy did not instruct Clay to pull back the tanks. He knew from Clay's cable that Clay would withdraw them himself once he had made his point.

Khrushchev later wrote that he had been in constant contact with Konev and that neither he nor Konev wanted the confrontation to get out of hand. He did not mention any contact with Ulbricht. One can assume that he, as well as Konev, was angry with the East German leader. According to Khrushchev's later memoirs, Konev reported to Khrushchev that the tanks had faced each other throughout the entire night. He recommended that the tanks pull back. Khrushchev wrote that he did not want to leave the tank crews sitting too long in the cold at the checkpoint.

He added: "I proposed that we turn our tanks around, pull them back from the border, and have them take their places on the side streets." He wanted "to give the Americans a chance to pull back."

Khrushchev wrote that if he ordered the Soviet tanks to advance, "it would mean war." If he ordered them to pull back, "it would mean peace." He chose peace. Then, "just as I had expected," Khrushchev wrote, the Americans also withdrew.[28]

The standoff ended by 10:30 AM. Once the Soviet tanks pulled back, Clay and Watson instructed the U.S. tanks to pull back as well. Shortly, all tanks had left the checkpoint. Clay felt that the U.S. tanks had done what he had told Kennedy in his cable. He did not want to humiliate the Soviet military, which he respected from his earlier days in Berlin. He wanted to leave them a way out. But he definitely wanted to cut Ulbricht down to size.

Clay had not expected or intended the confrontation to last, but had wanted to draw the Soviets to the checkpoint to make Khrushchev realize how dangerous some of Ulbricht's games might become. Khrushchev saved face for Ulbricht, but he could not have been happy to do it.

Khrushchev held Ulbricht responsible for the Checkpoint Charlie confrontation and saw it as an additional reason not to proceed with his plans for a German peace treaty. He was ready to let Ulbricht direct the situation in East Berlin, but he insisted on having control over relations with the allies and over anything that went beyond East Berlin itself. If there was to be a risk of war, it would have to be for a Soviet interest. Then, he would want to manage it himself.[29] The Soviet military had reacted nervously to the Checkpoint Charlie crisis, putting nuclear strike forces on special alert status. They may have felt that they were not fully in control of events and needed to be ready for anything that Ulbricht or the Americans might do.[30]

The Checkpoint Charlie confrontation proved to be a decisive moment in the battle for West Berlin. It showed that the allies and especially the United States would not continue to yield to East German pressure without a strong reaction. It played a major part in boosting the morale of the Berliners because it destroyed the image of the GDR as a sovereign force that could deal on an equal basis with the Western occupation powers and that could perhaps hope to seize power over West Berlin. Soviet tanks had to save Ulbricht only a few blocks from his office.

Clay regarded the confrontation as a success because it showed that the allies would not let themselves be bullied without putting up a fight. It showed that Washington would not desert West Berlin. It gave the city an essential shot in the arm, and it put an end to Ulbricht's hope that West Berlin could be neutralized or taken over by direct action. Clay hoped that the demonstration had shown Kennedy that he did not need to let his advisers and Macmillan paralyze him. An American scholar who read Soviet documents about the Berlin crisis appeared to confirm that analysis, writing that "the Checkpoint Charlie standoff . . . lessened Khrushchev's desire to provoke the west."[31]

Clay cabled Kennedy, saying "I believe that the Soviet government took the most cautious steps it could take to uphold its prestige." He added that the Soviets "did not send the East German army as they either considered it unreliable or that we might attack it," and he expressed the hope that this would mean a Soviet "retreat from their transfer of control to the East German government." He wrote that he had wanted to force the Soviet hand and that they had come out even sooner than he had expected. He concluded by saying that Ulbricht had been "humiliated" by the Soviet intervention.[32]

Clay wrote that he saw the events at Checkpoint Charlie and the Soviet decision to resume patrols on the Autobahn as signs that the Soviets would not want to escalate but would want to keep the Berlin situation under control just as much as the United States wanted to.

Three years later, in 1964, an American historian wrote that Kennedy had sent a secret message to Khrushchev through his brother Robert and Soviet intelligence officer Georgi Bolshakov promising to withdraw the U.S. tanks within twenty minutes if the Soviets withdrew first. In his own account of the incident, however, Robert Kennedy at first said only that he had asked Bolshakov for Soviet tanks to withdraw within twenty-four hours. He said nothing about having made any commitment to withdraw U.S. tanks, perhaps because he did not want to appear to be making any concessions to the Communists.[33]

Khrushchev always said that he had decided to withdraw the Soviet tanks because it was too cold and unpleasant for the tank crews to be stuck at the checkpoint and that he was sure the U.S. tanks would withdraw if the Soviet tanks did. He said nothing about any message from Kennedy being conveyed through Bolshakov.[34]

Clay never told me or anybody else (including his biographer) about any message to Khrushchev. Nor did he ever tell me that Kennedy had called and instructed him to pull back the tanks within half an hour after the Soviet withdrawal.[35] He always said that he withdrew them because they had done what he wanted them to do and because he had told the president he would do so. That has always been my impression from his attitude and behavior, especially because there was no additional call from Kennedy.[36]

Even if no Kennedy message to Khrushchev had ever been sent, both sides would have wanted to pull back. Khrushchev did not want to keep Soviet tanks facing American armor in the nominal capital of East Germany. Ulbricht also wanted Soviet tanks out of the area because they undercut his claim to sovereignty. Clay certainly had no reason to keep the tanks in place once they had brought the Soviets out of hiding. He did not need instructions.

Kennedy himself must have drawn some important conclusions by November 1961. His advisers had repeatedly told him that the United States had to avoid any confrontation with Moscow because the Soviets would always escalate to nuclear war. But at Checkpoint Charlie, as at Steinstücken and on the Autobahn, the opposite had happened. In fact, the Soviet tanks had come on the scene precisely to avoid the kind of miscalculation that Kennedy had been told to fear and that Khrushchev had dismissed in Vienna. At Checkpoint Charlie, Khrushchev himself showed that he did not want to escalate, and he saw that Kennedy would not always retreat.

When Clay returned to Washington in late November for consultation, the president drew him aside and thanked him for what he had done at Checkpoint Charlie and how he had done it. Under Secretary of State Chester Bowles sent Clay a cable transmitting the president's congratulations.[37] Kennedy, who had almost certainly begun to use the Berlin crisis to develop his own concepts about dealing with Moscow, undoubtedly saw some things that helped him later.

Khrushchev had already worried about Ulbricht before the Checkpoint Charlie incident. He had already written to Ulbricht to "avoid . . . steps which could exacerbate the situation."[38] Ulbricht, by launching the Checkpoint Charlie crisis on October 22, had obviously chosen to ignore Khrushchev's plea.

After the confrontation, Khrushchev stopped Ulbricht from sending a diplomatic note to "all the governments of the world" to complain about the "American provocation" at the "state border of the GDR." The note would also have boasted about how the GDR had defeated the "provocation."[39] According to East German files, the note was scrapped after Ulbricht phoned Moscow (presumably to ask Khrushchev for clearance to send the note). The Soviet leader was not ready to let Ulbricht establish his "state border" through the middle of Berlin, for that would have cut into Khrushchev's occupation authority over the entire city.

Ulbricht, for his part, objected to a Soviet publication that showed East Berlin as distinct from East Germany. He wanted to show that the eastern half of the city was now definitively and formally integrated into the GDR, but Khrushchev was not ready for that.[40]

American and German scholars who consulted Soviet military files in Berlin for the end of August to the end of December 1961, found expressions of continued Soviet frustration and concern about unilateral and potentially dangerous East German behavior.[41] For example, when Ulbricht at the end of October wanted to sow land mines around the borders of West Berlin, the Soviets complained that the incident along Checkpoint Charlie had already "created the danger of serious conflicts" and that land mines might "complicate the situation." They would "create convenient grounds for provocation by the Western powers."[42]

Most important, however, the Checkpoint Charlie incident showed Khrushchev that he had better manage any confrontation with the United States directly, not through a proxy he could not trust or control. It was a lesson that he was to apply the following year.

Having It Out

Khrushchev's decision to "postpone" the peace treaty, as well as his handling of the Checkpoint Charlie confrontation, led to a bitter argument between him and Ulbricht. On October 30, Ulbricht sent Khrushchev a note formally objecting to Khrushchev's decisions at the checkpoint. He also asked Khrushchev to issue a warning to Washington to stop the patrols along the Autobahn. Three days later, on November 2, Khrushchev and Ulbricht met in Moscow for a confrontation that proved decisive in the struggle for Berlin. Khrushchev told Ulbricht that the Soviet Union and East Germany could not afford the Western economic embargo that might well result from a peace treaty and from any further direct challenge to allied rights. He complained that Ulbricht had let the GDR become too dependent on West German trade.

Khrushchev went so far as to tell Ulbricht that Soviet and East German interests in the Berlin crisis were not identical. When Ulbricht angrily retorted "then all is clear," Khrushchev told him that he was no longer to harass allied military personnel in Berlin and Germany. He said that Ulbricht could tighten controls on civilian movement to West Berlin: "I am for order; let them know that running away is impossible." But Khrushchev in effect cut Ulbricht's power to do anything on his own that might affect allied rights.[43]

Although neither Clay nor any other U.S. official knew of Khrushchev's lecture to Ulbricht, Clay already believed that the Checkpoint Charlie confrontation had driven a wedge between the two Communist leaders. He had shown that Khrushchev had better keep his German satrap on a shorter leash.

Clay cabled the State Department to say that Governing Mayor Willy Brandt had told him that West Berlin morale was higher after the confrontation and that capital had begun returning. Brandt had said that the Berliners liked the U.S. show of force. They only wished it had come when the Wall was being constructed.[44] Clay also reported on a meeting with three bishops of the German Evangelical Church who told him that the increase in U.S. patrols on the Autobahn had inspired greater confidence among Berliners.[45]

Clay thus thought that he had won an important victory at Checkpoint Charlie. His tactics were having exactly the impact he wanted, both on Berlin morale and on the minds of the Soviet leaders. He thought that he was doing what Kennedy had wanted him to do in Berlin.

But Clay had won a hollow victory. Whatever his actions may have achieved in Berlin and in Moscow, they won him no friends in Washington other than Kennedy himself. Kennedy's advisers still thought that Clay had been excessively provocative by bringing up the tanks at Checkpoint Charlie. Some made a point of reassuring Soviet Embassy officials in Washington that Clay had acted improperly and without authorization. Macmillan sent Geoffrey McDermott, the chief of the British diplomatic mission in Berlin, to the Soviet Embassy in East Berlin to inform Pervukhin that Clay had lost authority and would soon be recalled.[46]

Thus, although the Checkpoint Charlie confrontation turned out to be an important turning point in the Berlin crisis after the Wall, showing Khrushchev that he could not trust Ulbricht and showing Kennedy that the Soviets might be just as worried about escalation as he was, it did not calm the Washington opposition to Clay.

The remainder of Clay's tenure in Berlin, no matter what he tried to do and no matter how much the president may have wanted to support him, became a holding action in which he found his views and actions under ever greater criticism from Kennedy's advisers, from Macmillan, and from U.S. military commanders in Europe. His position thus became increasingly frustrating, particularly because he believed that he had to remain in Berlin because of his promise to the president and his obligation to the Berliners. Clay held on, for he could do nothing else. But he was never to receive from Kennedy the kind of total bureaucratic and public support that would have helped him to do what he believed Kennedy had sent him to do.

CHAPTER NINE

꩜━◆━꩜

"The Game Continues"

On January 6, 1962, as General Clay was coming to meet with President Kennedy for a routine consultation, McGeorge Bundy wrote a long memorandum to the president in which he pointed out that Clay "has both major and minor differences with Washington."

Bundy wrote Kennedy that "Washington" worried whether some of Clay's actions, like the helicopter flight to Steinstücken or the confrontation at Checkpoint Charlie, might have been "provocative." He did not specify what he meant by "Washington," but he presumably meant to include himself, Dean Rusk, and Kennedy's experts on the Soviet Union.

Bundy concentrated on Clay's criticism that Kennedy's constant efforts to coordinate his policies with U.S. allies (and especially with the British) meant that the U.S. was always acting on the "least common denominator" approach instead of taking the kind of vigorous action that Clay believed necessary to save Berlin. Bundy specifically cited Rusk's feeling that Clay should not react to every infringement of allied rights but only to what Rusk termed "vital" rights.[1]

Bundy concluded:

The basic problem remains: it is the degree of confidence you and Clay have in each other. He is right when he says that slow or uncertain action

Kennedy meeting with Clay at the White House around the beginning of 1962. Courtesy of the John F. Kennedy Presidential Library

can be damaging. I fear you are right in feeling that Clay, acting on his own authority, would make choices you would not approve.

Bundy thought that Kennedy could discuss these matters with Clay during their talk, although, he remarked, "It may be better to stay on general grounds this time."

When Clay returned to Berlin he told me that he had been very pleased with his talk with Kennedy. He thought the president understood what he was trying to do and fully supported him. Kennedy had evidently chosen to stay on "general grounds" and had not reflected what Bundy had called "Washington" attitudes toward the general.

Despite those "Washington" views, Kennedy never put Clay on a tight leash. Moreover, he may by then have liked some of Clay's ideas better than Bundy or "Washington" liked them. Without clear direction, and with the president expressing private (if not public) support, Clay continued to do what he thought was right. Clay believed, as he told me, that Kennedy could not afford to lose Berlin.

About two weeks after his arrival in Berlin, Clay brought over James O'Donnell to be his special assistant. O'Donnell had known Clay during his first Berlin service and had remained in Berlin for many years as a correspondent. While he served in the Undersecretary's office at the State Department, he had worked with Marguerite Higgins to turn around the White House reaction to Ulbricht's border closure on August 13.

O'Donnell knew more members of the Berlin intellectual, journalistic, and political community than anybody at the U.S. Mission. He did not want a desk at the mission, but instead spent his time around the city talking and listening to his friends and other Berliners. He could brief Clay more accurately than anyone about what Berlin's principal opinion leaders as well as ordinary Berliners were thinking. He also had good friends in Washington and could tell Clay (as well as myself) what was being said and thought there. I was glad to have O'Donnell on board because he could get around Berlin better than I. He had also known Clay long enough to have a sixth sense about the general's mood; he often told me how Clay felt.

Clay tried to encourage American companies to invest in Berlin. He sat on many American corporate boards and knew all the leading business figures. He persuaded General Motors to set up a small spare parts plant in Berlin. He also persuaded several U.S. financial firms to open offices. Each of those openings, widely reported in the Berlin press, helped to rebuild confidence in the future of Berlin. He also appeared often in public to show Berliners that America would protect them.

By the beginning of 1962, Clay and O'Donnell saw that people were gradually returning to West Berlin and that investment was coming back. The post-Wall flight had stopped even if the city remained on edge. Nonetheless, Clay kept hearing about how some American and especially British officials were continuing to accuse him of being too provocative. He thus wrote to Rusk on January 30, 1962:

> It seemed essential to me when I arrived to take a few measures to demonstrate American intent to be firm on the ground in Berlin. It would not have occurred to me that I would have been sent here for any other purpose.[2]

Clay added: "Examining these few measures now, it seems incomprehensible that anyone should regard them as bold or, indeed as some of our allies do, as dangerous."

Pointing out that none of the bold steps he initiated had led to the "dreaded escalation which had been predicted by some," Clay noted that the Steinstücken helicopter flights had brought out about thirty refugees.

Clay wrote that allied, and especially American, firmness would actually reduce the likelihood that the Americans would have to react forcefully. Khrushchev would be less likely to make a mistake by trying new harassment if he could always expect a forceful U.S. reaction. Denouncing the "hysterical belief" that any incident in Berlin would provoke a war, Clay argued that he was as confident in 1962 as he had been in 1948 that "we can save Berlin without war only if we refuse to yield further at any point."

Clay nonetheless warned Rusk that he expected Khrushchev and Ulbricht to try additional forms of harassment because allied reaction had not always been as firm as he thought necessary. But he thought those could be handled if the United States was ready to meet any harassment head-on.

Clay informed Rusk that he was prepared to remain in Berlin as a symbol, but that this might not work for long if allied reactions fell short of what Berlin needed. The Berliners would begin to wonder what he was doing there and what the president had wanted to achieve by sending him. There is no record showing whether Rusk replied.

The Air Corridor "Reservations"

One of the effects of Clay's actions may have been that Khrushchev in January 1962 formally announced to his Presidium colleagues that they no longer needed a German peace treaty. The West, he said, would not agree to one. Moreover, he thought it was "better to have Berlin for aggravating the West."[3]

Because Mikhail Pervukhin, the Soviet ambassador in East Berlin, had warned Moscow that "the GDR leadership gives insufficiently deep consideration to questions regarding how to accomplish [Soviet objectives in Berlin] without causing a military conflict," Khrushchev told Ulbricht that "we would be idiots" to risk the Western reaction to a peace treaty. He indicated that he was not strong enough to force Kennedy to back down on Berlin.[4]

Nonetheless, Khrushchev told the Polish leader Wladyslaw Gomulka that "We . . . should keep applying pressure." He said that he would use "salami" tactics to undercut Berlin morale and ultimately to make the allies leave. He added that "the game continues."[5]

True to his word, and as Clay had predicted in his letter to Rusk, Khrushchev therefore soon began more harassment, but of a totally different type. On February 7, 1962, the Soviet controller in the Berlin Air Safety Center (BASC) told the Western allied controllers that the Soviet air force wanted to "reserve" all flight levels in the south flight corridor to Berlin up to 7,000 feet for "maneuvers" for several days. This would formally limit Western airline flights to altitudes between 7,000 and 10,000 feet.[6] (Although the 10,000-foot ceiling on the corridors was not part of any formal East-West arrangement, the Soviets had objected to allied flights above that altitude and Western airlines had not flown there for years.)

The three corridors served allied military aircraft and the civilian airlines of the three allied powers (Pan American Airways, British Airways, and Air France). Because of Berlin's occupation status, German airlines like Lufthansa could not use them. The aircraft could fly over East German territory without notifying the GDR authorities although they informed the Soviets in the BASC and in a flight control office at Tempelhof airport. Most civilian aircraft normally flew between 7,000 and 10,000 feet for efficiency, but did not want to be restricted in case of bad weather at those levels. Thus the Soviet "reservation" could jeopardize flight safety.

Khrushchev could not have picked a more sensitive issue. Any effort to limit allied and civilian flights in the air corridors directly challenged one of Kennedy's essentials. It also threatened morale in West Berlin because many Berliners relied on their ability to fly into and out of the city without being stopped or checked by the Soviet or East German secret police.

Ulbricht had long wanted to control air travel to and from West Berlin, but Khrushchev's decision to restrict allied civilian traffic in the air corridors may not have been designed to help Ulbricht. More likely, it reflected Khrushchev's wish to keep the Berlin crisis in his own hands because the East Germans had no role in the BASC. Any reservations would be made at Khrushchev's direction, not Ulbricht's. Nor did Khrushchev try to block the air corridors physically, with weather balloons, as Ulbricht had wanted to do earlier. Nonetheless, Khrushchev tried some dangerous maneuvers. Soviet jet fighters began to fly in or near the corridors at various altitudes and times. They occasionally came dangerously near civilian airliners but always avoided a collision.

One time, as Clay and I were flying to Bremen to attend the traditional annual dinner of the Schaffermahlzeit, Soviet fighters buzzed our flight. They were trying to make a point because they knew it was a special flight and would probably have known that space had been reserved in Clay's name. But they made no effort to harass the plane too closely. The Soviets respected Clay even if they did not like him.

The Soviets also occasionally dropped metal "chaff" in the corridors to confuse radar and to make it hard for pilots to know where they were. Fortunately, most of the pilots assigned to the Berlin flights knew the corridors and the ground features so well that they could not be so easily confused.

Khrushchev's actions did not intimidate the Berliners. They enjoyed showing the Soviets that they would not be stopped by chicanery. They suffered from some anxiety but not enough to stop them from flying whenever they wished. Clay believed that the air corridors had to be protected. He wanted Khrushchev to realize that he could not stop air traffic except by taking truly risky steps, which Clay believed Khrushchev would not dare.

To stop Khrushchev's maneuvers and to make Khrushchev realize that the allies would react forcefully to any harassment, Clay wanted to make a show of force in the air corridors. He wanted the U.S. Air Force to send fighter jets to escort some civilian aircraft. General Lauris Norstad, the U.S. military commander in Europe and the commander of NATO air and ground forces in Europe, opposed that recommendation. So did British Prime Minister Harold Macmillan. At their request, Kennedy vetoed Clay's recommendation, but Kennedy did support Clay's recommendation to have civilian as well as military flights continue to fly through the "reserved" sections of the air corridors. He also supported Clay's recommendation to send unarmed U.S. military aircraft, such as transports, through the corridors at Soviet-reserved altitudes.

General Clay and the author leaving Tempelhof airport for a trip to Bremen during which they were buzzed by Soviet fighters in the air corridor. Courtesy of the author

Kennedy also supported Clay against Norstad when Norstad wanted to assume control of civilian traffic so as to schedule it in accordance with Soviet reservations. Clay feared that Norstad would play havoc with airline schedules if he tried to adjust them to Russian threats. He also feared that Berlin morale would plummet if the Berliners learned that their flights were being scheduled in conformity with Soviet demands.

Macmillan presented a more serious problem for Clay because he could issue instructions to British air traffic controllers on the ground. For example, he ordered them to obey a Soviet request to notify the BASC of the exact time when British aircraft traveling through the corridors entered or left East German airspace. Clay opposed any such instructions because they would imply that the GDR might have some authority over the corridors. He wanted the air corridors kept above politics and above national borders. The French, like Clay, also opposed Macmillan's new practice. So did Kennedy after Clay informed him that he objected to what the British were doing. He was as sensitive as Clay to the importance of the air corridors.[7] The British then stopped the practice.

Khrushchev's maneuvers in the air corridors thus fell short of what he had probably wanted. The Western airlines did not comply with Soviet space reservations in the corridors. By the end of April, the Soviet reservations in the air corridors stopped as suddenly as they had begun. They had not succeeded in blocking or even delaying Western air traffic.

Khrushchev must have faced a difficult decision. He had presumably hoped and perhaps expected that Kennedy and the other Western leaders would respect the Soviet air corridor reservations. When they did not do so, he was left with the choice of shooting down a Western airliner or withdrawing the reservations. But shooting down a Western plane, civilian or military, would almost certainly have risked nuclear war.

Khrushchev did not believe that he was ready for that. His main intercontinental ballistic missile (ICBM), the R-16, had exploded on its launch pad in October of 1960. This had delayed his plans for a full panoply of intercontinental and medium-range missiles. Although the ICBM was finally being deployed by 1962, it could not be kept on constant alert because, unlike U.S. missiles, it used liquid rather than solid fuel. Khrushchev complained that he could not count on his intercontinental missiles to support Soviet policy in any East-West confrontation or in a fast-moving crisis.[8]

In April 1962, moreover, Defense Minister Rodion Malinovsky had given Khrushchev a depressing update on the nuclear ICBM balance between the Soviet Union and the United States. That briefing must have made him realize that he could not follow through on his "reservations" in the Berlin air corridors. Khrushchev's son later revealed that Khrushchev himself knew in 1962 that he was far behind in ICBMs with little hope of catching up quickly, if at all.[9] Kennedy knew of the Soviet weakness because a Soviet informer, Oleg Penkovsky, had passed that information to the United States in 1961.[10] Khrushchev simply did not have the power to force the Berlin issue.[11]

Clay believed that Khrushchev could not carry his gamble too far. But he worried because he thought the "reservations" showed "the risks the Soviet government is prepared to take to try to convince the West Germans that they cannot rely on allied protection and therefore should negotiate separately."[12] Nonetheless, Clay felt frustrated that Kennedy had not approved his recommendation for fighter escorts.

He told me that he thought Khrushchev would continue to try different maneuvers so long as he was not convinced that it would be risky. Clay felt that Khrushchev needed to realize that he was treading on dangerous ground whenever he challenged any American right in Berlin, and that he would have to pay a price for even trying.

In the U.S. Mission we had another concern: why had Khrushchev first tried to block the air corridors by his "reservations" and why had he later given up the effort without having reached whatever he might have wanted? We had no good answers to that question.

Clay's Frustration

Despite his success in persuading Kennedy to do what was necessary to keep the air corridors open, Clay remained bitter about General Norstad's actions and recommendations during the air corridor incidents. He could not understand why Norstad "couldn't make a decision as the U.S. commander without making it as the NATO commander." In effect, Norstad was "being pulled back all of the time by the fact that he was wearing a NATO hat." All of Norstad's decisions as NATO commander had to be approved by the British, in effect giving British officers in Norstad's command a veto over American civilian and military flights to Berlin as well as over Kennedy's policies. With Norstad acting as an alliance commander rather than as an American commander, he made the British view his own—especially because he probably agreed with it. That would perhaps have increased the president's inclination to accept it.

Macmillan, as bitter about Clay as Clay was about the British, considered asking Kennedy to recall Clay but did not do so because his new foreign secretary, Lord Home, advised against it. But Home did warn the U.S. ambassador in London, David Bruce, about Macmillan's attitude, and the British continued consistently to lobby against Clay and his policies through their ambassador in Washington, David Ormsby-Gore, and through Norstad himself.[13]

Macmillan played a dangerous double game of his own. He wanted Great Britain to be admitted to the European Economic Community, and he recognized that he would need Chancellor Konrad Adenauer's support for that. So he tried to use his influence over Kennedy and over Norstad to have them oppose Clay's policies without Macmillan's hand ever showing. Lord Home even specifically assured Macmillan in April 1962: "I think so far we have maneuvered so that when there is dirty work to be done the Americans do it."[14] Macmillan wanted to make sure that if Berlin was lost, the Americans and Kennedy rather than the British would get the blame in Germany. While talking sweetly to Kennedy, he was setting the president up to be the fall guy if things went wrong in Berlin.

David Bruce, the U.S. ambassador to Great Britain, understood Macmillan's tactics. He warned Washington that the British were "not unaware that if the West Berliners are forsaken, the monkey will be on the American back and not on their own."[15]

French president Charles de Gaulle also maneuvered to let the Americans take the blame for anything that went wrong. He did and said very little to support Berlin, claiming that French policy was not as important as American policy. But de Gaulle would not mind if Kennedy stumbled in Berlin; it would reinforce the French assertion that the Europeans and especially the Germans could not rely on the Americans. A Kennedy failure would enhance de Gaulle's stature in Germany.

Clay, who had long watched British and French policies in Berlin, knew what was going on as well as Bruce did. He wrote to Kennedy that the president should not let Britain or France dictate policy in Berlin:

"Failure on their part to react is taken for granted in Berlin; failure on our part could be disastrous."[16] If Berlin was lost, he feared, the Kennedy presidency would be lost. Nobody would blame Macmillan or de Gaulle.

Clay argued that a strong American stand was more important than allied unity, especially at the lowest common denominator. He believed the United States should take the lead and the others would follow. If they did not, that should not worry Kennedy.[17] But Kennedy's White House advisers still took Macmillan seriously, and Kennedy continued to treat Ormsby-Gore as a close friend instead of as a foreign ambassador selling a message.

Lawrence Legere, an assistant to General Maxwell Taylor at the White House, understood Clay's frustrations. He wrote to Taylor that Clay would have been the right man for Berlin if he had been "willing to act as some benevolent symbol" who would serve as "a bone tossed to Berlin to compensate for our do-nothingness after the Wall."

But, Legere wrote, Clay was a "high-principled, uncomplicated, rather inflexible, old War Horse." Moreover, "he has consistently recommended the full exercise of our rights." This could not work while the U.S. Berlin Task Force and the allied Ambassadorial Group were "acting like Generals making squad leaders' decisions for them."

Taylor sent Legere's memo to Bundy after writing on it: "Legere pretty much expresses my view." Bundy's notes do not show if he ever sent the memo on to Kennedy, but he probably did not.[18]

Robert Kennedy Visits Berlin

While Khrushchev's "game" continued, Robert Kennedy visited Berlin from February 22 to 24, 1962. He came with his wife, Ethel, and two of their children, Kathleen and Robert F. Kennedy, Jr., to look around Berlin and, as we learned later, to scout whether the president should himself visit the city. The president had told Clay that he wanted Robert's trip to go well. Clay had encouraged the trip because he thought it would boost Berlin morale and give a chance for Robert to see Berlin and to tell his brother the realities of the city.

Clay wanted to talk privately in Berlin with a senior American official who had the president's ear. He thought that Robert Kennedy represented the best chance for a member of Kennedy's inner circle to learn about Berlin and tell the president directly what he had seen. He had increasingly come to realize that Robert had more influence on the president's policies than Rusk or anybody else outside and even inside the White House.

Although Robert arrived on a bitterly cold day he drew a large crowd of Berliners on the way in from the airport. And he drew an even larger crowd, estimated at some 100,000, when he made a speech at the city hall in response to Willy Brandt's request. Much to Clay's astonishment, however, Robert felt that he had to call his brother from Clay's office to check some points about the speech, explaining "I don't want to say anything you don't mean." Clay told me that he found this extraordinary, as it seemed to show that the president after a year in office had still not formulated a Berlin policy that everybody understood and could follow. Clay was amazed that even the president's brother was not sure about U.S. policy.

The president and Robert discussed the speech and decided that Robert should follow a rather moderate tone in order to avoid raising Berlin expectations or risking a provocation toward Khrushchev. This led to a speech more suited to an academic audience than to a political rally, but the Berliners were happy to have the president's brother in town and they cheered everything he said.

Knowing of Robert Kennedy's presence, Ulbricht had floated some red balloons over West Berlin from East Berlin. Robert made a big hit by saying: "The Communists let their balloons come through, but they won't let their people come through."[19]

One of Robert's missions on this visit was to learn whether the president should himself visit Berlin. Henry Kissinger as a White House consultant had recommended such a visit in May 1961, before Kennedy's summit with Khrushchev, to underline the American commitment to Berlin. But Kennedy had hesitated then. Now, the president was apparently considering it quite seriously. Clay told me that he used the occasion to tell Robert that the president should very definitely visit Berlin. He said then, as he would say later in Washington to the president himself, that Kennedy would get a tremendous reception.[20]

Robert Kennedy's visit gave me my own first insight into the magic of the Kennedy name in Berlin. Because Clay had promised the president that he would watch over Robert, he asked me to help serve as an escort for him as well as for Mrs. Kennedy and their children. I went with the family to a Berlin school and was amazed to see hundreds of Berlin kids race into the playground during school intermission to see and touch the Kennedy children. A Secret Service officer and I each hoisted one of the young Kennedys on our shoulders to save them from being crushed. We carried them through the crowd of shouting youngsters and delivered them to their grateful mother and their waiting car. I had not understood until then the kind of Kennedy mystique that was beginning to grow in Berlin. It made me wonder how a visit by the president himself would go.

Kennedy's and Clay's Strategy and Tactics

The debates between Clay and Kennedy's advisers, and sometimes between Clay and Kennedy himself, reflected four very real differences in strategy and tactics.

1) Kennedy and Clay differed about Berlin's importance for Germany and Europe. Kennedy had been ready to divide Europe, Germany, and Berlin between the West and the Soviet Union. Kennedy had offered that in Vienna. Khrushchev had rejected Kennedy's offer because he not only wanted East Berlin but also wanted to support Ulbricht's drive to neutralize West Berlin. When he told Marshal Ivan Konev: "Go to Berlin, scare them," he still wanted to get the allies out of West Berlin.[21]

Clay thought that Kennedy's three essentials covering U.S. rights in West Berlin were too narrow. Although he fully agreed with those essentials, he thought American interests went far beyond them. He saw no point in preserving U.S. access to an empty city and having U.S. forces protect a shrinking population. West Berlin needed to be alive and to attract investment as well as young people and visitors. It should continue to be a beacon to the East, and America had to protect its interests in the East as well as the West. Unlike Kennedy in Vienna, he was not ready to write off Poland or Hungary or East Berlin.

Clay's tactics reflected his conviction that as long as the allies held a position in Berlin, and as long as the city was prosperous and alive, the future of Germany and all of Europe would remain open and the U.S. position on the continent would be secure. If Kennedy and the West were defeated in Berlin, either immediately or over time, the United States would lose much of its influence in Germany and in all of Europe.

Clay once told me that the Germans might choose neutrality if they became disappointed in the United States and the West. Khrushchev could and almost certainly would talk separately with West Germany and would try to use West German frustrations to make his own deals, trying to persuade West Germany to leave NATO. Some Germans might be ready to accept that. Berlin was an important key to German and European attitudes. Clay thus saw the battle for Berlin as a battle for Kennedy's entire European strategy, not only for the three essentials. As Rusk recognized, Clay wanted to defend rights that Rusk might not define as "vital."

The Nuclear Threat

2) The existence of nuclear weapons that could hit the United States shaped the arguments that Clay had with Kennedy's advisers as well as with the president himself.

Clay believed that U.S. military or civilian officials on the front lines should have full authority to handle any crisis. During and after World War II, they did. Neither President Franklin Roosevelt nor anyone else told General Dwight Eisenhower how to liberate Europe. President Harry Truman never gave Clay orders on how to handle the Soviet blockade of Berlin. He left Clay in charge and gave him full support.

Clay knew that the United States had a comfortable lead over the Soviet Union in nuclear missiles and did not need to fear a confrontation. He was a member of the President's Foreign Intelligence Advisory Board (PFIAB) and continued receiving top secret strategic briefings by special messenger even while in Berlin. He felt he could count on Khrushchev and the Soviets to act carefully and to pull back in a real crunch.

Clay thus made his decisions and recommendations on the basis of what he believed to be a well-informed judgment about the Russians. He had actually dealt with Russians as much if not more than Kennedy's experts on the Soviet Union. And he believed that he had considered Soviet reactions thoroughly when he made his own decisions and his recommendations to Kennedy. But Kennedy feared that any mistake or any confrontation even a continent away might lead to a nuclear war.

As the first president to face a Soviet Union armed with nuclear missiles and as the first president to be directly threatened with war by a Soviet leader, Kennedy would not yield the power of decision. He and the nation had too much at risk. He genuinely feared escalation and was dreadfully afraid that a confrontation over Berlin would lead to nuclear conflict. He wanted to control all U.S. actions to avoid that.

Kennedy's meeting with Khrushchev had left him deeply worried. He felt that Khrushchev could be irrational and was too mercurial to be predictable in a crisis. Even if Khrushchev did not have nuclear superiority, he might still do something crazy if he felt threatened. Kennedy obviously felt that he had to have Khrushchev's mental state in mind during any confrontation. Kennedy trusted neither Clay nor anybody else to understand his attitude because they had not seen Khrushchev in private meetings. Khrushchev had "impressed" him. He had not frightened Kennedy out of Berlin but had apparently made him worry whether he was dealing with a fully stable personality. The president believed that his summit with Khrushchev had given him a unique personal perspective and responsibility.

In a hypersensitive place like Berlin, where Kennedy feared that war could erupt at any moment, he wanted to manage every detail either himself or through persons in his immediate office. This frustrated Clay because he had known and served presidents who set broad policy lines and let field commanders carry them out as they judged best. But times had changed, and no president would let others make potentially cataclysmic decisions anymore.

How to Decide and Really Deter

3) Kennedy and Clay differed in their styles of decision-making. As one of my friends told me before I met Clay, his mind was like a "steel trap." He could and did make decisions almost instantaneously. Having managed the entire U.S. Army procurement system during World War II, having served as U.S. military governor in Germany and then going on to be chief executive of a major American corporation, Clay was accustomed to making big decisions and to making them fast.

Kennedy had never carried executive responsibility before coming to the White House. He liked to consult with many people and to hear a lot of opinions before making up his own mind. He conducted his policy meetings in seminar style because he would hear a wide range of opinions expertly presented.

Kennedy probably felt uncomfortable with Clay's lightning reactions to some of Khrushchev's and Ulbricht's moves. He might have wondered not only if Clay's tactics might risk escalation but whether Clay had considered all the alternatives. Clay usually had, but Kennedy needed more time to think. With most of his advisers routinely opposing Clay, Kennedy must sometimes have felt very lonely when he backed the general.

For Kennedy, the Berlin crisis became an educational experience. He had never had to face that kind of demand for instantaneous decision. He learned quickly, but he still needed more time than Clay to think things through.

4) Perhaps the most serious difference between Kennedy and Clay lay in their different concepts about how to handle Khrushchev's and Ulbricht's harassment. Clay believed firmly that the West needed to react harshly to the Soviets and East Germans. He once told me, "We have to make them sorry they tried." He feared that an American failure to push back hard would only encourage Khrushchev to try again, and to try ever more dangerous steps. Thus, he believed in going the Soviets and East Germans one better.

If Ulbricht harassed American drivers on the Autobahn, Clay would flood the road with patrols and convoys that would make the Soviets uncomfortable. If Ulbricht tried to close a checkpoint, Clay would bring in soldiers and tanks. This ran directly against Kennedy's concerns about escalation. He was not ready to push back hard when he could not be certain how Khrushchev would react. It also ran against Rusk's belief that the United States should only protect what he termed "vital" interests. It also made Macmillan anxious and angry.

Clay once warned General Taylor that Kennedy's failure to meet Khrushchev very firmly at all times would lead to a loss in Soviet respect for the United States. Khrushchev would feel confident to take steps that would involve what Clay termed "greater risks."[22] Thus Clay thought that the only way to end the Berlin crisis was to make Khrushchev believe that he was running incalculable risks by his policies and tactics. But on that score, Kennedy did not support him. The president may not even have understood Clay's thinking.

Kennedy's Middle Course

What kept Kennedy and Clay going in the same general direction even if not exactly on the same course was that Kennedy did not like to lose, and he particularly did not like the American public to think that he was losing. He admired Clay even when he may have felt uncomfortable with Clay's decisions or his style. Thus, despite the grumbling about Clay on Kennedy's staff, the president expressed his appreciation to Clay even when he did not necessarily agree with what Clay had proposed or done.

Kennedy wrote to Clay on March 1, 1962, that he had given standing instructions to see any message that Clay sent. He added, "On a number of occasions a cable from you has led me to order a review of policy or a new and somewhat different emphasis in existing activities. . . . We continue to count on you."[23] Two weeks later, even after he had vetoed Clay's proposals for fighter aircraft in the Berlin air corridors, Kennedy wrote Clay that he still wanted Clay's views although he had supported Norstad in that case. He added, "Your candid and determined comments are of great value. . . . It is a matter of great importance to me that your voice, which must always be heard, is on the line from Berlin."[24]

Kennedy might have written those messages only to keep Clay on board and to make the old general happy, but there was little reason to do that. More likely, his letters and his attitude reflected his wish—even greater than that of other chief executives—to hear more than one opinion.

Kennedy knew by 1962 what his main allies would say in any crisis: Macmillan would always look for a way out and de Gaulle would say and do nothing. All his advisers and his Soviet experts, whether at the White House, the State Department, or the U.S. Embassy in Moscow, would propose some form of compromise. The U.S. military would urge caution. Kennedy needed to have somebody who would forcefully present the opposite point of view, even if he might finally decide not to back it. He at least knew the full range of his options.

In Berlin we often had the impression that Kennedy would always choose the middle course whenever he had to make a decision. Although he spoke in inspirational language, he would feel most comfortable with a moderate choice. Clay certainly felt that Kennedy was always looking for consensus.[25] Clay offered options that Kennedy might not accept, but that gave him an idea of where the middle choice might lie. And there were times when Kennedy preferred to follow a tougher line with the Soviets, and Clay would tell him where that line lay.

Clay also often found that Kennedy would support his recommendations when he spoke directly to the president. Clay told me several times that Kennedy was more prepared than his advisers to confront the Soviets, although he still did not confront them as often as Clay would have wished.[26] Clay sang a different song than Macmillan, Bundy, and others, and Kennedy wanted to hear it and sometimes to follow it.

Kennedy definitely did not want Clay to resign in anger. He could not afford to have a senior Republican denounce his policies, even if Clay had promised not to act like MacArthur. Clay thus stayed on. He thought that he was making a contribution to U.S. policy and was helping to save Berlin, even if things did not always go his way.

Clay never spoke of his frustrations in public because he did not want to raise any doubts in the minds of the Berliners. He rejected several generous offers from publishers to write his memoirs of the Berlin Wall crisis because he would have had to express his doubts about American policy. But he clearly felt frustrated and would occasionally show it in his private moments. O'Donnell and I would sometimes talk about it but we knew that Clay would be the "good soldier" as long as he believed that he had a role.

Clay's Contribution

Although Clay may have felt frustrated in Berlin, he actually proposed or carried out a number of policies that changed the direction of the Berlin crisis and gave West Berlin a new lease on life despite the Wall:

- Despatch of a 1,500-man U.S. brigade to Berlin
- U.S. "courtesy" patrols on the Autobahn
- Helicopter flights to Steinstücken
- Patrols along the sector borders
- Retaliatory blockage of Soviet cars in West Berlin
- The Checkpoint Charlie confrontation
- A Firm U.S. policy against Soviet corridor reservations
- Encouraging U.S. investment in West Berlin.

Many of these steps seemed small, but they added up and they had a palpable effect in West Berlin. They gave the city new courage after the Wall and stopped the flight of capital and of young Berliners. They also had an impact on American relations with West Germany as a whole. Without them, Ulbricht might have realized his wish to neutralize West Berlin.

With Kennedy often supporting Clay, the suspicion that Bundy had expressed to Kennedy in August 1961, when he wrote "Maybe you are tougher than the line of thought I have sketched," had proved to be more correct than he may have realized at the time.

The relationship between the young president and the old general remains one of the fascinations of Berlin and of the Kennedy presidency. For several months, from the fall of 1961 through the spring of 1962, the two of them held the fate of Berlin in their hands, and beyond that the fate of Germany and Europe and perhaps of U.S. containment policy. They worked together, often closely, in the midst of crisis. At the end, despite the differences in their views, they saved Berlin and kept the German question open for others than Ulbricht and Khrushchev to decide.

The result of the Berlin Wall crisis would certainly have been very different if Kennedy had not appointed Clay to the city and if he had not supported Clay at least some of the time. As Khrushchev had said, the game continued.

Mainly, however, the Berliners themselves saved their city. It would have been easy for them to leave. But, contrary to Rusk's belief, they were ready to endure whatever was necessary to preserve their freedom. The West Berliners saw Ulbricht as another Hitler. The East Berliners saw him the same way, and they would continue to resist him and to flee whenever possible. That spirit forced Western leaders to help Berlin even when they had not at first intended to do so.

Clay Leaves Berlin

Khrushchev's policy appeared to shift in April and May of 1962. He not only stopped reserving space in the air corridors, he also stopped harassing and delaying allied traffic on the Autobahn. Soviet officials became more friendly. Marshal Konev left Berlin, a sign that Khrushchev did not believe he needed to keep such tight control in the city any more. We assumed it meant that the Soviets would no longer try novel forms of harassment and would also have told Ulbricht to lay off.

With the shift in Khrushchev's tactics, Clay wrote to Kennedy: "The Soviets and East Germans had to erect a wall to stop refugee flow but . . . hoped also that it would panic West Berlin and lead to allied disagreements, particularly with the Federal Republic of Germany."

Clay added:

> By meeting the harassments promptly with sufficient strength to nullify any real fears that might have developed in West Berlin and to convince the Soviet representatives that harassments to be effective would truly involve the risk of war, [the United States had shown] that harassment alone would not destroy West Berlin, had convinced the Soviets that they could not win and had forced them to relax their pressure.[27]

However, Clay warned, "I think we have won a battle but not the campaign, and that we now have an interlude in which we can get ready for the next battle."[28] Clay told me that he thought Ulbricht and Khrushchev still wanted to get control over West Berlin but he could not be sure what they would try next.

At the same time, with the end of the harassment in the air corridors, the mood in Berlin shifted noticeably. The crisis that had begun with the Wall eased. The United States had saved the Western position in West Berlin, even if East Berlin had been lost.

Perhaps equally important, although we did not know it at the time, was that Clay may have made Khrushchev realize that Berlin might not be the best place for a direct Soviet-American confrontation.

As his last official act, Clay spoke at Brandt's request before a May Day rally that Brandt had called. Over 700,000 Berliners, the largest crowd until then in West Berlin history, turned out for the speech. Clay told the Berliners that he was leaving because he had done his job, but that his heart remained in the city and that he would return if he was needed.

CHAPTER TEN

⊙═══╪═══⊙

"We'll Talk the Problem to Death"

On August 28, 1961, barely two weeks after the building of the Wall, McGeorge Bundy had urged President Kennedy to offer some new concessions to the Soviet Union:

> The main line of thought among those who are now at work on our negotiating position is that we can and should shift substantially toward acceptance of the GDR, the Oder-Neisse line, a non-aggression pact and even the idea of two peace treaties.[1]

This memorandum continued to ignore Henry Kissinger's recommendation that Kennedy should handle the Berlin negotiations with greater stress on potential German unification and on a referendum for the German people. Instead, it concentrated on trying to find ways to mollify Khrushchev.

Kennedy accepted Bundy's suggestions, urging Dean Rusk to be more forthcoming in his next meetings with Soviet Foreign Minister Andrei Gromyko and to ignore French and German reservations:

> I no longer believe that satisfactory progress can be made by Four-Power discussion alone. I think we should promptly work toward a strong U.S. position and should make it clear that we cannot accept a veto from any other power. . . . They must come along or stay behind.[2]

In dismissing "any other power," Kennedy most specifically meant West German chancellor Konrad Adenauer. He knew that Adenauer would be dead set against some of Bundy's proposals. But he, Bundy, and Rusk assumed that Adenauer would have to "come along."

With a congressional election coming up in November 1962, and after the public criticism he had received for letting the Wall go up, Kennedy thought it would be politically disastrous for him to pull U.S. forces out of Berlin. He did not even dare negotiate about it. Moreover, it risked destroying the Western position in the city. But the Wall had left him very little to negotiate about Berlin itself. He had to find topics other than the three essentials on which to offer concessions.

For Kennedy, Bundy's suggestions offered an ideal way to feed the Soviet beast by giving up some things that Adenauer might not want to surrender. The West Germans would not be voting in the U.S. election. With Harold Macmillan's backing, Kennedy decided to follow that route.

Gromyko Talks Tough

Rusk met with Gromyko three times at the end of September 1961 to talk about Berlin. Rusk stressed that he had no mandate to conduct formal negotiations because he had not consulted with other Western capitals, but he wanted to explore different ideas to see if it made sense even to try to negotiate.[3]

Rusk hinted broadly that Kennedy might be prepared to accept Khrushchev's long-standing proposals for reducing troops in central Europe and especially in Germany. He also suggested that Washington might recognize the existence of two Germanies. But he stressed that, in exchange for such concessions, the United States needed to keep its access rights to Berlin as well as its troops in West Berlin.

Gromyko told Rusk that the existence of two German states had to be accepted as an "inexorable, indubitable, immutable fact" that was not even subject to negotiation. He did not consider that a Western concession. But he also kept assuring Rusk that the Soviet Union would offer the "free city" of West Berlin all kinds of guarantees as well as free access. Of course, he added, such matters would need to be negotiated with the German Democratic Republic. After all, the West would have to "respect the sovereignty of the GDR." Moreover, the Soviet Union would defend the GDR if necessary.

Gromyko noted that the outlook was "very gloomy" if the West did not respect GDR sovereignty. But he never specified what GDR sovereignty might mean, either to Rusk or to other negotiators, although it appeared to mean that Ulbricht would insist on deciding who could or could not travel to Berlin.[4]

Clay worried about Rusk's negotiating style. He showed me a cable reporting a comment by Gromyko to Rusk that the Soviet position opposing West German links with West Berlin was "like a rock." Clay said that he wished that Rusk would just once say to Gromyko that some American position was "like a rock" instead of constantly hinting at potential further concessions. He feared that Rusk's tactics would only whet Soviet instincts to ask for more.[5]

Gromyko indeed emerged from his talks with Rusk totally convinced that he did not need to make any concessions. He wrote Ulbricht that the United States was "ready to do anything to avoid a confrontation between itself and the Soviet Union." That, he wrote, "was Rusk's principal purpose in the talks."[6]

After reading the record of the Rusk-Gromyko talks, even Bundy expressed concern. He warned Kennedy that Rusk appeared to offer "significant U.S. concessions in return for nothing more than a reassertion of rights that in our view are not open to discussion." Bundy questioned Rusk's suggestion that it might be possible to start real negotiations with the Soviets on the basis of his talks: "I believe we are on a dangerous slope of appeasement, and I am certain that this will be the view of the Germans, the French and the Republicans."[7]

Bundy was right. America's allies, including even the British, found Rusk's talks disturbing. They felt that Rusk had yielded too much. Foreign Secretary Lord Home wrote to Macmillan that the Americans "seem to be ready to consider almost everything." West German foreign minister Heinrich von Brentano said that the Germans would never have agreed to the soundings if they had known how far Rusk would go. French President Charles de Gaulle had already warned on September 2 that it would be a mistake to approach the Soviets for talks, and he now complained that the Americans were ready to hand everything to the Soviets on a silver platter. He told Adenauer, who certainly agreed, that the tenor of the talks proved that he had been right to oppose even opening them.[8]

Hoping to encourage Kennedy, Khrushchev weighed in on September 29 with a thirty-page letter in which he reiterated Soviet assurances about the "free city" of West Berlin. But he gave no sign that he was ready to yield on any single point. Instead, he offered to meet Kennedy again and wrote that he was "hoping for" a visit by Kennedy to the Soviet Union.[9]

Kennedy and Rusk knew very well that Konrad Adenauer would oppose the kinds of concessions that they were considering, particularly because Adenauer would be asked to yield some basic points of principle on which he had staked his political life. He would not and could not accept formal recognition of the GDR dictatorship or any kind of agreement that would infringe upon the NATO forces that protected West Germany. West German ambassador Wilhelm Grewe kept telling the White House not to expand the range of negotiating topics to "broader questions," but Kennedy and Rusk wanted to try new ideas and went ahead without telling him or Adenauer.[10]

Kennedy and Rusk proceeded in disregard of the fact that Washington was "a sieve," as Kennedy had himself described it. As we had also heard in Berlin, White House assistant Walt Rostow had once observed: "The Ship of State is the only ship that leaks at the top." Talkative White House officials, who liked to show journalists that they were in the know, kept telling the press that Kennedy was exploring new ideas on Berlin and Germany. They even specified what some of those ideas were.

Adenauer, reading these press reports, wrote to Kennedy on October 4 to warn him that "zones with special military status of any kind in Europe can be ominous and even impossible." A special military status for any West European country, "especially the Federal Republic," would be a "permanent invitation for the Soviet Union to intervene in the affairs of Western Europe." Such a status, he said, would thus be unacceptable. It would jeopardize any hope for West German security.[11]

A few weeks later, on October 21, Adenauer wrote to Kennedy again, arguing that not everything outside Kennedy's vital interests should be negotiated away.[12] This, he wrote, "applies particularly to the security interests of the Federal Republic" as well as to "the political and constitutional links between Berlin with the Federal Republic" which Adenauer described as "essential to Berlin's political and economic existence." Adenauer recalled plaintively that "the German people, after the catastrophe of the Hitler years and the war, had set all their hopes upon the West, the Atlantic alliance, and especially the United States." He wrote that the Germans had rejected Soviet 1950s "blandishments" offering to unite Germany if Adenauer accepted neutrality and expelled U.S. forces.

In exchange for the West German alliance, Adenauer recalled, the United States had agreed to support German unity through democratic elections. Although he knew that unification would not come soon, Adenauer insisted that there could be no negotiations on Germany's future borders or other German issues until a final peace treaty. Almost pleading, he asked once again to be consulted before Kennedy authorized any further negotiations about Berlin and Germany.

Like many Germans who had lived during the 1920s in the Weimar Republic, Adenauer feared that disappointment at the West could turn Germany toward the East, possibly toward an alliance with Moscow and toward another catastrophic dictatorship. He had set his policy and his entire political fate against that, but neither Kennedy nor the president's principal advisers except for Kissinger appeared to understand that.

Adenauer and Kennedy looked in different directions. Adenauer looked at the past, telling Kennedy that he expected the president to honor agreements that recognized the democratically elected Federal Republic of Germany as the only legitimate representative of the German people. Kennedy looked at the present. In the age of potential mutual nuclear annihilation, he was ready to disregard past commitments. If he could make a deal with Khrushchev on Berlin at the expense of West German interests, Adenauer would have to accept it.

Rusk had said that "We'll talk the problem to death," continually offering Khrushchev and Gromyko new proposals and concessions in order to keep them from attacking the three main U.S. interests in Berlin. Everything was on the table, whether Adenauer or de Gaulle liked it or not.

Prime Minister Harold Macmillan agreed with Kennedy's and Rusk's approach, and wrote to Kennedy in November 1961,

"The things which . . . I feel the [West Germans] ought to be prepared to accept are, first, the Oder-Neisse line, which is generally agreed; secondly, some formula which amounts to a considerable degree of de facto recognition of the GDR." In return, he reinforced Kennedy's essentials: "We must receive total satisfaction on the Western position in Berlin as well as unrestricted access.[13"]

In December 1961 Macmillan was even beginning to worry that Kennedy's insistence on keeping U.S. forces in Berlin might lead to war, so he suggested converting allied occupation rights in Berlin into some kind of trusteeship agreement. He thought such concessions offered a good chance for a deal on Berlin.[14]

As for the Germans, Macmillan's foreign secretary, Lord Home, thought that the most difficult problem would be "to decide how and when it is safe even to hint to them that we are thinking along these lines."[15] Macmillan and Home, like Kennedy, believed that Adenauer would have to agree on the points that they wanted to concede to Khrushchev. But they recognized that it would be an agonizing moment for Adenauer and for the alliance. Macmillan complained to Kennedy that de Gaulle was opposing Western concessions in order to get credit for being a good friend of Germany, leaving the Americans and the British to feel the brunt of German anger. But Macmillan was ready to face that.[16]

On August 26, even before Bundy's memorandum to the president, de Gaulle had warned Kennedy in a personal letter about three very specific points: first, that the opening of negotiations right after the Wall and under further Soviet pressure would be seen as "a prelude to the abandonment . . . of Berlin, and as a sort of notice of our surrender"; second, that Khrushchev would follow by making arrangements with "a number of our allies of today" (a thinly veiled reference to de Gaulle's constant fear of a deal between West Germany and the Soviet Union); and, third, that France would not join in talks "which are in fact demanded by Moscow."

Because de Gaulle's ambassador in Washington was better briefed than Grewe, de Gaulle knew enough to warn Kennedy that the ideas being bandied about in Washington for negotiations with Khrushchev "might result in the neutralization of West Germany" and that the future of Europe would be in jeopardy if Germany did not remain firmly attached to the West.

De Gaulle told Macmillan in November that France "was concerned above all, and perhaps even more than her British and American allies, to ensure that Germany was tied to the West." He feared leaving the Germans with "a sense of betrayal."[17]

De Gaulle had reason to worry. If Khrushchev could neutralize West Germany, France would be on the outer border of the West. Macmillan could count on the English Channel to protect Great Britain, and the United States could count on the Atlantic. But France would have only a narrow neutral strip of West Germany between it and the Soviet army. De Gaulle proposed periodic summit meetings between France, Great Britain and the United States to review talks with the Soviets. Kennedy rejected that idea. He did not want his negotiations to be hemmed in by others and especially not by the French.

However, de Gaulle gave Kennedy the opening the president wanted when he wrote that Kennedy was of course free to explore whether there might be any room for negotiations.[18] De Gaulle then expected Kennedy to engage in such "exploration," and he was sure that this would destroy Adenauer's confidence in the United States and force him to turn to France.

In effect, de Gaulle was setting a trap, hoping to win Adenauer to side with him against Kennedy. But neither Kennedy nor Rusk saw the trap. They were pleased to have de Gaulle's clearance for what they kept describing as their "probes" to see if "real" negotiations might be possible.

To try to ease Adenauer's concerns, Kennedy wrote to the chancellor that Rusk would not actually engage in negotiations with Moscow, but that he would engage only in diplomatic probes to learn if formal negotiations offered any promise. Adenauer replied that Kennedy should limit topics to Berlin itself and not offer to change arrangements for Germany as a whole. But a talk between him and Kennedy on that topic proved so tense and difficult that both agreed to destroy the notes.[19]

On December 22, 1961, Khrushchev did what de Gaulle had feared. He told the German ambassador in Moscow, Hans Kroll, that he would regard reconciliation of the German and Russian peoples as his crowning achievement in foreign policy. He asked for direct talks with Adenauer on Berlin, but Adenauer refused, fearing that such talks would create havoc in the Western ranks. He also did not believe that Khrushchev would offer anything meaningful.[20]

More U.S. Tries at Diplomacy

At about the same time, and without knowing of Khrushchev's move toward Germany, Bundy concluded that the time had come to try again for talks with Moscow about Berlin. In January 1962, he wrote Kennedy that "we should promptly decide to initiate genuinely private and bilateral talks." Although he still thought that the Soviets were far from serious negotiations, he hoped to learn if Khrushchev would accept the Western presence in Berlin in exchange for new Western proposals on Germany.

Kennedy agreed and went even further: "Should we not pretty soon allow Thompson to open up the discussions a little more?"[21] On February 15, Kennedy wrote to Khrushchev that a breakthrough on Berlin might lead to agreements on such other matters as "German frontiers, respect for the sovereignty of the GDR, prohibition of nuclear weapons for both parts of Germany, and the conclusion of a pact of non-aggression between NATO and the Warsaw powers."[22] These were all points that Moscow had been demanding, in some cases for years, and which presidents Harry Truman and Dwight Eisenhower had always rejected out of hand.

Recognizing that these proposals went well beyond any previously agreed to Western negotiating positions, Kennedy and Rusk continued to describe their talks as "probes." They hoped that this formula would avoid an outright clash with de Gaulle and Adenauer.[23] But Gromyko, terrified of losing his position by agreeing to any concessions, found it safest to dismiss everything that Kennedy or others offered to him.[24] He refused even to discuss a number of topics, such as the status of Berlin as a whole, or to fix a firm agenda for negotiations. No matter how hard Kennedy might try, de Gaulle and Adenauer would not really have needed to worry that the president could make a deal behind their backs.

Gromyko grimly repeated his mantra: the West had to remove its forces from Berlin, to respect the sovereignty of the GDR, to accept East Berlin as the capital of the GDR, to recognize German borders as they had been fixed by the Soviet Union, to limit troop levels in central Europe, and to accept a nuclear-free zone in Europe. He sometimes added that the West also had to sign a non-aggression pact. He even began some meetings by rejecting out of hand any new ideas that Thompson might have raised at the previous meeting. He explained that he was trying to save time.[25]

As Thompson's talks with Gromyko dragged on, French Foreign Minister Maurice Couve de Murville said that Khrushchev would regard Kennedy with contempt for offering such concessions.[26] De Gaulle himself continued to regard the probes as useless and dangerous.[27] When Kennedy called him to ask him to approve a NATO communiqué supporting the probes, he demanded that the communiqué be edited to show that only some NATO members agreed.[28] He wrote to Kennedy that he would be prepared to talk about a true settlement for Germany, but that Khrushchev was clearly not interested in that.[29]

Adenauer fretted. He feared that he was not being properly briefed and that Kennedy continued to negotiate behind Germany's back on issues that had little to do with Berlin itself but that would deeply affect the future of Germany.[30]

On the other hand, British foreign secretary Lord Home urged the negotiators to hurry because the Soviet position might get harder over time.[31] Macmillan went even beyond Kennedy's position, saying that the West should no longer insist on its rights in Berlin but should be ready to renegotiate those rights.[32]

Kennedy's advisers then persuaded the president that he might need to grant the GDR a role in controlling access to West Berlin. Offering to negotiate about one of his essentials, Kennedy proposed a new thirteen-member "International Access Authority" to control the ground routes as well as the air corridors to West Berlin. The members of that authority on the Eastern side were to be East Germany, East Berlin, the Soviet Union, and two East European states; on the Western side, the three Western occupation powers and West Germany as well as West Berlin; in the middle, three neutral states such as Sweden, Switzerland, and Austria. Offering to yield allied control over access to Berlin, Kennedy wrote—as Gromyko had demanded—that the International Access Authority would respect "the sovereignty of the GDR."[33]

In order to win Khrushchev's support for his International Access Authority proposal, Kennedy mentioned it to Khrushchev in a letter of February 15, 1962. He stressed to Khrushchev that the authority would have East German participation. Kennedy also wrote Khrushchev that "I feel very strongly that we must make every effort and explore every possibility to avoid the development of a major crisis over Berlin, replete with all the dangers of war."[34] That sentence as well as the tone of the letter almost certainly reinforced Khrushchev's belief, dating from the Vienna summit, that Kennedy would do anything to avoid the risk of war over Berlin (and perhaps over anything else).[35]

Kennedy and Rusk may have hoped that their warnings about war would persuade Khrushchev and Gromyko to negotiate, but they apparently had the opposite effect. Clay had wanted to make Khrushchev worry, but the Soviet leader was becoming ever more certain that the United States would ultimately capitulate in order to avoid a confrontation. In an interview with the Russian journalist Aleksei Adzhubei, Khrushchev's son-in-law, Kennedy reiterated his fear of escalation. He also told Adzhubei that he could understand Soviet worries about Germany, but assured him that Germany would not be united.[36]

The Adzhubei interview, when published in Moscow and picked up in the West, led to a bitter joke in Berlin that "Kennedy is neutral toward America's enemies, friendly toward neutrals, and hostile toward America's friends."

Willy Brandt thought that the proposal for an International Access Authority was a "monstrosity." If thirteen states had to decide on the rules governing access to Berlin, and if a large number of those states were subject to Ulbricht's pressure, West Berlin would die.[37]

Henry Kissinger, disagreed strongly with the proposal. He thought it was dangerous. He warned Kennedy that the Germans might "pick up their French option."[38]

Gromyko immediately rejected the International Access Authority along with other U.S. proposals, dubbing it "a violation of GDR sovereignty." Ulbricht had told Khrushchev that he wanted "one hundred per cent control over access to West Berlin," and Gromyko echoed that line. No other state, and certainly not the ones listed in the U.S. proposal, should have any role at all.[39]

Kissinger Briefs Adenauer
on Nuclear Strategy

Despite his resignation, Kissinger had stayed on for "special missions" at Kennedy's request. He thus undertook the delicate task of briefing Adenauer in Bonn on U.S. defense plans for Western Europe, an important element in trying to persuade the chancellor that West Germany did not need to have a separate atomic arsenal.

Adenauer had wanted nuclear weapons in the 1950s because he feared that the West could not defend West Germany with conventional forces. President Eisenhower had agreed with Adenauer, but Kennedy did not. Kennedy wanted Kissinger, whom Adenauer knew, to reassure Adenauer that American protection could guarantee West German security and that he did not need his own nuclear weapons.[40]

Adenauer began the conversation with Kissinger by asking how the professor spent his time as a White House consultant. When Kissinger said that he spent three-quarters of his time at Harvard and one-quarter in Washington, Adenauer showed his deepening cynicism about the White House by replying: "Then I will believe only three quarters of what you say."[41] Nonetheless, Adenauer began to listen with deepening intensity as Kissinger described how the mix of U.S. conventional and nuclear forces could defeat any potential Soviet attack against Germany. He described in detail how those forces would target Soviet weapons and troops in Europe and within Russia itself.

Kissinger, who had long studied and had even helped design American nuclear strategy, particularly stressed that the United States would not permit the Soviet Army to advance across all of West Germany. Instead, U.S. weapons would block the Soviet attack. Adenauer, who had long worried about that point, appreciated the reassurance. He later thanked Kennedy for the briefing on U.S. strategy in Europe, and said that it had lifted a deep worry from his mind.[42]

Kissinger's presentation was the most thorough U.S. strategic briefing that Adenauer had ever received, so highly classified that the chancellor asked his assistants to destroy the notes and the U.S. Embassy did the same. But, while it increased Adenauer's confidence in American military strategy, it did not convince him to support American diplomatic tactics over Berlin. The allies remained deeply deadlocked.

The "Principles Paper"

As Kennedy grew more concerned about Soviet air corridor harassment and about the lack of progress in his probes, he decided to offer Khrushchev a full further range of concessions on Berlin and Germany in a paper titled "Draft Principles, Procedures, and Interim Steps." The paper went through several drafts, one of which Rusk passed on to Gromyko as a "personal informal paper" on March 11, 1962, before either the French or German governments had seen it.

The final "Principles Paper," dated April 3, offered more concessions to the Soviet position than any previous American or allied position. It incorporated a number of points, including proposals for final German borders, for recognition of the GDR, for limits on armaments within Germany, for a NATO–Warsaw Pact non-aggression treaty, and for mixed West and East German technical commissions. The Principles Paper also repeated the proposal for an International Access Authority. In exchange for these concessions, Moscow was to respect allied rights in Berlin. By packaging all those points together and expanding them further, Kennedy hoped to draw Soviet interest. He had high expectations for the paper.

Rusk wrote Kennedy proudly that the State Department had made a special effort to be sure that the Principles Paper contained "new language, which is indicated by underlining, that is largely either drawn from Soviet texts or formulated to take at least verbal account of expressed Soviet views." Indeed, most of the paper was so underlined, to show Khrushchev how much Kennedy was prepared even to use Soviet terminology.[43] Rusk warned Kennedy that he would now need to show the paper to the British, French, and Germans because he would be presenting it shortly to Soviet ambassador Anatoly Dobrynin as a formal negotiating proposal—moving beyond "probes." He thought there would be no trouble with the British, who already knew of the paper. He did not expect concurrence from the French. Incredibly, he wrote that "we would also hope to have the Germans on board."

Whatever Rusk had written, he and Kennedy knew that many of the proposals in the Principles Paper, and especially the joint committees of the two German states, were anathema to Adenauer. The chancellor might be surprised and distressed by what he would see.[44]

Kennedy was practicing "smorgasbord diplomacy," putting one offer after another on the table to see which Khrushchev would pick. Rusk and the White House had said nothing about any of this to Ambassador Grewe, who was undoubtedly becoming alarmed by American press reports that hinted at American negotiations with Moscow while the White House and State Department were telling him nothing.[45]

Macmillan, as Rusk expected, approved the Principles Paper enthusiastically. The French, also as expected, reacted harshly. Claude Lebel of the French Embassy in Washington objected to the paper and particularly to the International Access Authority. He told Assistant Secretary Foy Kohler that the paper was dangerous. He warned that the use of Soviet language would have a negative impact on German opinion. Lebel said that offers about the future of Germany were potentially explosive. The Principles Paper adopted the East German line when it did not mention either free elections or reunification. He said that he hoped that the United States would not hand over such a paper because that would seem like a negotiation and not like the probes that Kennedy and Rusk had cleared with de Gaulle. Kohler made no commitment about that. He still planned to give the paper formally to Dobrynin.[46]

What Lebel did not say, and may not have known, was that de Gaulle might actually welcome the Principles Paper. The paper served de Gaulle's strategic objective to win Adenauer to his side. By refusing to negotiate on the basis of the Principles Paper, de Gaulle would cast himself as the most consistent and committed friend of Germany. Kennedy's diplomatic tactics on Berlin would turn West Germany toward France.

On April 11, 1962, one month after Rusk had passed an informal draft of the Principles Paper to Gromyko, Kohler gave the formal paper to Grewe and asked him to get Adenauer's approval within twenty-four hours. When Grewe protested that this amounted to an ultimatum unworthy of a friendly alliance, Kohler gave him forty-eight hours. He protested that he could not give Grewe more time because he had already made an appointment to give the paper to Dobrynin.

Adenauer reacted furiously to the ultimatum as well as to the proposed terms for negotiations. Assistant Secretary of Defense Paul Nitze was the first to feel Adenauer's wrath. On April 13, in a previously scheduled meeting in Bonn, Adenauer denounced the Principles Paper to Nitze. It meant recognition of the inhumane GDR dictatorship. He observed bitterly that there would not be enough moving vans in West Berlin to carry those who would want to leave if the West made such a proposal. Directly criticizing Thompson, Rusk, and Kennedy himself, Adenauer told Nitze that the U.S. role as sole Western negotiator was "unsatisfactory."[47]

On April 14, Adenauer followed up his talk with Nitze by writing a short, sharp note to Kennedy:

Up to now the repeated efforts to open negotiations with the Soviet Union about Berlin have failed. The latest proposals of the State Department contain decisive elements concerning not only Berlin but also Germany itself, proposals that go far beyond anything that has been proposed to date. I have considerable objections against some of these proposals. I ask you most urgently, my dear Mr. President, to call an immediate pause to these proceedings in order to permit reexamination of all proposals concerning Berlin in common with the three occupation powers."[48]

Adenauer's anger and his brusque language reflected his firm conviction that the Principles Paper jeopardized the future of Berlin, of European security, and of Germany's membership in the Western alliance. The principles, Adenauer complained, dealt not only with Berlin, where the United States still had occupation rights and a residual authority to negotiate, but with Germany as a whole, on which Washington no longer had such authority. He believed that only the West German government had the right to negotiate about the borders of Germany, and that only a united German government could legitimately agree to them.

Adenauer later wrote a memorandum for the record in which he gave more detailed vent to his rage:

> "We want Berlin negotiated separately, not as part of a global deal in which it becomes a mere bargaining object."
> "Gromyko rejects Western proposals because he knows Rusk will come up with others. The West loses ground each time."
> "Kennedy and Rusk keep talking about 'West Germans' and 'West Germany' instead of referring to us as 'Germans.' That equates us with the dictatorship in East Germany."
> "The Americans are not keeping us informed about the negotiations. We know nothing and are not consulted."[49]

Adenauer noted that Kennedy had proposed accepting Soviet demands for German neutralization that had been made in the 1950s, but Kennedy had not asked for German unification which Moscow had then offered in exchange for neutralization. Kennedy was not even asking for things that Moscow had long been prepared to concede. He and Rusk had obviously not studied the history of diplomacy about West Germany.

Adenauer also noted that some Kennedy proposals, especially his readiness to accept an East German role on the access authority, jeopardized Berlin's security and freedom. Walter Ulbricht would certainly not permit any person who had ever criticized the GDR, or any refugee, to travel into or out of Berlin. The city would become an empty shell.

Once Adenauer had objected so totally to the Principles Paper, Kennedy had no choice but to abandon it. He could not negotiate about Germany without having Adenauer on board. Kennedy and Adenauer had reached a total deadlock. A day later, the deadlock turned into a crisis of confidence. The text of the Principles Paper appeared in the German press and in the *New York Times*. Kennedy, now furious in turn, accused Adenauer of leaking the text. Adenauer flatly rejected the charge.

Whether Adenauer had leaked the paper or not (and many people believed that he had authorized the leak), it certainly served his purpose. The proposals to recognize the GDR and to transfer American access rights to Khrushchev and to neutral nations through an International Access Authority generated such an uproar in the United States, in Europe, and in Berlin that the shamefaced president had to withdraw them immediately. American political figures and commentators almost unanimously criticized the very notion of offering major concessions while the Soviets were harassing allied air traffic, reinforcing the Wall, and shooting refugees. They did not want American rights to be turned over to others. Nor did they want to recognize the East German dictator who had just built the Wall.

Once again, as after August 13, the White House mailroom filled up with black "Chamberlain" umbrellas. In the cold harsh light of day, Kennedy's diplomacy looked more like Neville Chamberlain's appeasement of Hitler than like the noble spirit of Camelot that Kennedy's friends liked to evoke. Kennedy realized that he had made a bad domestic political blunder as well as a diplomatic mistake by listening to Macmillan, Rusk, Kohler, and his White House advisers. Contrary to his expectations, Americans did not want to make concessions about Germany and about Berlin.

Kennedy must also have had to admit to himself that the whole exercise had been pointless. Gromyko had rejected the Principles Paper when he had first received the "informal" draft. He had told Thompson that he would accept the International Access Authority only if it included the total withdrawal of U.S. forces from West Berlin. Kennedy risked destroying the Western alliance and his own presidency for no good purpose.

The Berlin desk officer at the State Department, who had not even been told about the Principles Paper before reading of it in the press, later wrote that West Berlin might well have become a neutral city within ten years if Khrushchev and Gromyko had been smart enough to accept the paper. Ulbricht could have used the International Access Authority to determine who could or could not travel to West Berlin. And, given the likely West German reaction, Khrushchev would have faced a much weaker American and West German strategic base on continental Europe.[50]

Khrushchev had his own objections to the Principles Paper. Although Kennedy and Macmillan were prepared to make concessions that could indeed have allowed a neutral West Berlin over time, they did not concede to the ever impatient Khrushchev the immediate victory that he wanted.

Kennedy never replied to Adenauer's letter. Instead, after allowing some time for cooling off, Kennedy wrote to the chancellor on May 16 and suggested that relations return to where they had been earlier. Adenauer, having won his point and scuttled the probes and the Principles Paper, agreed.

Stalemate

However Khrushchev might have reacted to Kennedy's diplomacy, he must have had a deep sense of frustration about Berlin by the spring and summer of 1962. He still had a bone in his throat. Clay had prevented Khrushchev and Ulbricht from winning West Berlin by direct action. Adenauer had blown the whistle on Kennedy's probes. Khrushchev could not stop allied and civilian aircraft from flying along the Berlin air corridors without shooting some down, which he dared not do without the forces to back it up. And Kennedy had made it clear that he would not remove U.S. forces from Berlin.

Ulbricht had tried to do his part to destroy the confidence of the Berliners. He had continued building the Wall and the barriers to show that they were truly permanent and unbreachable. In November and December of 1961, he had expanded the Wall to a thickness of six feet at the Brandenburg Gate and placed a number of ditches filled with metal "dragon's teeth" along frequently visited border points like Potsdamer Platz. He had fortified all crossing points so that cars had to snake their way through a series of concrete baffles to get through. He continued to bulldoze a "death strip" inside East Berlin everywhere along and beyond the Wall, to make certain that nobody could get near it from East Berlin

Ulbricht's massive concrete barriers reinforcing the Wall at the Brandenburg Gate to make clear that East and West Berlin are now fully separate. Courtesy of Landesarchiv Berlin

or East Germany without being seen and shot. That "death strip" was constantly supervised from watchtowers; fully lit at night, it was patrolled by Vopos and border police with dogs.

Ulbricht had tried to persuade Khrushchev to sign the peace treaty in the spring of 1962, but Khrushchev had refused, arguing that it would provoke a West German embargo against Eastern Europe and perhaps some U.S. reaction. Khrushchev still could not afford the kind of massive aid that the East European economies would need. He also complained to his colleagues in Moscow during the spring of 1962 that he did not have the correct balance of power to compel Kennedy to make the right concessions.[51]

Kennedy was equally frustrated. Rusk's hope of talking the Berlin issue "to death" had not worked as he had hoped. Khrushchev and Gromyko would not accept anything short of Kennedy's abject surrender. Adenauer had stopped Kennedy from making Germany pay for a deal with Khrushchev. The Wall still stood and Soviet demands still stood.

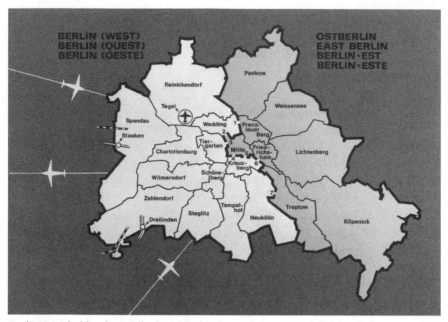

Berlin Divided by the Wall, showing the three air routes and the Autobahn exits to the West, with the Dreilinden checkpoint (Bravo) for the Western military in southwest Berlin and Checkpoint Charlie at point 4 south of the Mitte borough in central Berlin. Courtesy of Landesarchiv Berlin

The worst of the post-Wall crisis appeared to have passed, but neither Khrushchev nor Kennedy could feel satisfied with the situation. Nothing had been solved, either from the Soviet or the Western standpoint.

The exhausted Berliners felt the same way. They would have been happy to settle into the summer doldrums in 1962 after the tumultuous twelve months that had begun with Ulbricht's Wall and had ended with Khrushchev's air corridor "reservations" and the open debate about the Principles Paper. But they knew that they could not count on it.

The Mysterious Pipelines

By July and August, after Clay had left Berlin and I had returned to my previous duties of watching developments in East Germany, several American intelligence agency officials told me that they had noticed something worrisome from their aerial photography: the Soviets had begun to lay long oil pipelines from East to West across East Germany. They had not made their usual effort to camouflage the pipelines.

The pipelines ended near two highly strategic points on the inner-German border, the city of Magdeburg opposite the British Army of the Rhine and the Fulda Gap opposite the American Seventh Army. Both also faced major West German military units.

Soviet troops often ran oil pipelines into and within East Germany during their autumn maneuvers because the pipelines could supply their forces faster and easier than gasoline trucks could. But the noticeably large number of those pipelines and their positions closer than usual to the border of West Germany and to Berlin left us puzzled. An American military intelligence officer in Berlin told me: "If their purpose is to persuade us that they are preparing to jump off, this is how I think the Soviets would go about it." The Red Army apparently planned to mass forces along the West German border and perhaps near Berlin during the fall. Moreover, Khrushchev wanted us, the West Germans, and the British to know it. We could not help but wonder why.

We were even more puzzled when, by the first week of October, major Soviet troop deployments to those areas began. We felt that the Soviets were preparing to make a massive show of force along the border with West Germany, but we could not figure out why.[52] We again felt, as we had in the summer of 1961, that Khrushchev was up to *something*, although we did not know what. We suspected, however, that it would again be bad.

CHAPTER ELEVEN

"This May End in a Big War"

On July 5, 1962, almost three months after Khrushchev had stopped making "reservations" in the Berlin air corridors and after Adenauer had derailed Kennedy's efforts at negotiations, Khrushchev sent a strikingly new and different proposal on Berlin to Kennedy. He called it a compromise proposal for a solution "of the West Berlin occupation regime."[1]

In that letter, Khrushchev for the first time spelled out his precise terms for a United Nations role in West Berlin, an approach the Soviets had sometimes mentioned but never in detail:

- UN forces should be stationed in West Berlin to replace the Western occupation troops. Those UN forces should be "police formations and not combat troops."
- UN initial strength should not exceed the number of Western occupation troops in Berlin as of July 1, 1962. They should be drawn from the three Western powers, from one or two Warsaw Pact states (Khrushchev suggested Poland and Czechoslovakia), from some neutral states, and perhaps from one or two "small" NATO states. All would be under United Nations, not Western, command.
- The numbers of those police forces would be cut by 25 percent by the end of the first year after the "abolition of the occupation." Another 25 percent cut would follow in each of the next three years, leaving no more foreign forces of any kind in West Berlin.

After that, Khrushchev wrote, "West Berlin will be considered as an independent political entity, that is, as a free city." There would be no more subversive activities against the GDR or other socialist countries. "Naturally," he continued, any claim by West Germany on West Berlin "must be declined." Free access to West Berlin was to be negotiated with the GDR with due respect for its sovereignty. A "special temporary international body" would arbitrate any dispute about access. Next would come a general German peace settlement, providing for a cut in forces in central Europe and no nuclear weapons for West or East Germany, as well as a NATO–Warsaw Pact non-aggression treaty.

The letter, especially noteworthy because of its detailed plans for the deployment of UN forces and subsequent steps, showed that Khrushchev had something new in mind. He was presenting the most carefully scripted proposal he had ever made on Berlin, almost as if he were opening a new diplomatic push. Most strikingly, the peace treaty would apparently follow other changes, not precede them. Khrushchev concluded by proposing a meeting between himself and Kennedy and extending an invitation for the president to visit the Soviet Union to sign the deal.

On July 17, Kennedy rejected Khrushchev's proposal by writing that it ignored American vital interests, such as U.S. forces in Berlin, an issue that was central to the negotiations. He said that he had tried to compromise and to be "practical" in his approach by not raising topics that he knew to be unacceptable to the Soviets, such as free elections, but what Khrushchev was proposing was not really a compromise. To finish on a positive note, Kennedy offered to discuss some (but not all) of the topics listed in the "informal" version of the Principles Paper that Rusk had given to Gromyko in March, which Gromyko had rejected.[2]

Khrushchev then tried a different approach on September 28, offering to put the German problem "on ice" until after the U.S. congressional elections scheduled for November.[3] This seemed as if he was trying to be helpful to Kennedy, agreeing to White House counsel Ted Sorensen's request through Soviet ambassador Anatoly Dobrynin for Khrushchev to exercise restraint prior to the elections so as to avoid helping the Republicans.[4]

The Soviets then stopped further diplomatic discussions on Berlin, saying that it seemed pointless to restate established positions. (That must have amused anyone who had ever suffered through Andrei Gromyko's infinite capacity for repetition.) Instead, Soviet officials began telling Western diplomats they believed the discussions in the spring had settled most issues and that the entire Berlin question could be concluded after the U.S. elections. They would accept Kennedy's offers in the probes and in the Principles Paper (perhaps regretting that they had rejected them earlier).

Khrushchev had a more threatening tone when he asked U.S. Interior Secretary Stuart Udall to meet with him while the latter was visiting Moscow in September. He insisted firmly that he would not allow U.S. forces to remain in Berlin. But, "out of respect for your president," he said, he would wait until November before pressing his demands. Khrushchev also told Udall that he would give Kennedy a choice of "going to war or signing a peace treaty." He added that, contrary to earlier times, "now we can swat your ass."[5] He would make sure that Kennedy solved the Berlin problem.

> Even more menacingly, Khruschev added, "We will put him in a situation where it is necessary to solve it."[6] Showing utter contempt for Kennedy, Khrushchev told Udall, "As a president, he has understanding, but what he lacks is courage."
>
> He added that Adenauer and de Gaulle would also have to "get wise in a hurry," for "war in this day and age means no Paris and no France."

Udall, who had not asked for a meeting with Khrushchev, could not quite understand why the Soviet leader had called him in to receive that message. But he reported it to the president when he returned to Washington.

At about the same time in September, Khrushchev warned Hans Kroll, the West German ambassador to Moscow, "We have already prepared everything for a free city of West Berlin" to come right after the American elections. He added that Kennedy would then be forced to make an historic decision: "We now have the freedom to choose when to implement this act."

> Obviously reveling in what he was saying, Khrushchev added, "Kennedy is waiting to be pushed to the brink—agreement or war? Of course, he will not want war; he will concede."[7]

Deeply worried by Khrushchev's sharp tone, Kroll immediately reported the conversation to the West German Foreign Office, which in turn warned Washington. There is no record that the warning ever reached Kennedy or even Bundy. It may have remained in the State Department.

Gromyko followed up in a White House meeting on October 18, 1962. He told Kennedy forcefully that West Berlin represented "a rotten tooth which must be pulled out" and that Western troops would have to leave the city.[8] That meeting was to be the one in which Kennedy had to bite his tongue to avoid telling Gromyko that he had intelligence showing a Soviet missile deployment to Cuba. Gromyko, who already knew that Khrushchev was deploying medium-range missiles to Cuba, spelled out Soviet plans to Kennedy: Khrushchev would do nothing until after the American elections. After those elections, he would come to the United Nations in November and would hope to meet with Kennedy to "settle the Berlin matter."[9]

Georgi Bolshakov, Robert Kennedy's Soviet intelligence contact, had also played his assigned part in the diplomatic buildup when he met with the president at Robert's suggestion in late August. President Kennedy told him that he was worried about the number of Soviet ships going to Cuba, but Bolshakov assured him that there were no offensive weapons on those vessels. He asked Kennedy to suspend overflights by U.S. spy planes over Cuba because they were creating difficulties for Castro. Kennedy agreed and issued an order to suspend the flights. The flights did not resume until October, when CIA director John McCone (who had been out of town) was astonished to learn of Kennedy's order and immediately countermanded it.

Bolshakov later met with Robert in early October and again offered the assurance that any Soviet weapons going to Cuba were defensive. He said that Robert could tell the president that on Khrushchev's own authority.[10]

Missiles in Cuba

Within three weeks after Khrushchev's September 28 letter and two weeks after Bolshakov's assurance to Robert Kennedy, U.S. intelligence flights over Cuba saw unmistakable signs that Moscow had begun to prepare deployment of medium-range ballistic missiles on the island. Those missiles represented a major threat to the balance of power between the United States and the Soviet Union.

Observing that "this is a matter we can't ignore" in one of the meetings Kennedy convened to discuss the threat,[11] Dean Rusk pointed out that, according to intelligence estimates, those missiles would double the number of warheads that could reach the United States. Khrushchev was obviously trying to overcome the shortfall in intercontinental missiles that he had complained about in the spring.

The landing and deployment of Soviet missiles in Cuba began what has become known as the Cuban missile crisis. After long debate in the ExComm (the Executive Committee of the National Security Council that Kennedy had formed to deal with the crisis), the president first had to decide when and how to tell Khrushchev that he had found the missiles. He then chose a naval "quarantine" to prevent Moscow from deploying any more missiles and warheads. After that, he had to compel Khrushchev to remove the missiles as well as some Soviet nuclear-capable bombers that Khrushchev had also sent to Cuba.[12]

Faced with Kennedy's demands, Khrushchev said, "This may end in a big war."[13]

Kennedy threatened a major U.S. attack against the missiles in Cuba, forcing Khrushchev to choose between humiliating defeat and nuclear obliteration. Khrushchev chose defeat, removing his missiles and bombers from the island. For the first time in his dialogue with Kennedy, Khrushchev in one of his letters wrote of the death, destruction, and anarchy that nuclear war would cause.[14] That was the kind of language he had derided when Kennedy had used it.

To end the crisis Kennedy instructed his brother Robert to call on Dobrynin and to assure him privately that the United States would withdraw U.S. missiles from Turkey after Khrushchev withdrew his offensive weapons from Cuba. Robert said, in Dobrynin's words, that if the missiles in Turkey represented "the only obstacle to a settlement," then "the president saw no unsurmountable difficulties."[15] Robert said that the U.S. missiles would leave Turkey in four to five months (as indeed they did). He also told Dobrynin that the president "had ordered their removal some time ago."[16]

President Kennedy thus used the same technique in Cuba that he had reportedly used during the Checkpoint Charlie confrontation in Berlin, asking Khrushchev to retreat in public against a secret pledge to make a later U.S. concession. But the bargain had to stay private. Robert told Dobrynin that he might himself want to run for president in the future and he could not win if it was known that he had made this kind of deal.[17]

On October 28, after the end of the crisis, Khrushchev wrote to Kennedy that he had intentionally not mentioned the U.S. missiles in Turkey. "All the proposals that I presented," he said, "took into account the fact that you had agreed to resolve the matter of your missile bases in Turkey." Khrushchev expressed his appreciation that Kennedy had told Robert to convey these thoughts.[18]

Dobrynin delivered this letter to Robert on October 29. But Robert returned the letter the next day, saying it claimed a concession that he had not made. By refusing to accept the letter, Robert Kennedy reinforced the president's public insistence at the time that Khrushchev had withdrawn the Cuban missiles against nothing more than Kennedy's promise not to invade the island. This made the withdrawal a total Kennedy triumph just before the congressional elections.

Khrushchev later wrote in his memoirs that the withdrawal of U.S. missiles in Turkey had been part of the Cuban deal, and some American scholars have accepted that reasoning.[19] He had never written of such an American concession for the withdrawal of Soviet tanks from Checkpoint Charlie.

Berlin in Khrushchev's Cuba Plans

Khrushchev left a number of clues suggesting that he saw Berlin as a key objective for putting missiles into Cuba, and perhaps even as his main objective:

- Gromyko's categorical October statement to Kennedy that Khrushchev would come to the United Nations after the U.S. elections in November and would then expect to settle the Berlin matter, presumably after Khrushchev had announced the presence of the missiles in Cuba.

- Khrushchev's detailed July letter to Kennedy proposing to replace U.S. troops with UN police forces as one of a number of steps on Berlin that Khrushchev would probably have planned to reiterate to Kennedy and before the United Nations in November when he made his prospective visit to the United States. After all, Khrushchev must have noted, Kennedy had himself proposed neutral members for the International Access Authority. And Khrushchev had been informed that Arthur Schlesinger, Jr., an assistant to the president, had told a West German journalist: "What's wrong with transferring West Berlin to the custody of the United Nations?"[20] So the UN proposal would have fitted right into Khrushchev's new Berlin offer.

- Khrushchev's menacing prediction to the German ambassador, as well as his warning to Udall that "We will put [Kennedy] in a situation where it is necessary to solve [the Berlin problem]."

- A private remark to Walter Ulbricht that Gromyko made at a stopover in East Berlin, on his way back from Washington in October, that the Soviets were well on their way to changing the status of West Berlin and moving toward an access regime that would respect GDR sovereignty.[21]

- A public speech by Gromyko during his visit to East Berlin demanding very firmly that U.S. forces leave Berlin. Although Kennedy had revealed the missiles in Cuba two days before that speech, Gromyko may not yet have realized that it was Khrushchev who would retreat. Notably, Gromyko was the last Soviet official to demand American withdrawal in such a firm and uncompromising tone.

- Last but by no means least, the oil pipelines across East Germany. Those, like the Soviet troop deployments to the West German border in October, confirmed Khrushchev's hint to Udall that there would be a direct military threat in November against West Germany and perhaps even against France.[22] Khrushchev knew from press reports that Adenauer had been responsible for blocking Kennedy's concessions in the Principles Paper, and he might have expected Adenauer and even de Gaulle to become more accommodating on Berlin if large Soviet forces stood on the West German border and all around Berlin while Soviet missiles were deployed in Cuba. In Khrushchev's words, they would "get wise in a hurry."

The timing of Khrushchev's elaborate Berlin and Cuban preparations and tactics coincide remarkably. In April 1962 Khrushchev had
abandoned the "reservations" in the Berlin air corridors when Defense
Minister Marshal Rodion Malinovsky had briefed him on the severe
Soviet lag behind U.S. ICBM deployment. Khrushchev replied, "Why
not throw a hedgehog at Uncle Sam's pants?", suggesting that Cuba
might make a useful base for the intermediate-range missiles Moscow
already had in large numbers. After that, he would no longer need to
worry that, as he had said, he did not have the force to compel U.S.
concessions.

During the same month, Adenauer had blocked the negotiations over
Berlin, probably disappointing Khrushchev who must have kept expecting further offers. After that, Khrushchev had neither a military threat
nor a diplomatic track going on Berlin. Thus, presumably, after further
consideration by Khrushchev and his staffs, a formal Cuba deployment
decision by the Soviet government was made at the end of May.[23] Just
before that time, Soviet harassment in Berlin eased and both General
Clay and Marshal Konev left Berlin. Khrushchev had decided to move
the Berlin confrontation to the Caribbean.

The steps that followed, like laying the pipelines across East Germany
during the summer, would normally have grown out of decisions taken
by Khrushchev and the Soviet Presidium in late May and in June. The
summer would have given time for all the steps that Khrushchev needed
to take and did take.

Khrushchev had obviously expected Kennedy to accept the Soviet
missiles in Cuba as the Soviet Union had accepted U.S. missiles in Turkey. He told his son Sergei that the United States would "make a fuss,
make more of a fuss, and then agree."[24] Given his view of Kennedy as a
"boy in short pants," and recalling Kennedy's frequently expressed worries
about the risk of escalation and miscalculation, he would probably never
have expected Kennedy to threaten war. But Kennedy had surprised
Khruschev by changing his pattern of behavior.

After taking his preparatory steps and deploying the missiles,
Khrushchev presumably planned to come to New York to make a moderate speech inviting the UN General Assembly to send UN police to
replace the Western forces in West Berlin. With the threat of nuclear
war hanging over the world, this demand might have seemed reasonable

to most UN members. Kennedy would have been hard put to oppose it fully.

With his UN police force offer, with his renewed insistence on U.S. withdrawals from Berlin, and with Bolshakov's assurances, Khrushchev had thus prepared for a decisive diplomatic campaign on Berlin after the American elections.

We obviously did not know all that in Berlin at the time. But we realized later that the mysterious Soviet pipelines across East Germany had probably been part of Khrushchev's plan for a November move against Berlin.

Of course, Berlin might not have been Khrushchev's only objective. Fidel Castro told the French correspondent Claude Julien that Khrushchev had earlier told him the missiles would "reinforce socialism on the international scale."[25] A number of other Russians thought that Khrushchev wanted to exploit the new balance of power everywhere, not only in Berlin.[26] Nonetheless, the timing of Khrushchev's decisions as well as his and Gromyko's statements and actions indicate that Berlin would have been his first and perhaps most important objective. Khrushchev could well have decided that the only way to get U.S. forces out of Berlin was to put Kennedy under direct pressure.

Khrushchev told the East German Sozialistische Einheitspartei Deutschlands (SED) congress in January 1963 that the missiles would have compelled American leaders "to make a more sober assessment of objective reality."[27] Khrushchev would have achieved a neutral "free city" of West Berlin. He would have been well on his way to splitting the Western alliance. He would also have reestablished his authority within the Communist world against the Chinese challenge. He would have won a major and perhaps decisive battle in the struggle over Germany and even Europe.

Khrushchev himself, in his speeches and in his writings, never gave a satisfactory answer regarding his purpose in placing missiles in Cuba. Anastas Mikoyan, visiting Cuba after the missile crisis, offered no reply to Fidel Castro's anguished questions about it. The explanation that Khrushchev wanted only to defend Cuba itself rings hollow. He could have defended the island better with Soviet troops and anti-aircraft missiles. The missiles pointed at America clearly had more than a defensive purpose.[28]

Kennedy's Fears for Berlin

Kennedy described the horns of his dilemma over the missiles in Cuba to the Joint Chiefs of Staff:

> We do nothing: they have a missile base there with all the pressure that brings to bear on the United States and damage to our prestige. If we attack Cuban missiles, or Cuba in any way, it gives them a clear line to take Berlin. . . . We would be regarded as the trigger-happy Americans who lost Berlin."[29]

Thus, if Kennedy accepted the missiles, he might lose Berlin because the U.S. position in the balance of power would have collapsed. Throughout the entire Cuban missile crisis, he appears to have believed that the missiles were primarily intended to force him to yield on Berlin. On the other hand, if Kennedy attacked the missile bases, Khrushchev might retaliate by seizing Berlin. Either way, the city would be lost. Finally, however, Kennedy concluded that "we've got to do something" about the missiles.[30]

As Kennedy kept saying in the ExComm meetings, any decision that he made could have an effect on Berlin in one way or another. But he could not be sure what Khrushchev might do. Regarding his experts on the Soviet Union, he remarked: "[Khrushchev's] action in this case is so at variance with what all the Soviet experts have predicted that it is necessary to revise our whole estimate of his level of desperation, or ambition, or both."[31]

During the crisis, Kennedy realized that he could no longer trust anybody's predictions about Khrushchev and would have to go by his own instincts. Those, supported by his concern about the likely American domestic reaction, told him to get the missiles out. He could not carry out his responsibilities, in Berlin or elsewhere, under such a threat.

Tommy Thompson, who had returned from Moscow to the State Department as its leading Soviet expert, recommended that Kennedy stop military traffic to Berlin during the confrontation on Cuba. Kennedy rejected that recommendation. He had decided to show no sign of fear or weakness.[32]

Some ExComm members proposed trading Berlin for the missiles in Cuba, although they recognized that this plan raised some difficult political questions. Bundy mused, perhaps contemplating a deal: "If we could trade off Berlin, and not have it [be] our fault." But Kennedy said that the United States could not hope to escape responsibility for the loss of Berlin no matter how he might cast the deal.[33]

Kennedy was determined not to accept any Soviet military moves against Berlin during the missile crisis. He wrote to Macmillan, as he wondered openly about his options: "Any time he takes an action against Berlin, we take action against Cuba. That's really the choice we now have." He added: "If [Khrushchev] takes Berlin, then we will take Cuba."[34]

As the ExComm discussion evolved, it became clear that Kennedy's worries about Berlin helped to lead him toward the decision to "quarantine" rather than attack Cuba. He also recognized, however, that Khrushchev might match Kennedy's quarantine of Cuba with a blockade of Berlin. When he instructed the U.S. Navy to stop Soviet vessels that were approaching the quarantine line, Kennedy warned the ExComm: "We must expect that they will close down Berlin. Make the final preparations for that."[35]

The risk of a Soviet blockade of Berlin loomed very large in Kennedy's mind throughout the entire Cuban missile crisis. To meet that risk, Kennedy asked Assistant Secretary of Defense Paul Nitze to chair a special ExComm subcommittee to consider all Berlin issues and to prepare for a blockade. He said, "We don't want Berlin squeezed."

Kennedy also asked General Maxwell Taylor to ask General Lucius Clay to be on standby in case Kennedy wanted to send him to Berlin to coordinate U.S. actions in the event of a blockade.[36] Robert Kennedy reflected all those worries about a blockade of Berlin in the book he wrote in 1968 about the Cuban missile crisis.[37]

To help protect West Berlin, Kennedy even cited it in his speech to the nation on the Cuban crisis, warning Khrushchev not to act there:

Any hostile move anywhere in the world against the safety and freedom of peoples to whom we are committed—including in particular the brave people of West Berlin—will be met by whatever action is needed.[38]

Khrushchev may have confirmed what Kennedy thought. He later wrote that he would have retaliated in Europe for an attack on Cuba:

To tell the truth, I have to say that if the Americans had started a war at that time we were not prepared to adequately attack the United States. In that case, we would have been forced to start a war in Europe. Then, of course, a world war would have begun.[39]

Khrushchev reinforced that argument by asserting: "The Americans knew that, if Russian blood were shed in Cuba, American blood would surely be shed in Germany."[40] That would almost certainly have meant an attack against the Western position in Berlin, which is what Kennedy feared.

But it is not at all certain that Khrushchev would have attacked Berlin even if U.S. forces had attacked Cuba.[41] When Soviet Deputy Foreign Minister Vladimir Kuznetsov suggested an attack on Berlin as a diversion from Cuba, Khrushchev replied, "Keep that sort of talk to yourself. . . . We don't know how to get out of one predicament and you drag us into another." He did not want to widen the confrontation. As his son Sergei reported, Khrushchev considered any action in Berlin during the missile crisis to be "unduly dangerous."[42]

That would explain, as we noticed in Berlin, why the Soviet forces that had been sent to East Germany and to the West German border in early October began to withdraw as soon as Kennedy had made his speech revealing the missile threat. Khrushchev was presumably trying to show Kennedy that he wanted to avoid any kind of confrontation.

Thus the Soviets made no move against Berlin, either by a blockade or by any other form of military action. But Kennedy and the ExComm members worried about it from the beginning until the very end of the missile crisis.

The Allies and Berlin

Kennedy wrote to Macmillan during the first stage of the Cuban crisis that "Khrushchev's main intention may be to increase his chances at Berlin." He referred to Berlin as the main site for the confrontation.[43] He explained to Macmillan that "we have not done more than we have" because of his worry about the "obvious Soviet tit-for-tat" in Berlin and especially the seizure risk in the city. Macmillan also worried about Berlin, noting that, "If Khrushchev were stopped, with great loss of face, in Cuba, would he not be tempted to recover himself in Berlin? Indeed, might not this be the whole purpose of the exercise—to move forward one pawn in order to exchange it with another?"[44]

Kennedy rejected Macmillan's offer to go to Moscow to mediate with Khrushchev or to call a special conference or summit to deal with Cuba. He feared that Macmillan would want to keep talking while Khrushchev was completing his missile deployment. He was prepared to listen to Macmillan on Berlin, but not on Cuba.[45]

Although Macmillan offered a lot of advice, most of which Kennedy did not accept, de Gaulle supported Kennedy absolutely. When Dean Acheson, who had been sent to brief him, offered to show him photographs of the Soviet missiles in Cuba, de Gaulle said that "a great nation" did not act if there were "any doubts about the evidence."[46]

Adenauer also gave Kennedy total support. He even welcomed Kennedy's tougher line with Khrushchev, although he was worried when Kennedy warned that he was "carefully watching the possible link between this secret and dangerous action with the situation in Germany and Berlin."[47]

When Acheson arrived in Bonn to brief Adenauer, he found the chancellor already determined to support the strongest possible American action. Adenauer thought that the Federal Republic needed U.S. military superiority over the Soviet Union for German security and for Berlin's, and that meant no Soviet missiles in Cuba. When Acheson told Adenauer that Kennedy was considering invading or bombing Cuba, Adenauer said that he would support any such decisions. "Absolutely," he said: "the missiles must go!" But he also organized the German government to be ready to handle any emergencies in Europe, including a possible blockade of Berlin and even a nuclear war.[48]

The Reaction of the Berliners

Having become finely attuned to Soviet tactics over the years, the Berliners immediately understood what the Cuban crisis meant for them. As soon as they heard of Kennedy's quarantine, they saw a Berlin connection. Whether or not Khrushchev had seen Cuba as part of the battle for Berlin, the Berliners certainly saw it that way.

Every Berliner I saw during the crisis cheered Kennedy's speech. They believed that they were totally safe once Kennedy confronted Khrushchev and demanded the withdrawal of the missiles. They fully expected Khrushchev to comply. And they told me that Kennedy was fighting *their* battle as much as his own. Therefore, they thought that the Cuba crisis would actually help them because it would force Khrushchev to retreat.

The Berliners did not fear any Khrushchev moves against Berlin to balance the American moves against Cuba. They believed that Khrushchev would not dare to have two simultaneous world crises. Gromyko admitted as much when he wondered before the Supreme Soviet in January of 1963 "how the whole matter might have developed if yet another crisis in central Europe had been added to the critical events around Cuba."[49]

Some Berliners still had the hoarding instinct that they had developed during World War II and the Berlin blockade. They stocked up on food, water, batteries, basic kitchen supplies, and other staples, but many knew that the city had large stockpiles of everything and they did not make panic purchases.

When Allan Lightner, the senior State Department official in Berlin, first received a copy of Kennedy's speech on the Cuban quarantine, he called urgently on Willy Brandt to give him a copy of the speech and to point to Kennedy's remark about defending West Berlin. Brandt asked Lightner to tell Kennedy that he was grateful for the president's commitment. He stressed that Kennedy should not worry about the Berliners, who were prepared for any consequence no matter what might happen.

When Kennedy wrote to Brandt that there might be a confrontation with the Soviets and that there might be possible repercussions for Berlin, Brandt replied as he had to Lightner, stressing that the president should not take any possible repercussions against Berlin into consideration but should handle the crisis according to his own interests and best judgment. Kennedy wrote back that he appreciated Brandt's attitude.[50]

Brandt privately feared that there might be a Berlin blockade, although he did not think it likely. He thought that the risk of war in Europe was small. Nonetheless, he and his assistant Egon Bahr wondered privately whether they should call on the East Germans in the army and police to disobey any orders they might receive to attack West Berlin. Bahr thought that might actually have succeeded (*"funktioniert"*). As things turned out, they did not need to launch such a call. "We were spared," Bahr said later.[51]

When Khrushchev retreated from the Cuba confrontation, every Berliner I knew told me that it meant the end of the threat to their city. Kennedy's unconditional triumph had settled the matter for the Berliners. Having never doubted that Kennedy could push back the Soviets once he decided to do it, the Berliners were reinforced in their conviction that they did not need to yield to Khrushchev as long as Kennedy remained firm. And, as usual, they wished Kennedy had acted that way all along.

Kennedy's Cuban action won him genuine admiration and appreciation in Berlin. The Berliners liked the way Kennedy handled the situation. They did not know about the deal for the missiles in Turkey, but it probably would not have mattered to them. What mattered was that Kennedy had acted as they had hoped he would from the beginning, and that he had thus saved the freedom of West Berlin as well as protected America's global interests. Of course, they thought that Ulbricht might still try one or more maneuvers to harass or intimidate the allies and the Berliners, but they believed that he would be careful not to get too far out on a limb because he would know that Khrushchev could no longer offer him the kind of support he had offered earlier.

The American victory in the Cuban crisis thus had an even more dramatic effect in Berlin than Clay's Checkpoint Charlie confrontation. It really ended the Berlin crisis because Khrushchev's threats had lost credibility. Kennedy's insistence on secrecy about the U.S. missile pullback from Turkey made the impact in Berlin all the greater.

No More "Boy in Short Pants"

The Cuban missile confrontation had a dramatic impact on the Berlin crisis, as the Berliners said. Although the Soviets and especially the East Germans occasionally tried further harassment, they were more careful and less assertive than before. And, when there was harassment, as in some Autobahn identification disputes in 1963, Kennedy met it much more firmly than before.

Contrary to what he had so often said and written to Khrushchev, Kennedy had shown that he was not afraid of escalation or of confrontation. To Khrushchev, that appeared to be the measure of a man. Kennedy passed that test in the Cuban crisis. From Khrushchev's talks with his son, it was clear that he was surprised. Khrushchev had almost certainly expected Kennedy to accept the Soviet missiles or at least to hesitate long enough to give Khrushchev time to install them fully.

Up to that point, Khrushchev's image of Kennedy had probably still been the one he had formed at the Vienna summit, and that might have been confirmed by Kennedy's and Rusk's persistent warnings about escalation during their efforts to compromise on Berlin. As he had told his son, he still thought of Kennedy as a young man "in short pants."

By the fall of 1962, however, Kennedy had probably realized that he could prevail in confrontations with Khrushchev. Khrushchev had not disrupted the transit of the U.S. brigade to Berlin after the Wall was erected; he had withdrawn his tanks at Checkpoint Charlie; and he had not enforced his "reservations" in the air corridors. Kennedy must have learned from his Berlin confrontations that he could defy the Soviets without having to fear escalation. He was a different man from his Vienna days, but Khrushchev had not realized it until now.

Kennedy also acted against a matter of great interest to Khrushchev, a Soviet physical presence in West Berlin. Khrushchev wanted that presence in order to support his claim that West Berlin was an independent entity. In 1962, the Soviets had begun to refurbish a large building in the British sector that had held their trade mission before World War II. They wanted to convert it into a cultural center with a large auditorium and a consular office. Macmillan was ready to let the Soviets hold a big ceremony to inaugurate the building, but Kennedy heard of it and asked Macmillan to block Soviet plans. Macmillan then did.[52]

When Adenauer met with Kennedy in Washington a few weeks after the Cuba crisis, he was delighted to hear that Kennedy would stop the probes he had attempted to use for negotiations about Berlin. Adenauer wrote to de Gaulle that the Cuba crisis had been instructive for the Americans.[53]

The Cuban crisis also had an effect on U.S. and Soviet negotiating style. Khrushchev acted less assertively. He wrote to Kennedy on December 11 that only one question—the U.S. troop presence in Berlin— remained to be settled, and he promised rather mildly that a Berlin agreement and a withdrawal of U.S. forces would lead to an improvement in Soviet-American relations. He uttered no threats. In his letters to Kennedy over the following months, Khrushchev's tone became consistently more gentle, and each letter had a less demanding text on Berlin.[54]

Kennedy in turn acted more firmly. When Khrushchev claimed that the Soviet Union would accept the conditions that Rusk had offered to

Gromyko in the informal draft of the Principles Paper, Kennedy replied that Rusk and Gromyko might be good diplomats but they had never settled everything. In effect, Kennedy took advantage of Gromyko's rejection of the Principles Paper to walk back from the concessions he had offered in early 1962. He did not want to relive his own embarrassment when the Principles Paper had leaked. As far as he was concerned, any deal along those lines was dead.[55] He wrote Macmillan only a few days later, saying that he wondered whether it had been a mistake always to treat Soviet leaders "with consideration and courtesy."[56]

In a White House meeting, Kennedy even said that he saw no useful purpose in continuing a dialogue on Berlin with Moscow if the Soviets did not make meaningful proposals. Thompson reiterated the traditional view of the U.S. Soviet experts that the West had to negotiate with Moscow in order to prevent a dangerous crisis over Berlin, but Kennedy no longer paid attention to that kind of talk.[57]

Cuba reinforced the Checkpoint Charlie lesson. It showed, as Clay had written to Kennedy a year earlier, that "escalation works both ways" and that Khrushchev also had reason to fear it. Khrushchev himself said later that the situation in Berlin had quieted down after the Cuban missile crisis.[58]

Khruschev must have been genuinely surprised by Kennedy's stiff reaction over the Cuban missiles. He must have seen it as a complete reversal of the rather cautious way in which Kennedy had reacted to harassment in Berlin, and it certainly appeared to go against Kennedy's own frequently expressed fear of the risks of nuclear confrontation.

Khrushchev had thus made a massive blunder by wanting to threaten the United States directly. He had moved the crisis from Berlin, where he had a local advantage, to the Caribbean, where Kennedy had one. He had also changed the politics of his threat. Kennedy could perhaps think of offering concessions on Berlin and Germany without paying too high a price in the United States. He could not do the same on Cuba, especially on the eve of congressional elections.

Clay's Private Assessment on Cuba

When I met with Clay in New York right after the Cuban missile crisis, he told me that he believed Khrushchev would never have dared to put

missiles into Cuba if Kennedy had earlier reacted more forcefully to Soviet moves against Berlin. He thought U.S. tactics on Berlin had encouraged Khrushchev to try more dangerous adventures because Khrushchev
had really believed that Kennedy would not push back hard. He suggested, though he did not say it in so many words, that the whole crisis
might have been unnecessary.

Clay undoubtedly remembered the times that he had warned Kennedy
about the "greater risks" Kennedy would face in the future if he did not
meet Khrushchev firmly on every single harassment over Berlin. He may
have also recalled the time when he had warned that the apparent eas-
ing of the Berlin crisis in May of 1962 only represented "an interlude in
which we can get ready for the next battle."

Clay had always thought in wider terms even when he was dealing
specifically with Berlin. He had never expected Khrushchev to ease his
threats until one of them had been so solidly rebuffed that he would not
dare to try again.

But Clay added that Kennedy's policy in the missile crisis had hit
exactly the right note and that there was no longer any reason to worry
about what Khrushchev might do next on Berlin. The threat to Berlin
was over.[59]

Indeed, Kennedy did apply in Cuba some of the things he had learned
in Berlin. His handling of the Berlin crisis helped him handle the Cuban
crisis. It had become part of his learning experience. His decision to send
the brigade to Berlin in August 1961, his refusal to pull back at Checkpoint Charlie, and his readiness to defy Soviet air corridor "reservations,"
must have shown him that he did not need to yield to Khruschev. But
Khrushchev had not recognized the change in time. Kennedy had not
pushed back as hard as Clay would have liked, but he had at least learned
that he could react firmly to Soviet moves.

Khrushchev had correctly foreseen that the Cuban confrontation
would decide the future of Berlin, but it did not come out as he had expected. In the distant waters of the Caribbean, thousands of miles from
the Brandenburg Gate and Checkpoint Charlie, the struggle over Berlin
and Germany had turned in Kennedy's favor and to the advantage of the
Berliners.

CHAPTER TWELVE

"Treaties Are Like Maidens and Roses"

In May 1962, shortly after Konrad Adenauer's angry split with Kennedy over the Principles Paper, Charles de Gaulle invited Adenauer to come to France for a state visit. De Gaulle obviously knew how to strike when the iron was hot.

De Gaulle had first invited Adenauer for an informal visit to his private home in Colombey-les-deux-Eglises shortly after the general returned to power in 1958. De Gaulle had then said to Adenauer that his home was "too small" for "such a great man" as Adenauer. [1] He had convinced Adenauer that, for the first time in centuries, France would not try to weaken Germany but would instead look for cooperation. [2]

The two men had begun a warm friendship, which deepened when de Gaulle paid a return visit to Germany right after Khrushchev's ultimatum and told Adenauer that he would protect Berlin against Khrushchev. He also promised to keep Adenauer briefed on the state of East-West talks about the city. Two years later, in a meeting at Rambouillet Castle in France, de Gaulle had proposed a strong Franco-German alliance as the centerpiece for a new Europe. Adenauer accepted that proposal enthusiastically. He believed, perhaps even more than de Gaulle, that they needed to forge a new and lasting alliance.

Charles de Gaulle Makes His Move

Adenauer replied to de Gaulle that the invitation for a state visit was a great honor. He added, as de Gaulle well knew, that the invitation had come at an opportune time.[3] On July 9, 1962, in honor of Adenauer's state visit, French and German troops marched side by side on the French military parade grounds at Mourmelon, and hundreds of tanks conducted joint maneuvers while Adenauer and de Gaulle watched. Seventeen years after the end of World War II, only de Gaulle could have commanded this to happen in France. He hailed Adenauer as the man who had led Germany to freedom, prosperity, and respectability. In a gesture that invoked the Emperor Charlemagne—the last ruler who had joined the French and German peoples—de Gaulle and Adenauer knelt next to each other in the great Gothic cathedral at Reims while the archbishop preached on reconciliation. Adenauer, deeply moved, remained a long time on his knees.

Two months later, de Gaulle paid a return state visit to West Germany, the first friendly visit to Germany by a French head of state in over 1,000 years. It turned into a triumphal tour that took de Gaulle through most major German cities. He made a powerful impact on the estimated 500,000 Germans who came to see him during his visit. He left Berlin off his schedule in order to concentrate on Franco-German relations instead of East-West tensions, according to his Foreign Minister Maurice Couve de Murville.

In several of his speeches, de Gaulle called the Germans "*ein grosses Volk*" ("a great people"), something the Germans had not heard from any other foreigner, and not even from any German, in a long time. The magazine *Der Spiegel* wrote that de Gaulle's visit was a triumph: "De Gaulle came to Germany as President of France and he leaves it as Emperor of Europe."[4]

Having learned German in his youth and as a prisoner of war in Germany during part of World War I, de Gaulle made his speeches in German throughout his trip. He must have made an enormous effort to memorize his German texts because he refused to wear glasses at any public ceremony. De Gaulle stressed that the French and German peoples had the opportunity, and even the obligation, to build a common Europe together. He clearly signaled, publicly as well as privately, that a new era of Franco-German friendship was at hand. With those comments, he fulfilled Adenauer's lifelong dream.

U.S. State Department reports on de Gaulle's visit to Germany were forwarded to the White House for McGeorge Bundy's personal attention. Washington was worried that de Gaulle was winning Adenauer away from his close link with the United States. The French ambassador in Washington, Hervé Alphand, rubbed salt in the wounds by telling Rusk that one reason for de Gaulle's success was his ability to speak in German.[5]

Kennedy had fallen into the trap that de Gaulle had set by agreeing to let him try the "probes" for a settlement on Berlin. Kennedy had gone so far in those probes, especially by offering concessions that went against Adenauer's most important policies, that he had given de Gaulle an opening. Now, de Gaulle was using Kennedy's policies on Berlin to forge a new German link that could challenge the American role on the continent.

Unlike Kennedy and Harold Macmillan, de Gaulle was not looking for a deal with Khrushchev on Berlin. Nor was he trying to make Germany pay for a deal on Berlin. He continued to insist that the West could make no concessions to Khrushchev until the Soviet leader proved he was really ready to negotiate. While Kennedy was trying to trade away things that Adenauer regarded as his historic legacy, de Gaulle was assuring Adenauer that he would honor German interests.[6]

De Gaulle's vision of the future for Germany was not a deal with Khrushchev but an unbreakable Franco-German link that would anchor a new Europe independent of both America and Russia. With that link solidly in place, Europe could recover its greatness and both France and Germany would be secure.

Adenauer had a less lofty goal. He did not want to create a great and powerful Europe, but he needed trustworthy friends to protect his rump state. Kennedy's negotiating style had convinced him that Kennedy was a weak president surrounded by dangerous advisers. John McCloy had told Adenauer that those advisers had never made any decisions except which of their fellow professors should get tenure.[7] Adenauer clung to de Gaulle as the alternative.

The Elysée Treaty

While de Gaulle was courting Adenauer, Harold Macmillan was negotiating for Great Britain to become a member of the European Economic Community (EEC). Kennedy supported Macmillan's application because he thought Britain's membership would strengthen EEC links with the United States.

De Gaulle harbored deep suspicions about British intentions. He thought that the British and the Americans, whom he saw jointly as the despised "Anglo-Saxons," did not share the traditions or the interests of the continental European states. He pressed a hard bargain with Macmillan, trying to make Britain end its privileged links to such Commonwealth states as Canada and Australia if it wanted to join Europe.

Kennedy used a speech on July 4, 1962, to announce a "Declaration of Interdependence" with Europe and to propose a grand design for a close transatlantic partnership that his advisers called the "dumbbell." He wanted an architecture that would bring the United States, Great Britain, and the European continent into a single structure.

However, Secretary of Defense Robert McNamara unilaterally canceled an Anglo-American air-to-surface nuclear missile program called Skybolt on which Great Britain had hung its nuclear deterrent plans. Trying to repair the damage, Kennedy met with Macmillan at Nassau just before Christmas in 1962, and agreed to provide American Polaris nuclear missiles for Great Britain.

Neither Kennedy nor Macmillan had briefed de Gaulle or Adenauer on their strategic plans. In fact, Macmillan had kept de Gaulle in the dark about his discussions with the Americans when de Gaulle hosted the prime minister at Rambouillet right after McNamara's decision to cancel Skybolt. Macmillan had not replied when de Gaulle invited him to join a European defense system but had gone to Nassau on the very next day to sign the Polaris agreement with Kennedy. De Gaulle was furious that Macmillan had rejected the European option in favor of an American system without telling him in advance.[8]

Nothing could have better confirmed de Gaulle's suspicions that Great Britain would act as Kennedy's Trojan horse in the EEC. It convinced him—if he even needed convincing—that Britain would always put its relations with the United States ahead of its relations with Europe. At a press conference on January 14, 1963, he announced that he would veto Britain's application to join the EEC. The U.S. Embassy in Paris commented that de Gaulle had acted with surprising "brutality."[9]

Kennedy had wanted Adenauer to support British membership in the EEC. In remarkably sharp messages, Rusk had warned Adenauer that the United States expected him to support Great Britain and that there would be serious consequences for Bonn if Germany should help France to make British entry "unreasonably difficult."[10] Rusk used harsher language with Adenauer than he ever used with any other U.S. ally (or with Gromyko). Adenauer resented Rusk's perceived tendency to treat him as a lackey, and he also objected when Bundy told him that the Europeans should learn to accept U.S. leadership. Although he did not want a Europe that was separate from America, he did not want Washington to dictate his actions.[11]

Nor did Adenauer like Macmillan's attitudes on Europe. He believed that Great Britain did not want the European Community to move beyond a free trade zone, whereas Adenauer favored total European unity.[12] He had warned Kennedy that Macmillan's attitudes on Europe made support for British membership "very difficult."[13]

Macmillan's constant push for concessions on Berlin reinforced Adenauer's skepticism toward the prime minister. As one British observer wrote, Macmillan's views on Berlin "squandered . . . the possibility of German support for Britain's stance on Europe." The British government had been "irrevocably tainted" in Adenauer's eyes.[14]

De Gaulle and Adenauer did not have the same approach to Europe. De Gaulle spoke in myths; Adenauer dreaded myths. De Gaulle believed in the nation state; Adenauer despised the nation state. De Gaulle was romantic; Adenauer was practical. De Gaulle wanted a Europe that would be directed by its leading states; Adenauer wanted a Europe that would transcend states. De Gaulle saw the Atlantic and the Channel as moats; Adenauer saw them as bridges.

The Berlin crisis reconciled these radically different approaches because it convinced Adenauer that he could rely only on de Gaulle. And de Gaulle consciously took advantage of Adenauer's doubts about Kennedy and Macmillan, stressing that only he really protected the interests of Germany and Berlin. The chancellor proved unable and unwilling to resist.[15]

Moreover, de Gaulle did more than speak kind words. He briefed Adenauer from time to time on new proposals being discussed by Washington, London, and Paris. He thus cast himself as the protector of Berlin's security and German interests. By resisting the British and American tendency to suggest ever more sweeping concessions to Khrushchev, de Gaulle put the chancellor in his debt. Much to the annoyance of Kennedy and Rusk, de

Gaulle did not offer Berlin or Germany the kind of military protection that U.S. forces did, but he offered Germany the respect and support that Adenauer craved after the wreckage and disgrace left by Hitler.

Thus, eight days after de Gaulle's veto of Great Britain's EEC application, when Adenauer came to Paris on a long planned visit, he and de Gaulle signed a treaty for Franco-German cooperation that became known as the Elysée Treaty (where it was signed). The two old men wanted to set their nations on an unalterable new course. Kennedy was losing the battle for Germany to de Gaulle.[16] De Gaulle would have preferred an executive agreement to a treaty, but Adenauer insisted on a formal agreement in order to cement the Franco-German alliance as part of his historic legacy. He saw it as the culmination of his work and even of his life.[17]

Kennedy reacted in shock to the Elysée Treaty. He feared the dawn of a new axis between Paris and Bonn with a possible extension to Moscow. Deeply suspicious of de Gaulle, he must have thought that the entire Western alliance system might come unglued. The treaty could put an end to Kennedy's grand design and perhaps to the Bonn-Washington tie that many Americans had helped to foster after World War II.[18]

Dean Acheson, George Ball, and John J. McCloy, three veteran members of the American foreign policy establishment, also feared that the Elysée Treaty would challenge the American role in Germany and Europe. With Kennedy's encouragement, Acheson and McCloy denounced the treaty in personal meetings with Adenauer. They warned that it would jeopardize the U.S. commitment to German security.[19] Ball told the German ambassador that the United States might have applauded the Franco-German treaty at any other time, but not with "the coincidence between the signing of the treaty and General de Gaulle's action." He thought that the treaty seemed to serve "de Gaulle's design for Europe—a design quite different from ours." He said that he hoped the German parliament would take action to "allay these apprehensions."[20]

Adenauer had written to Kennedy to inform him of the Elysée Treaty and to describe those elements that he thought would strengthen the entire free world as well as European integration. He had expressed disappointment over Macmillan's failure to win British entry into the European Community, but he added that he would continue to work for a "positive result from the negotiations."[21] Kennedy probably did not believe him.

At a press conference in 1961, Kennedy had quoted Napoleon's remark that he won all his successes because he fought without allies.[22] There were moments in 1963 when he must have thought of that.

To try to influence Kennedy, Adenauer had a long background interview on March 11, 1963, with the American columnist Joseph Alsop, who was close to the Kennedys (among other things, the Kennedys had gone to Alsop's Georgetown house after Kennedy's Inaugural Ball). Adenauer told Alsop that the two great ambitions of his political life had been to tie Germany firmly to the United Sates and to France. He did not believe that either of those ties should jeopardize the other. The Elysée treaty did not and would not do that.

Adenauer also reminded Alsop that France had made a treaty with the Russian czar in the 1890s after the German emperor Wilhelm II had refused to renew Chancellor Otto von Bismarck's Reinsurance Treaty with Russia, and that de Gaulle himself had made a treaty with Stalin in 1944. He said that he wanted to prevent any new deal between France and Russia. He would rather have France on Germany's side. He also did not want Germany to become a loose cannon rolling around between alliance systems.[23] Adenauer made similar comments to other influential American journalists, including Joseph Kraft and Daniel Schorr, trying to explain his actions to American opinion makers.

Kennedy could not grasp the emotional and human weight that Adenauer attached to Franco-German reconciliation. He mainly saw a threat to his "dumbbell" plans for a trans-Atlantic alliance. The Elysée Treaty seemed incompatible with that.

Kennedy, Acheson, and McCloy found ready listeners in the German body politic. Many Bundestag members did not want to tie Germany too closely to Paris. The opposition members of the Bundestag, the Social Democrats, were delighted to have a chance to show that they were better friends of the Americans than Adenauer. Bundestag members who had long worked for closer German-American ties felt that the American commitment to defend Germany was essential to keep Berlin out of Soviet hands.[24] But the Bundestag could not and did not want to reverse Adenauer's signature. A majority feared that de Gaulle might react in rage if they rejected the treaty outright, so they decided to split the difference. They approved the treaty by a substantial margin, but they added a preamble that stressed the continuous German commitment to the Atlantic alliance and the United States:

> Nothing in this treaty alters the rights and obligations of the Federal Republic of Germany, . . . especially the close partnership between Europe and the United States, . . . the common defense within the framework of the North Atlantic Treaty, . . . or the unification of Europe with the entry of Great Britain and others who wish to join.[25]

De Gaulle was deeply disappointed by the preamble. Trying to cover that disappointment by making light of it, he paraphrased Victor Hugo: "Treaties are like maidens and roses; they last as long as they last." And, by implication, one could not really expect them to last forever.[26]

Adenauer, who had spent his life cultivating roses in his garden above the Rhine, said that he knew from personal experience that roses were "the hardiest of flowers." He said that he would carry out the terms of the treaty no matter what the preamble might say. And he did precisely that, inviting de Gaulle to Bonn in July 1963 for the first of what were to be many Franco-German summits under the terms of the treaty.[27]

For Kennedy the Elysée treaty represented a net loss and a sobering challenge. His Berlin diplomacy had risked the American position in Europe. He had to change that, and quickly.

Planning Kennedy's Visit to Berlin

On January 18, 1963, well before the controversy about the Elysée Treaty, Adenauer had heard that Kennedy would be visiting Rome in the late spring. He immediately wrote to the president to invite him to come to Germany and Bonn on the same trip. Willy Brandt followed up with an invitation for Kennedy to visit Berlin.

There was some debate in the White House about whether such a visit to Berlin might prove "provocative" to Khrushchev. But George McGhee, the new American ambassador in Bonn and a close Texas friend of Vice President Lyndon Johnson, pushed hard for it. He wrote that Kennedy had to counter de Gaulle's growing influence in Germany and that Berlin was the best place to do it. Kennedy himself must have felt more comfortable about accepting the invitation after discovering he had been able to handle Khrushchev during the Cuban missile crisis. He clearly no longer worried as much as before about provoking Khrushchev.[28]

Marguerite Higgins again weighed in, citing Khrushchev's several visits to East Berlin. She wrote: "If Kennedy does not show his face in the free part of Berlin after Khrushchev has himself praised the enslaved part of Berlin, what will the world, and especially the Kremlin, think of Western determination?"[29]

For Kennedy, de Gaulle's visits to Germany as well as the Elysée Treaty had served as a wake-up call. Although he had been able to work with sympathetic Americans and Germans to change the treaty's tone through the preamble, the president realized that he could no longer take Adenauer and Germany for granted. Any look at U.S. military bases in Europe made clear that Germany remained at the center of America's strategic position on the continent and that the United States could no more afford to lose Germany to de Gaulle than to lose Berlin to Khrushchev.

Dean Rusk wrote to Kennedy that "German-American relations must be kept within the Atlantic framework" (rather than de Gaulle's framework). He thought that a Kennedy trip to Germany would provide a chance to influence Germans at a crucial time when "attitudes for the future will be shaped." Although Kennedy should not give the appearance that he was engaging in "a popularity contest with de Gaulle," that was precisely what Rusk was asking him to do.[30]

Rusk added that Kennedy must visit Berlin as well as West Germany. In particular, Rusk warned that de Gaulle would be planning a trip to Germany and perhaps Berlin in the late summer of 1963, after the Elysée Treaty had been ratified, and that "the President should not be placed in the position of seeming to compete with . . . de Gaulle." Kennedy had to get there first.[31] Having seen and heard all the recommendations, and especially the frequently expressed fears about de Gaulle's growing influence in Germany, Kennedy decided to accept both Adenauer's and Brandt's invitations.

Once Kennedy had decided to visit Germany and Berlin, the State Department provided the White House with a scope paper on what the president might expect and should achieve during the visit. In that paper, the department stressed the importance of Kennedy's visit as a counter to de Gaulle's growing influence in Germany. In the paper's first paragraph, the department reminded the White House of de Gaulle's state visit to Germany in September 1962.[32]

The State Department warned that Kennedy's trip would be made "against the backdrop of a scheduled further visit by de Gaulle to Germany in early July." But it left some room for hope, pointing out that de Gaulle had not visited either Frankfurt, Wiesbaden, or Berlin during his visit. Because Kennedy would be visiting those cities, he would be seen by Germans who had not seen de Gaulle. That would give him a chance to outscore de Gaulle. The State Department suggested that Berlin might be the subject on which Kennedy might win Adenauer and Germany back, after having been the subject on which he might have lost them.

The scope paper even urged Kennedy to speak of German reunification, which Kissinger had suggested in 1961 but which Kennedy had never done because it might have seemed provocative to Khrushchev. The department suggested that the president should meet German political and emotional "requirements" by raising the topic in Berlin. It still warned, however, that Kennedy should not sound overly provocative on this point.

Edward R. Murrow, head of the U.S. Information Agency, also urged Kennedy to counter de Gaulle in Germany and Berlin. Having once made Kennedy recognize the danger represented by the Wall, Murrow again recalled the "world importance" of Berlin. Murrow suggested that Kennedy quietly emphasize that the U.S. contribution to Western defense and security outweighed all others.[33] Kennedy's preparatory briefing papers were thus full of references to the threat from de Gaulle and hardly mentioned any threat from Khrushchev.[34]

Although Kennedy's White House advisers still continually told him that he should not appear too provocative toward Moscow, Kennedy's own attitude on Berlin must have shifted after the Elysée Treaty. He could now see that the city could be important for his goals in Europe. He also had to keep Adenauer on his side to prevent de Gaulle from taking Germany (and with it Berlin) into the French vision of Europe. The chancellor had long believed that Kennedy could end the threat to Berlin only by making Khrushchev realize that he faced the risk of war. That was how Kennedy had ended the threat from Cuba. Now the chancellor should realize that Kennedy understood this could work in Berlin as well.[35] With Western Europe shaping its future, Kennedy's treatment of the Berlin crisis during his visit would offer him his best chance to influence that future.

Waiting in Berlin

As Kennedy's visit drew closer, those of us in the U.S. Mission in Berlin followed the plans by reading State Department cables or listening to the ever-lively Washington rumor mill. We could not help but be amused that the same U.S. officials who had been very anxious to avoid any actions on Berlin that might offend Khrushchev had suddenly become great defenders of Berlin when de Gaulle challenged the American position. But we hoped that it would make the president say things that would finally end Ulbricht's threat to the city.

We could see the whole Berlin problem shifting before our eyes. Although we did not see the Gaullist threat as the White House apparently saw it, particularly because de Gaulle had not visited Berlin, we welcomed Kennedy's concern.

Most of all, we could see a deepening appreciation in Berlin for the president himself ever since the confrontation in Cuba. Kennedy's firm position on the Soviet missiles and his assurance that he would not forget Berlin during the crisis had made a profound impression on everybody we met. We wondered if this could help in his competition with de Gaulle. We awaited Kennedy's visit eagerly. So did the Berliners.

CHAPTER THIRTEEN

⊙━━◆━━⊙

"We'll Never Have
Another Day Like This"

As he prepared for his Berlin visit, John F. Kennedy wanted very much
to say some things in German to match Charles de Gaulle. He hoped to
say several sentences and perhaps an entire paragraph in German. The
White House called the American RIAS director Robert Lochner, who
had lived in Germany much of his life, to Washington to help coach Kennedy in German. Margarethe Plischke, who taught German at the U.S.
State Department Foreign Service Institute, was also called to help.[1]

Practicing Kennedy's German

Kennedy's speechwriters and potential interpreters had drafted a number
of phrases and even whole sentences that they wrote out for Kennedy
in phonetic German. Lochner and Ted Sorensen thought the following
sentence would please the Berliners:

> "I am proud to be in free Berlin, the city which is a shining symbol, not
> only for Europe but for the whole world."

Kennedy's phonetic guidance ran as follows:

> Ish FROYA mish in daim FRY-en bear-LEAN tsu sine, dair SHTAT,
> dee ine LOISH-tendess sim-BOWL IST, nisht NOOR fear oy-RO-pah,
> sondern fear dee GANTSA VELT.[2]

217

Other sentences ran along similar lines with phonetic spelling, but Kennedy had no gift for foreign languages. It soon became painfully (and perhaps mercifully) clear that he could not utter a full German paragraph or even a long sentence without embarrassing himself and making his audience wonder what he was trying to say. Having not spoken German as a youth, he could not make certain German language sounds successfully even with the most punctilious phonetic spelling and preparatory coaching.

Kennedy's draft speech for Berlin thus had no German phrases. But he still wanted to say something that would have an impact on his audience and would match de Gaulle.[3] He knew that his best chance was at the city hall.

Different concerns pressed in on Kennedy. McGeorge Bundy had advised him to praise the Berliners for their courageous stand but still to speak in terms that Khrushchev would regard as unprovocative. Averell Harriman was then negotiating a nuclear test ban treaty with Khrushchev. Kennedy's visit should open the door for wide-ranging diplomacy with Moscow.[4] Moreover, after the Elysée Treaty Kennedy needed to persuade the Berliners and the Germans that his concept of a trans-Atlantic world linking America and Europe was better than de Gaulle's concept of a separate Europe. It was a tall order for a single day.

In the final schedule for his Berlin visit, Kennedy was to make three speeches. The first was to be a short statement at a German labor congress. He had been invited to speak there by American union leader George Meany, and he had to accept. The second and most important speech was to be a public address at the West Berlin city hall. The third was to be a more academic speech at the Free University of Berlin.

The speeches that Sorensen drafted reflected Kennedy's three goals. They praised the Berliners, restated America's commitment to Europe, and avoided any provocation of Khrushchev. Bundy had carefully reviewed various drafts and finally approved the city hall text that General James Polk had labelled "terrible" during Kennedy's flight to the city.[5]

All the careful preparation for the visit went by the board, however, when Kennedy and his retinue actually arrived in West Berlin. The president's advisers had not reckoned with the Berliners themselves. Although General Lucius Clay had told them to expect a powerful reception, they were unprepared for the overwhelming waves of humanity or for the sheer noise that engulfed the presidential party from the moment that the motorcade left Tegel airport.

The Berliners greeted Kennedy very differently from the way they would have greeted him in the fall of 1961 or the spring of 1962. By June of 1963 he was no longer the man who had let the Wall go up but the hero of the Cuban missile crisis and the man who had saved West Berlin from Ulbricht and Khrushchev. They wanted to thank him. Over a million Berliners came to welcome him along his thirty-five-mile route through the city. Perhaps half a million had already come to the city hall hours in advance to hear his speech.

I had been assigned to help take care of Kennedy and his party during his Berlin visit. I sat as monitor in the first bus that followed his limousine and the police escort. Members of the White House staff in the bus initially snickered at the Berliners who had gathered just outside Tegel airport. Some said that such crowds had undoubtedly also cheered the Nazis. Others said that Germans would do anything for a parade. But I noticed that the throngs of cheering Berliners began to affect the White House staffers as the bus slowly inched its way through the city behind Kennedy's open Lincoln convertible. The unbridled shouts and applause from the vast hordes of people gradually made the visitors realize that this reception differed from anything that they had ever experienced. They fell silent, almost hypnotized.

The Berliners had come to see Kennedy and to cheer him. They stood five to ten deep along the sidewalks, they hung from trees, from lampposts, from traffic lights, and from construction cranes that they had placed conveniently for the occasion. They crowded on balconies, on beer wagons, on trucks, and on any platform that gave a better view, like the flat roofs of service stations. They waved handkerchiefs, scarves, placards, sheets, and anything else that they could handle.

When any group got its first glimpse of Kennedy's car, they would go wild. They shouted "Ken-ne-dy!" at the top of their lungs and tried to get past the police escort to touch the president or to throw flowers and confetti into his car. Kennedy stood for most of the trip on the right side of the car, with Willy Brandt standing next to him and Konrad Adenauer on the left side of the car. Kennedy wanted to be sure to invite Adenauer to join him, wanting to avoid the problems that the failure to invite Adenauer to accompany Vice President Johnson in 1961 had helped to cause.

The motorcade did not go only to the Wall and to the notorious sites of East-West confrontation, but also through parts of the thriving center of West Berlin. Brandt had not wanted Kennedy to see only the signs of East-West struggle but also the evidence of West Berlin's defiance and prosperity.

Kennedy stopped for the first time at the Kongresshalle, a conference center, where Meany had invited him. By then, Kennedy had begun to react to the power of the masses. His speech to the trade union, often spontaneous, not only cited the importance of worker rights in the free West but also included the statement "West Berlin is my country." He obviously did not mean that he spoke as the commander-in-chief of the U.S. occupation sector of Berlin, but that he felt at home in the city. He had never said anything that personal about Berlin before.

Then Kennedy's motorcade proceeded to the sites that had become famous because of the Wall and the clashes at the sector border. Kennedy saw Bernauer Strasse, where people had jumped to their deaths before their windows could be barred. He saw the Brandenburg gate, where the Wall had been reinforced to a height of eight feet and a width of six feet, and he saw Checkpoint Charlie, where the tanks had faced each other.

As Kennedy got out of his car and stood at improvised observation platforms to look into East Berlin, he caught a glimpse of some East Berlin women who were surreptitiously waving at him and trying to avoid being seen by the Vopos who had been instructed to keep them from waving to the president. He also saw an improvised sign which read in English, "We greet Kennedy also for the East Berliners." Reporters wrote that in his several visits to the Wall, he showed a grim and determined face.[6]

"Ich bin ein Berliner"

After the long drive through the city, Kennedy needed to relax before making his speech to the crowd waiting at the city hall. He went into a side office in Brandt's suite and changed his shirt. He then lay down on a couch for about ten minutes without his national security staff around him. He was suffering from back pains induced by standing and waving for miles. But he could not rest too long because he could already hear the roar of the expectant crowd that overflowed the square and even the adjoining streets as far as the eye could see.

By then, Kennedy had fully realized that he needed to make a rousing political statement to match the mood of those who had come to welcome him. He had to reflect the intensity of the surroundings in which he was to stand and speak. For the first time, Kennedy had seen the Berliners and the Wall with his own eyes and in human instead of diplomatic terms, not as a chip to be bargained with Khrushchev but as a city and a people. He needed to use his short break to improve his speech.

Kennedy had begun redrafting in his mind even as he was driven through West Berlin. By the time he had finished absorbing the events of the day, he had obviously decided to say words that had never been planned in Washington. He also wanted to say them in a memorable way.

Despite his pronunciation problems, Kennedy now wanted more than ever to say something that would resonate in Berlin. He had remembered from his days as a student how citizens of Rome would proudly say *"Civis romanum sum"* ("I am a citizen of Rome") and he thought that the matching German phrase *"Ich bin ein Berliner"* ("I am a Berliner") would make the right impact on the crowd. He decided to include that sentence in his speech.[7]

Kennedy looked over his speech notes, which had by then been put on cards from which he could read more easily. He threw away most of the cards and wrote on some of the others. He practiced his pronunciation again with Lochner. He particularly rehearsed the phrase *"Ich bin ein Berliner"* with Lochner, but also to a lesser degree the phrase *"Lasst sie nach Berlin kommen"* ("Let them come to Berlin"). Those phrases were not in the text that had been drafted for him nor on any of the cards that he had in front of him, but he wanted to use them.

Heinz Weber, Chancellor Adenauer's interpreter, joined the group. He had been designated to translate the city hall speech because he had more experience than Lochner interpreting political texts. He guided Kennedy on some of the same German pronunciation points as Lochner and took notes on the German remarks that Kennedy wanted to make.[8]

Kennedy discussed a subtle but tricky stylistic point with Lochner and Weber. Theoretically, if Kennedy were to say *"Ich bin ein Berliner"* he could be interpreted as saying "I am a jelly doughnut," which is what a *"Berliner"* is in some German slang (although not so much in Berlin itself). They wondered whether he should say *"Ich bin Berliner,"* which might be a way of saying that he was a citizen of Berlin without any implication that he was a doughnut. But Lochner and particularly Weber advised against that because it would imply that Kennedy had been born in Berlin. Neither thought that the crowd would imagine for a moment that Kennedy was describing himself as a jelly doughnut.[9]

To make sure that he would remember the pronunciation, Kennedy wrote both phrases phonetically in red ink on special note cards that he attached to his speech. He wrote "*Ich bin ein Berliner*" as "Ish bin ine Bear-LEAN-er" and "*Lasst sie nach Berlin kommen*" as "Lust z nach Bearlin comen."[10] With those preparations made, and with Weber and Lochner behind him, Kennedy was ready to speak to the crowd, which had continued to shout "Ken-ne-dy!" while he was in Brandt's office.

By the time Kennedy came to the podium to speak, he had totally rewritten the original draft speech in his mind. He dropped all the careful phrases that his advisers had planned. He used almost none of their prepared remarks except at the end. For the most part Kennedy spoke freely. He rarely glanced at his text. He praised the fighting spirit of the Berliners, coming down fully on their side. His speech left the realm of standard rhetoric and rose to the level of powerful political theater.[11]

Kennedy began his speech, as he had rewritten it, by comparing Berlin with ancient Rome. Starting from his own earlier recollection, he said that the proudest boast that people could once make was to say "*Civis romanum sum.*" Now, however, the proudest boast that anyone could make was "*Ich bin ein Berliner.*" He praised the Berliners for their courage and their determination to remain free.

Kennedy then launched into a fulminating attack on the Communist system, saying: "Many people in the world don't understand, or say they don't understand, what is the great issue between the free world and the Communist world." To them, he would say, "Let them come to Berlin." Others might see Communism as the wave of the future, or might think that one could negotiate with the Communists, or that Communism's promise of economic progress compensated for its cruelties but, Kennedy reiterated, "Let them come to Berlin." He repeated that phrase four times in English for effect, finally also saying it once, as he had planned, in German: "*Lasst sie nach Berlin kommen.*"

Kennedy admitted that democracy might not be perfect, "but we have never had to put up a wall to keep our people in." He denounced the Communist system as an offense against humanity. Finally, drawing on

The crowd that came to cheer Kennedy's Berlin city hall speech on June 26, 1963. Courtesy of the John F. Kennedy Presidential Library

the few note cards that he still carried from his prepared text, he spoke of how the Berlin Wall separated families, husbands and wives, brothers and sisters, and other people who wished to be together. He could take plenty of time to study his notes because the Berliners frequently interrupted his speech for long stretches of applause.

Kennedy then spoke of Germany as a whole, again drawing on his prepared note cards and saying that in eighteen years of peace and good faith, "This generation of Germans has earned the right to be free, including the right to unite their families and their nation in lasting peace." He promised that this would happen, both for the city of Berlin and for the

German nation and the European continent. It was the first time he had spoken of German unification, a topic he and U.S. negotiators had long avoided so as not to offend Khrushchev.

Kennedy ended his speech by returning to the beginning and by specifically pronouncing even himself a Berliner:

> All free men, wherever they may live, are citizens of Berlin, and, therefore, as a free man, I take pride in the words "*Ich bin ein Berliner.*"

With that remark, Kennedy fully associated himself with Berlin and the Berliners even more than he had with the statement "West Berlin is my country" addressed to the trade union that morning.

The speech that Kennedy gave at the city hall did not look or sound at all like the words that had been written and carefully vetted for him in Washington.[12] More important, Kennedy's remarks had a totally different tone from the draft that Weber had been given.[13] Fortunately, as an experienced political interpreter, Weber knew how to translate what he heard, not what he read.

Loud and prolonged cheering frequently prevented Kennedy from continuing because he had perfectly captured the defiant mood of the Berliners against Khrushchev's and Ulbricht's brutalities and threats. The crowd would first cheer his English remarks. They would then cheer again when Weber gave the translation. Like any good politician, Kennedy had spoken the words that his listeners wanted to hear. They had not come more than half a million strong to get an academic lecture. They had certainly not come to hear about the need to compromise with Khrushchev and Ulbricht. They had come to welcome a young president who had protected them, who had beaten Khrushchev back at Checkpoint Charlie and in Cuba, and who would inspire them. That was precisely what they got.

Kennedy dropped phrases tinged with caution or with a warning tone, such as the draft's reference to a "hard journey" ahead or that the Wall would fall "sooner or later." Instead, he spoke of hope for the future. Kennedy also matched the spirit of the speech with some of his actions on the speaker's tribune. He went out of his way to praise the Germans and Americans who had held the line in Berlin, citing particularly Adenauer, Brandt, and Clay.

Kennedy calls Clay to the podium in Berlin to show his support for the general. Courtesy of Jean Edward Smith

Kennedy even called Clay to the front of the podium and the two stood together and waved as the crowd roared. He said that he was proud to stand next to Clay and that he knew that Clay would come back to Berlin if needed. These gestures, like the speech itself, went directly against the advice and spirit of what had been prepared for him and against the continuous criticisms of Clay from State Department and White House staff. But they certainly pleased his audience.[14]

Horst Teltschik, who was later to help Chancellor Helmut Kohl negotiate the unification of Germany with Soviet President Mikhail Gorbachev, still remembers going to the city hall square at 8 A.M. that morning with about half a dozen university friends to be in a good spot for Kennedy's speech. Several hours later, as the crowd swelled, they had to link their arms at the elbows to avoid being separated. At times they feared being crushed. But they did not mind. Kennedy's speech still re-mains in Teltschik's memory as one of the greatest experiences in his life, as it was for many Berliners at the city hall square.[15]

Even those Germans who only heard the speech on the radio, like Klaus Scharioth, later Germany's ambassador in Washington, have never forgotten either the speech or the moment when Kennedy gave it. Scharioth said that, like all Germans, the speech inspired him, and that it convinced him to dedicate himself to public service.[16] Those who were in the square or in the city hall that day still speak of it in awe. So do Berliners or Germans of that generation who heard it. Even Germans of later generations—and many Americans—can quote "*Ich bin ein Berliner*" as if it were part of their standard vocabulary.[17]

Despite Ulbricht's instructions to keep East Berliners away from the Wall and despite his prohibition about looking at Kennedy's motorcade, East Germans and especially East Berliners also wanted to hear Kennedy's speech. They could follow the full visit on Western radio and television, which most of them heard although they could not watch Kennedy in person.

Most East Berliners reacted as enthusiastically as the West Berlin crowds. The wife of a Politburo member of the East German Communist Party telephoned the wife of another Communist official and described the speech: "*Das war fabelhaft*" ("That was fabulous"). The friend agreed, showing that the speech could even affect Berliners who were supposed to be dedicated Communists.[18]

Not everybody in his audience liked Kennedy's speech as much as the people in the square did. Bundy and Sorensen stood toward the back of the balcony and looked on uncomfortably. They did not approve of what the president was saying. They were even shocked by parts of it. They did not think Kennedy's tone would promote negotiations with the Kremlin. After the speech, Bundy told the president that "I think you went a little far." Bundy had liked the earlier more diplomatic text, which he had cleared.[19]

Sorensen, who did not recognize much of his own draft, agreed, al-though he had grown accustomed to having Kennedy give the speech he wanted to give no matter what had been written for him. Both of them recognized that Kennedy might well have been inclined to rewrite that text in his head once he had seen and felt the enthusiasm of the crowd, but they had not realized how much he would change the words, the tone, and the political message of the speech. Bundy urged Kennedy to adjust his later and more formal speech at the Free University of Berlin in order to make that speech more conciliatory toward the Soviet Union. Bundy wanted to make sure that Khrushchev understood Kennedy's wish for negotiations even if the president had said what he had needed to say to rally the Berliners.[20]

Kennedy did sound more conciliatory in that policy speech.[21] In the part of his text addressed to Khrushchev, Kennedy stressed the importance of negotiations. He also told his audience that they, like himself, would have to deal with Moscow and that nothing would happen quickly. He warned that German unification would require patience and a readiness to deal with "realities as they actually are and not as we wish they were."

Still, Kennedy's words at the Free University had a tone aimed at his Berlin and German audience. He spoke of the prospect for German unification. Although he added that peaceful unification of Berlin and Germany would be "neither quick nor easy" because others would need "to see their own true interests better than they do today," he had said what many Berliners and particularly East Germans regarded as magic words. Against the realities of "the police state regime" in East Germany, he summoned "the realities of Western strength, the realities of Western commitment, the realities of Germany as a nation and a people, without regard to artificial boundaries."

Although Kennedy did make some changes in his later speech to leave an open door to Khrushchev for their arms control negotiations, he did not accept Bundy's assertion that he had gone too far. He felt that he had seized the moment at the city hall. He understood better than his advisers the kind of language that he needed to use. Kennedy must also have realized as he toured the city that the United States should regard the attitude of the Berliners as something to be welcomed rather than dismissed, derided, or feared as it had been by many in his administration.

Thus Kennedy discarded his balanced tone. He sang a paean to freedom. Following de Gaulle's model by saying some words in German, he even trumped de Gaulle. He captured not only the imagination but also the unique role of the Berliners when he hailed their pride in being able to say "*Ich bin ein Berliner.*" Nothing like it had been heard in Berlin before, and nothing like it has been heard there since.

Even more important was Kennedy's decision to use the phrase twice, claiming at the very end of his speech that he himself took pride in being able to say "*Ich bin ein Berliner.*" This put the president of the United States squarely into the Berlin camp. For weeks, excited Berliners could speak of little else.[22]

Kennedy could not have issued a clearer warning to Khrushchev not to try any more harassment in Berlin. By personally associating himself with Berlin and the Berliners, he issued the most categorical defense of the city and of his three "essentials" ever. Whether or not he intended the statement as a commitment, it could hardly be interpreted as anything else.

Kennedy's triumph went further than anybody in Berlin had dared to hope. Brandt and Bahr had expected the visit to be a success but they had not imagined that Kennedy and the Berliners would form such a powerful and immediate bond. Kennedy's youth and charisma, his decision to stand up in his car and to wave to the crowd, and later his city hall speech, went beyond whatever Brandt and Bahr could have hoped. Bahr would say later that he had never in his whole life seen such a huge number of Berliners acting so enthusiastically, not even at the moment of German unification.[23]

Kennedy's New Policy

In one visit and in one speech, Kennedy reversed his policy toward Germany and Berlin. He and his advisers had first seen Germany and Berlin as elements to be fitted into a new global agreement with Khrushchev. They had tried hard to reach that. But Khrushchev and Foreign Minister Andrei Gromyko had rejected that. Kennedy then changed direction. Abandoning his early attitude, when he and Rusk just wanted the problem of Berlin to go away, Kennedy had returned Germany and Berlin to the center of American policy in Europe.

After two years of trying to negotiate about Berlin, Kennedy had come to realize that West Berlin could actually be an asset, not a liability, in the wider struggle for Europe. Having watched Khrushchev and de Gaulle struggle for Germany and Berlin, Kennedy understood the stakes. He thus returned the city to the core of the Atlantic alliance system.

Kennedy's speech at the Berlin city hall marked his final reconciliation with the paradox of Berlin and Germany. The speech rang as an act of defiance, a final declaration of independence from any worries about Soviet threats, carrying the Cuban message one step further. His speech also became part of the lore of Berlin and of Kennedy himself. No other Kennedy speech is cited as often or as proudly, except perhaps his inaugural address.

By putting his personal guarantee over the city, Kennedy had also put an end to the Berlin crisis. There were still occasional harassments over Berlin access or other matters after that visit and that speech, but no major challenges and no more threats. Brandt believed that Kennedy's speech had simply made it too risky for Khrushchev to try to act against the city. Khrushchev also told Ulbricht to lay off, as Berlin officials later learned, although Ulbricht could not resist playing occasional games until he was removed by the Soviets ten years later.[24]

Bundy may have thought that Kennedy's speech at the city hall ruined the message he wanted to deliver in his other speeches. But it had, in fact, reinforced that message. Kennedy told Khrushchev that he wanted to negotiate a new relationship but that Ulbricht could no longer disrupt the peace of Berlin without Khrushchev himself having to pay a price. That drove home the point that Clay had made at Checkpoint Charlie. After Kennedy's visit and his speech, America and Berlin became linked more firmly than they had been even after the blockade or Checkpoint Charlie. No American president could ever back away from the words that Kennedy had spoken. None did.

It mattered not that Kennedy had started his presidency with a cool attitude, under which the Berliners were to accept the place to which they had been consigned in the greater White House scheme of things. It mattered only that he finally understood the human and emotional needs of the city and of its people. He could not then change what had happened with and at the Wall, but he could and did at least show that he did not like it any more than they did and that he had not given up the hope to change it in the future.

As Kennedy and his elated entourage flew to Ireland from Berlin, he told Sorensen, "We'll never have another day like this as long as we live."[25]

CHAPTER FOURTEEN

"Our Hope Is the *Ami*"

The new American ambassador to West Germany, George McGhee, wrote that President Kennedy's visit to Germany, and particularly Kennedy's speech in Berlin, would have a dramatic effect on German-American relations.

McGhee did not concentrate on Kennedy's message about the evils of Communism or on "*Ich bin ein Berliner*." Instead, he wrote that Germans at all levels now fully recognized what the Atlantic alliance meant for them. McGhee felt that the Germans would henceforth "be more cautious about engaging in excursions with France."[1]

As McGhee noted, many Germans, moved by Kennedy's speech in Berlin, linked it with his speech at the Frankfurt Paulskirche. There, Kennedy had repeatedly stressed the importance of the Atlantic alliance. He had stated, "The future of the West lies in the Atlantic partnership—a system of cooperation, interdependence and harmony."

Kennedy also added: "Our commitment to Europe is indispensable—in our interest as well as yours," for "war in Europe, as we learned twice in 49 years, destroys peace in America." In a direct challenge to de Gaulle, the president said, "Those who would doubt our pledge—those who would separate Europe from America or split one ally from another—could only give aid and comfort to the men who make themselves our adversaries and welcome any Western disarray."[2] Kennedy's visit to Berlin had rein-forced that message.

McGhee also thought that the Germans had noticed how Kennedy's personal courtesies and tributes to Adenauer had "almost visibly melted [Adenauer's] reserve." That, as well as Kennedy's decision to invite Ad-enauer to join him in Berlin, would improve Kennedy's relations with those Germans who had long resented Kennedy's evident disdain for the chancellor.

By the summer of 1963, as he watched the Federal Republic of Ger-many slide into the Gaullist camp, Kennedy recognized that he could win his German listeners only by committing himself fully to the future of Berlin. Kennedy used the enthusiasm he had generated in Berlin to support what he said in Frankfurt. When Kennedy met Khrushchev's thrust toward Cuba, he reinforced his position in Berlin. When he spoke in Berlin, he reinforced his position in Germany and Europe.

Khrushchev's and de Gaulle's Visits

Two days after Kennedy's tour of West Berlin, Khrushchev came to East Berlin to help celebrate Walter Ulbricht's seventieth birthday and to chair a meeting of Communist leaders. He and Ulbricht decided to rival Kennedy's visit with his own. The East Berlin press dutifully spoke of a "hurricane of enthusiasm" with 600,000 East Berliners shouting "Nikita, Nikita!" to acclaim the Soviet leader. East Berlin's *Berliner Zeitung* called his visit a "triumphal tour through the capital" and wrote that "the hearts of Berliners beat in response to him."[3]

But Khrushchev could not compete with Kennedy. He and Ulbricht tried to match Kennedy directly, touring East Berlin while standing together in an open car, but they did not attract the vast crowds that Kennedy had attracted. Western journalists who got into East Berlin told us that Khrushchev's "crowds" consisted of thin lines of party functionar-ies brought in by bus, and that the speech with which he tried to rival Kennedy—given in front of East Berlin's city hall—also evoked little reaction. Khrushchev's counter to Kennedy's "*Ich bin ein Berliner*" turned out to be "*Ich liebe die Mauer*" ("I love the Wall"), a phrase that was hardly likely to arouse enthusiasm among the many East Berliners who saw the Wall as a prison.

A Central Intelligence Agency report on Khrushchev's visit wrote that Khrushchev had used it to tell Ulbricht to undertake no new initiatives and to reinforce a message he had earlier given the East German leader: "An important reason for not pressing ahead with Berlin . . . is the outcome of the Cuban crisis."[4] The CIA reported that Khrushchev had already told the East German Communist Party Congress in January 1963 that the Wall had contributed to the stabilization of the GDR and reduced the importance of a peace treaty. The CIA concluded that the Soviets "do not intend to reactivate the Berlin issue for a long period." The report continued, saying that Khrushchev, having changed his view of Kennedy's determination, had told the Soviet Communist Party Central Committee in a secret speech in December 1962 that the Soviet Union had been forced onto the defensive and that this had to be reflected in its policy on Germany and Berlin. Even Ulbricht now said that the Berlin question should be solved "step by step."

Within two weeks after Kennedy's visit, de Gaulle also came to Germany for a consultation under the terms on the new Franco-German treaty. He and Adenauer agreed on various cultural programs and agreed to some cooperation on military hardware as well as placing some military units under each other's command.

Ambassador McGhee reported with some pleasure that the French ambassador in Bonn said that de Gaulle's visit had produced "not much" in terms of results. Yet de Gaulle thought it important because he still feared that the Germans "might approach the Soviets." The French president thus wanted to use his visit to continue to hold Germany close to the West.[5] De Gaulle had nonetheless seen Kennedy's visit to Berlin as "a plebiscite in favor of the United States."

De Gaulle realized that Adenauer's successors would not pursue the old chancellor's policies.[6] Although he had returned to Paris proclaiming that a good beginning had been made for Franco-German cooperation under the Elysée treaty, the results of his visit had been relatively spare. He recognized that most Germans would not join his drive for independence once the United States had again committed itself firmly to Germany and Berlin, as Kennedy had now done.[7]

There was indeed no hiding the impact that Kennedy had made, especially in Berlin. De Gaulle did not even try to make any public appearances during his visit. Although he had played a strong card in Germany during most of 1961 and 1962 while Kennedy was floundering, Kennedy's stand in the Cuban crisis and his spectacular tour of Berlin had reinforced the German-American alliance. French officials in Berlin told me that it would have been "grotesque" for de Gaulle to have made a visit to Berlin right after Kennedy. De Gaulle had outmaneuvered Kennedy in the competition for Germany while Kennedy was trying for a deal with Khrushchev, but Kennedy was stronger once he made up his mind to treat Germany as an ally instead of as a pawn in his game with Moscow.

Disappointed, de Gaulle said in July 1964 that, despite pleasant contacts with Germany he had "remained a virgin." He added that France "is pursuing, by her own means, that which a European and independent policy should be."[8] By committing himself fully to Berlin and to Germany, Kennedy had outflanked de Gaulle and countered Khrushchev.

Nixon's Visit to East Berlin

One month after Kennedy's visit to Berlin, his old political rival Richard M. Nixon came to the city for several days on a personal visit with Mrs. Nixon and some California friends. I was asked to serve as his escort because he wanted to visit East Berlin. The Nixons and I spent some time in East Berlin on the afternoon of July 25, walking around the center of the city. The East German state police followed us everywhere to make sure that nobody got close to us. Nixon had hoped to see the city quietly, but the East German police were not letting him.

That evening, after dinner, Nixon called and asked me to go back to East Berlin with him and Mrs. Nixon and their friends. He wanted to see it without being surrounded by police. We took a taxi to Checkpoint Charlie and then walked through on foot as if we were ordinary tourists. We had the good fortune that the border guards did not immediately fix on Mr. Nixon's name and we could go into East Berlin without being noticed.

It was already dark and quite hazy by the time we walked into East Berlin along Friedrichstrasse toward the Unter den Linden boulevard. The only light came from some weak overhead street lamps about twenty yards apart. We thus walked from one faint pool of light into the dark and then into another faint pool of light.

As we entered one pool of light, we saw a man dressed in a dark and rumpled suit coming toward us from across the street. Recognizing us as

Westerners, he made the traditional hand-to-the-mouth gesture familiar in Europe as a sign that he wanted a cigarette. Nixon's friend gave him one and lit it for him. Nixon's friend, by way of conversation, said: "That is Mr. Nixon, the former Vice President of the United States." I translated it. The man looked at us curiously, peering through the penumbra as if he was not quite sure of what he had heard, but recognizing us as Americans.

Leaning forward toward Nixon, he said in a low but firm voice: "*Unsere Hoffnung ist der Ami*" ("Our hope is the American"). It did not sound like a plea but like a simple statement of fact.

Nixon was about to reply, but the man suddenly froze and began edging backward away from us. He made a little gesture with his hand as if to show that we should leave. I looked around and saw two East Berlin Vopos entering our pool of light, probably heading for the checkpoint to begin their tours of guard duty. I told Nixon that we should continue on our way, which we did.

As I looked back, I could see the guards still walking toward the checkpoint, wanting to get to their job on time. The man we had met was continuing to edge backward, leaving the pool of light into the darkness. It seemed like a scene from Dante's *Inferno*.

We walked further until we found a small pub with traditional dark wooden walls and sat down at a table. As we were drinking some beers, a few of the men in the pub, recognizing us as Americans, lifted their glasses in a silent toast. We responded in kind, but we did not want to engage them in conversation because it might have been dangerous for them. For about twenty minutes we had a pleasant evening, obviously among friends although they said nothing to us.

Suddenly a group of about three to four men in hats and trench coats entered the pub. All conversation stopped. They were clearly state police who had been alerted by somebody—we did not know who—that some Americans were at the pub. To avoid any scene, we paid our bill and left. We found a taxi back to the checkpoint and the men in trench coats followed us there in a black East German Wartburg car.

I have often wondered what that evening meant. As we discussed it among the Nixons and their friends, we all agreed that Khrushchev and Ulbricht had not won the Berliners although they had built the Wall and secured the GDR regime. At least some East Berliners, and we suspected many, still felt a sympathy for the United States. Why else would any man have said to some perfect strangers that their hope was the *Ami*?

Ulbricht had perhaps relieved one symptom of East German discontent by blocking refugees, but he had not ended the deeper discontent itself that his regime inspired. As it turned out, his successors never ended it either.

After the Wall

As I and others at the U.S. Mission remained in Berlin after Kennedy's visit, we could see that the Wall had not only divided Berlin but also divided Europe. But that divide did not run where Ulbricht had hoped, along the western border of the GDR. Instead, it ran through the center of the former capital of Germany. Khrushchev had let Ulbricht save his regime, but he had not given Ulbricht what Ulbricht wanted most: control over West Berlin. And he could not do more. After Cuba, he was no longer ready to challenge Kennedy.

Konrad Adenauer recognized the new line. He had secured West Germany and had staked his political career on the alliance with the United States, but it did not lead to German unity as he had hoped. Some Germans could accuse him of having duped them. Some, like Willy Brandt, could say that he had chosen the wrong road. But fifteen years after World War II, when many Americans and Europeans still regarded all Germans with deep suspicion, he believed that his first task had been to restore Germany's reputation.

In October 1963, in his last official letter before retirement, Adenauer wrote to Kennedy that he had always wanted to link the German people indissolubly with the West. He added proudly, "I am pleased that this goal has been reached."[9] Kennedy had taken that for granted, but it still mattered to Adenauer.

On November 22, 1963, five months after Kennedy's triumphal tour of Berlin, Willy Brandt learned that the president had been assassinated. In deep shock, he joined tens of thousands of Berliners who assembled spontaneously on the square before the city hall. Many carried torches to mourn the death of the American president. Brandt made a brief speech in which he said:

The Americans have lost the president of whom it was believed by so many that he would be able to lead us firmly along the road to a just peace and a better life in this world. But we in Berlin grieve because we have lost our best friend.[10]

When Brandt went to Washington to join in the memorial service, Mrs. Kennedy asked to see him. She told him that the president had held a special place in his heart for Berlin and that he and his family loved to watch the movie of his visit to Berlin. While Brandt was at the service, the Berlin government renamed the square in front of the city hall "John F. Kennedy Platz."

In recalling Kennedy, Brandt often said that he had been particularly impressed by Kennedy's June 10, 1963, speech at American University in Washington. There the president had spoken of peace as "the most important topic on earth" and as a rational goal for rational men. Linking that with Kennedy's speech at the Free University, where Kennedy had spoken about reconciliation with the East, Brandt saw a summons for the Germans to try to find their own solutions.

Willy Brandt and Egon Bahr

Brandt wrote later: "My political deliberations in the years that followed were substantially influenced by [the Kennedy] experience, and it was against this background that my so-called *Ostpolitik*—the beginning of détente with Russia—took shape." He wanted to begin "the task of entering into a new relationship with the great power in the East." This, Brandt wrote, "in a nutshell defined our crucial task in foreign policy during the years to come."[11]

President Kennedy's Berlin and Frankfurt speeches had told the Germans that he would continue to defend the freedom and viability of West Berlin and would also defend West Germany, but he would no longer negotiate with Khrushchev about Berlin or the German question, and he would not go out of his way to unify Germany. Those tasks were now for the Germans themselves to handle, and Brandt wanted to do precisely that.

Brandt decided that Kennedy had dropped the German question into German hands. Brandt was ready.[12] Brandt saw a chance to express his vision in a speech at Tutzing in Bavaria only a month after Kennedy's visit. In that speech, he said that force could not bring Germans together again. It could not end the pain of German division and of the families split by the Wall and the death strip. Instead, they had to try new ideas and new approaches, dealing with enemies as well as friends.

In this spirit, Brandt drew several conclusions that were to become the foundations of his and later West German policy:

1. Reunification is a foreign policy problem that can be solved only with the Soviet Union, not without and not against it.
2. The despicable regime in East Germany cannot be destroyed; one must work with it.
3. These thoughts are uncomfortable and go against our deepest feelings, but they are unavoidable.[13]

Brandt essentially reversed Adenauer's priorities. Whereas the chancellor stressed the importance of early German reunification, Brandt put that on the back burner. He thought that the only hope for German unity was to make sure that it did not appear to threaten any other state. Germans never could and never should give up the hope for reunification, but other things had to come first.[14]

Although Brandt's speech was important, Egon Bahr's remarks the following day stole not only Brandt's thunder but all the headlines. For Bahr in his speech spoke of "*Wandel durch Annäherung*," a revolutionary phrase that stunned German and international discussion.

Like so many German phrases, *Wandel durch Annäherung* cannot be easily translated into English. Its meaning can perhaps be best given as "transformation through accommodation." It implies that parties or states engaged in conciliation might be profoundly if unwittingly transformed in the process. Bahr thus hinted that the East German regime might be changed by contact with the West. But others could worry that the West might change as well. What did Bahr mean? Would Ulbricht's dictatorship become more humane if one recognized it? And what might "accommodation" mean in the context of Berlin and Germany?

East Germany's Foreign Minister Otto Winzer saw the danger in Bahr's phrase. He denounced it as "*Aggression auf Filzlatschen*" ("aggression in felt slippers"), for the GDR could not accept any kind of transformation without risking its very existence. It would have none of that. Still, the Russians were interested. The Soviet ambassadors in both Bonn and East Berlin invited Brandt to meet, hoping to learn what he might do if he became chancellor. Although generally noncommittal, they told Brandt that Moscow wanted to improve its relations with West Germany. Even Gromyko told Brandt when both were in New York that Moscow did not see the West Germans as "the eternal enemy."[15]

Brandt also tried to ease the suffering of families split by the Wall. Through intermediaries, he informally asked East German authorities in late 1961 if it would be possible to have family reunions for West and East Berliners in East Berlin. Ulbricht showed no interest, not even in reunions for family emergencies.[16]

Then, quite suddenly, on December 5, 1963, Brandt got a message from the GDR Council of Ministers offering to talk about passes for West Berliners to meet relatives in East Berlin during the upcoming Christmas and New Year season. Brandt immediately agreed. So did the allies and the new West German chancellor, Ludwig Erhard. After a series of hurried negotiations over many meetings in East and West Berlin, the GDR finally accepted a face-saving formula that "both sides have established that it is impossible to reach agreement on joint definitions of localities, authorities, and official posts." Each side could use the terminology it wished, and Brandt did not need to recognize the GDR officially.[17]

West Berliners, still believing in a united city, wanted far more passes than anybody had expected. Many waited six to eight hours in the cold to apply. The East Germans, prepared for about 30,000 visitors, got almost 800,000, a total of over 1.2 million visits because some came several times. Although the West Berliners could officially meet only East Berlin family members, other relatives came from all over East Germany. Brandt hailed it as a humanitarian triumph, estimating that over 4 million people had seen each other during the weeks around Christmas and the New Year. Ulbricht also was pleased because of the fees that the GDR received for the passes and the funds that the West Berliners spent in the East.

West Berlin and the GDR reached similar agreements over the next three years, as well as agreements covering visits for emergency family situations. But in mid-1966, Ulbricht stopped the agreements. He no longer accepted the face-saving clause that skirted irreconcilable debates about terminology. East German documents show that Sozialistische

Einheitspartei Deutschlands (SED) leaders argued fiercely about the pass agreement. Some objected that the face-saving formula failed to recognize GDR sovereignty over East Berlin. The documents do not show Soviet views, but Brandt believed that Moscow, still embarrassed about the Wall's "black eye" for Communism, had pressed for agreements.[18]

In 1969, openings for negotiations on Berlin and on many other topics appeared for both the United States and Germany. Newly victorious, President Nixon used his inaugural address on January 20, 1969, to proclaim the beginning of an "era of negotiation." Henry Kissinger, then Nixon's assistant for national security, told Soviet ambassador Anatoly Dobrynin that the new president wanted a new relationship with the Soviet Union. Importantly for Berlin, Nixon introduced the concept of "linkage." Washington would not negotiate on subjects that Moscow wanted to discuss, such as recognition for the GDR, unless it could also talk about topics that the West wanted to discuss, such as Berlin.

In West Germany, the election in September 1969 turned on *Ostpolitik* (relations with the East), with Brandt accusing the Christian Democratic Union (CDU/CSU) government of having forfeited chances for progress with Moscow. Brandt did not win a majority, but got enough votes to form a government in coalition with the Free Democratic Party (FDP). He would now have a chance to pursue the policies he wanted, with Nixon prepared to help.

Brandt knew that he could not end the division of the German state, but he could perhaps ease the division of the German nation. At least he would try; and he also wanted to do something for Berlin. As all eyes turned toward the new team in Bonn, he made no secret of his wish to test new ideas, and others made no secret of their readiness to listen. The Soviets had already signaled that they wanted better relations with West Germany and would make concessions on Berlin as well as other topics. This led to violent arguments between Ulbricht and the Soviet leaders who had deposed Khrushchev in 1964.[19] Vladimir Semyonov, the new Soviet deputy foreign minister, came to East Berlin to tell Ulbricht to change his policy. He particularly upset Ulbricht when he said that Moscow had agreed with Nixon and West German leaders to try to improve the situation in and around Berlin.[20]

In his government declaration on October 28, Brandt acknowledged that there were now "two states" on German soil, the closest that West

Germany had ever come to recognizing the GDR. But he added that his government would not extend full recognition. He also reminded his listeners that Germans, like others, had the right to self-determination.[21] Brandt's speech showed Moscow that he had given up Adenauer's hope for early unification of Germany and Berlin. It also showed that he had not given up the long-term dream of bringing the German nation back together. He gave up unification as a policy but kept it as a goal. Brandt knew that Ulbricht would not accept such a bargain, but he hoped that Khrushchev's successor Leonid Brezhnev and his colleagues would accept it.

In the talks between the Soviets and the West Germans, the Soviets made their interest clear to Brandt by introducing a secret channel into Soviet-German diplomacy. They chose two Soviet intelligence agents, who went by the names of "Leo" and "Slava," to give Brandt and Bahr a direct line to the top levels of the Soviet leadership whenever Gromyko became excessively obdurate. Leo and Slava helped Brandt and Bahr to overcome many hurdles in the negotiations, including those posed by Ulbricht himself (whom Leo and Slava called "the man with the beard"). Ulbricht even visited Brezhnev personally once to ask him not to sign any agreement with West Germany that did not include formal legal recognition of the GDR, but Brezhnev still went ahead. He believed that "we must build our house in Europe, and that cannot be done without Germany."[22]

On August 12, 1970, Brandt and Soviet premier Alexei Kosygin signed the Moscow Treaty, a key step in German détente policy. Soviet readiness to meet so often and so long with the West Germans showed an important change in the order of things. Western ambassadors in Moscow continued to wonder what it might mean. The French ambassador, Roger Seydoux de Clausonne, told Bahr that the political landscape of Europe had shifted.[23]

Nixon's focus on linkage became a key element for Berlin. It would mean that Moscow had to make progress on Berlin if it wanted to make progress with Washington on any topic. This differed from Kennedy's policy.[24] Nixon had certainly not forgotten Berlin.

Having visited the city many times, having seen the Wall and met with East Berliners as well as West Berliners, and having been directly told that "*unsere Hoffnung ist der Ami*," he understood that he had to meet the needs of the city. He also understood that the city evoked powerful emotions and that any Berlin crisis would destroy the positive political atmosphere necessary to détente. When he visited Berlin on February 27, 1969, barely a month after his inauguration, he proposed four-power talks about the city. After reaffirming the U.S. commitment, he said that Berlin should become a place for "negotiation . . . and reconciliation."[25]

Nixon formally offered to negotiate about Berlin in a March 26 letter to Kosygin. At his suggestion, the American, British, French, and Soviet ambassadors in Bonn then began intense talks. Brezhnev wanted those talks to succeed because he wanted no crises in or around Berlin. He did not want his foreign policy disrupted by incidents on the access routes.[26]

On September 3, 1971, the four ambassadors initialed the draft text of what became known as the Berlin quadripartite agreement. It dealt with the three main elements of the Berlin question, finessing issues that could not be solved and finding compromise solutions wherever necessary. In that agreement, the West won important concessions, including specific pledges that transit traffic would be "unimpeded." This was probably the item that most disturbed Ulbricht, for he had wanted authority over access ever since Khrushchev's initial ultimatum in 1958. The West also won Soviet agreement that ties between West Berlin and West Germany were to be "maintained and developed." Bahr felt particularly pleased about this Soviet concession because he had won it even though the Americans told him that he should give it up for lost. Once again, Leo and Slava helped. In return, Moscow could place a consulate general in West Berlin.[27]

The associated accords included agreements on transit traffic between West Berlin and West Germany as well as on travel and phone calls between East and West in Germany. Millions of persons took advantage of the new provisions over the following years. The agreements also made it easier to send mail and to make phone calls.[28] Willy Brandt's détente policies had created openings in the Wall even if he could not tear it down.

Under Soviet pressure, Ulbricht formally resigned as GDR president on May 3, 1971, just before the Quadripartite Agreement was to be signed. He announced, "There is no prescription against advancing years." The SED central committee anointed Erich Honecker, the builder of the Wall, as SED first secretary.

In 1978, General Lucius Clay died. He was buried on a bluff above the Hudson River at West Point. The Berliners wanted very much to build a special memorial to him, but that would have been inappropriate at the site. They therefore decided to place a stone placard on his grave with the following inscription:

"WIR DANKEN DEM BEWAHRER UNSERER FREIHEIT" ("We thank the defender of our freedom").[29]

Clay's passing, like the quadripartite agreement on Berlin and the German détente agreements with Moscow, marked the end of an era. The Americans had held the line during that era, protecting West Berlin and even Berlin as a whole as best they could during the time of German division. By the late 1970s, however, the Germans had moved ahead ever more on their own. With the help of the allies, and especially of the Americans, they had also been able to ease the human burdens of Germany's division to some degree. For Berlin itself, however, the *"Amis"* still represented the hope that the East Berliner had expressed to Nixon, because it was U.S. insistence that produced the kind of quadripartite agreement that made a true difference to the Berliners.

Yet the Wall remained in place. It was no longer as impenetrable as it had been, but it still confined many East Germans and East Berliners into what they rightly perceived as a jail. Sooner or later, it would have to go.

CHAPTER FIFTEEN

"We Are the People"

Mikhail Gorbachev, who had succeeded Brezhnev and a series of aged Communist leaders as the chief of the Soviet Communist Party in 1985, told the Council of Europe in July 1989 that the social and political order of European states was "entirely a matter for the peoples themselves and of their choosing." He excluded the possibility of using force within the "common European home," either "by one alliance against another, within alliances, or anywhere else."[1] He had already made clear that Communist regimes would have to make peace with their own people and not count on the Soviet army to keep them in power.[2]

Gorbachev's attitude unleashed a tide of revolution in Eastern Europe. Hungary led the way in opening its borders to the West by May 1989. Within days, East Germans who wanted to flee the GDR were on their way. They could get East German exit visas for visits to East European states even when they could not get them for Western Europe. They began driving their boxy little Trabant cars to Hungary in order to go from there to Austria and West Germany. Bonn granted a liberal credit (rumored at DM one billion) to Hungary and tens of thousands of East Germans could suddenly come to the West.

Prague was even closer to East Germany. The West German embassy there suddenly found itself inundated by East Germans wanting permits to come to the West. When the embassy could no longer hold the refugees, West German foreign minister Hans-Dietrich Genscher worked out an arrangement with East German foreign minister Oskar Fischer to let the East Germans come to the West. But Erich Honecker insisted that the refugees go out by train through Dresden, where they would receive official GDR exit permits to make their flight appear to be a GDR decision.

As Dresden residents learned that a train for West Germany would come through their city, tens of thousands flocked to the station to try to get on the train. Although Communist leaders held an unprecedented dialogue with the would-be refugees and were able to persuade them to leave the station, the demonstrators had left their imprint throughout all of East Germany. The city of Prague, in honor of the refugees, painted an abandoned Trabant car in imitation gold and placed it in one of the squares of the old city.

At that very moment, Gorbachev himself arrived in East Berlin for the fortieth-anniversary celebration of the GDR, held on October 6 and 7. Although he listened patiently to Honecker's recital of GDR accomplishments, he used his official speech to stress the importance of change in the Socialist system. He and Honecker barely spoke to each other at the ceremony.

The following day, Gorbachev threw the fat into the fire by stating, almost in passing during a brief meeting with the press, that "life punishes him who comes too late." Although Gorbachev later insisted that he was voicing his fear that he could not reform the Soviet Union as fast as necessary, all East Germans heard it as a slap at Honecker for resisting change. The sentence coursed like lightning through Berlin and East Germany, especially as it was repeated and debated endlessly on West German radio and television. It convinced East Germans that Gorbachev sympathized with them.

Leipzig, the biggest city in East Germany, became the biggest center of dissent. For some months during the summer and fall of 1989, ever larger crowds had attended Monday night services for peace at the Nikolaikirche (Church of St. Nicholas) in the old center of Leipzig. They had begun to walk around the center of the city after those services, carrying candles and praying for peace and freedom. They had scheduled a particularly large march for the night of Monday, October 9, 1989.

Honecker wanted the East German police and army to put down that march by force. The police authorities distributed extra blood plasma. Eighty companies of regular and mobile police as well as additional militia units were called up. Honecker instructed the police that they should be prepared to use firearms if truncheons did not keep the crowd under control. But the East German police and army were on their own. During his visit to East Berlin, Gorbachev had issued strict orders forbidding the Soviet army to move against any demonstrators. One person present at his meeting with the Soviet army commander said that Gorbachev's orders were "like iron."

At this moment, as the course of East German history veered toward mass repression, a powerful figure arose from the sidelines. Kurt Masur, the bearded, barrel-chested conductor of the Leipzig Gewandhaus Orchestra, stepped in to avert a bloodbath. He called a pastor, a well-known cabaret artist, and some SED party officials. At his urging all agreed to issue a joint appeal for calm.[3] He also asked the East German police commander to pull back his forces from the route that the marchers would take.

Masur's message and person carried the day. That evening, after church services, 70,000 demonstrators marched by candlelight through the Leipzig city center. They flowed slowly through the dark streets of the old city and to the main square. They sang hymns as they marched. From time to time they shouted "*Wir sind das Volk*" ("We are the people") or "Gorby, Gorby." The marchers changed the face of East Germany. They had shown the authorities that they had to respect the power of the assembled people.

Berlin could not wait long. At the beginning of November, almost a million East Berliners convened at the Alexanderplatz for the largest gathering ever held in East Berlin. Speaker after speaker reiterated the same reform and freedom themes that other rallies had addressed in Dresden, Leipzig, and other East German cities. They also demanded the right to travel.

The rally in Berlin shifted the priorities of the East German revolution. The East Berliners had a very specific and very intense grievance: the Wall. Like other East Germans, they wanted freedom of expression, basic human rights, and real elections. But the Wall topped their agenda. From the moment Berliners began to demonstrate in earnest, the East German government had to address the Wall more urgently than anything else.

The Wall kept most East Berliners in a prison. Although some (especially the elderly) could leave under arrangements negotiated with West Germany, and although even more could and did receive occasional family visitors from the West, most could not get out. They could not visit family or friends who lived so near and yet seemed at times to be on another planet. They could not see movies or rock concerts half a mile away. They could not take their children to the old Berlin zoo, which happened to be in West Berlin, or to see the popular West Berlin soccer team. Not a day passed without a sense of frustration and, for many, a sense of pain. When they demonstrated, they carried placards that said "*Mauer Weg!*" ("Away with the Wall!")

After ever more demonstrations and many internal debates, and knowing full well that they would get no backing from Gorbachev against a revolt, the Communist SED leaders decided that they had to accommodate the demand for travel. They did so not only to placate the demonstrators but also to respond to angry East European governments that no longer wanted to be way stations for East German refugees. Late on Thursday morning, November 9, the GDR ministries for interior and state security finished drafting the text of a law that would ease travel regulations. The new law provided that East Germans could apply for private trips abroad without offering any explanation and that the application would be approved quickly in all but exceptional cases. The legislation was to go into effect at 4 A.M. the following day, November 10.[4]

The draft next went to Egon Krenz, who had replaced Honecker. He glanced at it and liked it. He hoped it would ease the pressure from the streets. He read the text quickly to some other politburo members and got immediate approval. He then gave the text to Günter Schabowski, the press spokesman, and hurriedly asked him to announce the new law. He told Schabowski, "*Das wird ein Knüller für uns*" ("That'll be a hit for us").

Krenz did not brief Schabowski on the details of the law nor that it was to enter into force only on the following day. Schabowski did not have time to glance at the text before going into his daily briefing for the German and international press. At the end of the briefing, an Italian journalist asked Schabowski whether the GDR had passed a new travel law yet. Schabowski said that it had done so, permitting East Germans to travel more freely. Pressed for details, he scratched around among his papers and found the text. He read it out loud, reiterating that the new law would make it possible for East Germans to travel out of the country at any time and through any border point. He did not stress that people would have to apply for exit permits before they could leave. The journalists concluded that the GDR would now let people travel freely. Schabowski, no better informed than they, agreed.

Tom Brokaw of NBC News asked if this meant the Wall was open. Schabowski said yes. In reply to a question about the timing of the new rules, he said "*Ab sofort*" ("immediately"). Not realizing that he had dropped a bombshell, he went home for dinner and a rest.

Schabowski's announcement headlined the early evening East and West German news broadcasts. Western media excitedly reported that East Germans could now come west at will. East Berliners did not hear the official text, but only the news. They did not understand quite what the new rules might mean but many decided to go to the Wall to find out. West Berliners, equally curious, also moved toward the Wall by the thousands. So did Western radio and television crews and print reporters.

Such border checkpoints as Bornholmerstrasse and Invalidenstrasse, located near large East Berlin workers' apartment complexes, drew large crowds within minutes. The workers shouted at the guards that they had heard the announcement from Schabowski and now wanted to get through as he had promised. They shouted "*Tor Auf!*" and "*Sperren Weg!*" ("Open the door!" and "Remove the barriers!"). Knowing that they could not ignore anything that a senior official such as Schabowski had said, the guards called their headquarters for guidance. They said that they could not ask people to come back the next day because Schabowski had said the border would be opened immediately. All had witnessed the fraying of SED authority. They were not about to go down fighting.

Around 10:30 P.M., the guards at Bornholmerstrasse let the most persistent demonstrators through. They thought they did it cleverly, by stamping exit visas on the workers' identification cards, in effect expelling them as unwanted. But when the "expelled" workers burst into West Berlin, they shouted to the Western television reporters that they had gotten out and were free to go where they wanted. Brokaw and others announced that the GDR was letting people leave.

That news hit every apartment in central Berlin and every home in the GDR within minutes. Others wanted to follow those who had gone through.

As the crowds grew larger by the minute, the guards decided by 11:30 P.M. to let everybody through. They reported to their headquarters, that "We are flooded, we have to open up," and "We are being overrun." More than 20,000 East Berliners had raced out at Bornholmerstrasse by midnight.[5] Conditions were similar at other checkpoints.

Schabowski himself, horrified when he heard radio reports of the crowds building up at Bornholmerstrasse and afraid that the guards might shoot at the demonstrators, had raced to the checkpoint but could not get through the traffic until after the guards had begun letting people pass. He was grateful that both the guards and crowds had acted sensibly. He later wrote that "the true miracle of November 9, 1989" had been that the confusing situation at the checkpoints had not led to bloodshed.[6]

Thousands of West Berliners stood waiting on the other side of the checkpoints. Guards at one checkpoint after another threw up their hands and let everybody go in both directions.

By two minutes after midnight, according to official GDR reports, all checkpoints along the entire border between East and West Berlin had opened. East German state authority had ceased to exist along the Wall.

Only the Brandenburg Gate remained closed. It had no crossing point. But on that night it represented much too tempting a target. By midnight, hundreds of young Berliners began converging upon the gate from opposite directions. Once at the concrete barrier, the young pulled themselves and each other up. Carrying their ever-present boom boxes, they danced on the Wall in the garish glare of the searchlights intended to prevent refugees from scrambling across in the dark. Adding rhythm to the dance, some hammered away at the concrete barriers for souvenirs. The police could not clear the area around the gate until 4:30 in the morning.

Berlin had never seen such a night. Few slept. Once the East Berliners got into West Berlin, they called friends and relatives. Many went to the homes of people they knew but had not seen in years, hugging young relatives whom they had never known in person. They embraced and laughed and wept. Or they merely walked or drove around West Berlin to see with their own eyes what they had seen on television.

Krenz understood that he could never close the Wall again without generating a mass revolt. He let the people continue to go where they wished. They received DM 100 as "welcoming money" from the West Berlin government and walked around West Berlin to visit, to shop, and to look. By the weekend, millions had come not only from East Berlin but from all over East Germany. They bought things that they could never buy at home. Grandmothers stood before fruit stands, weeping uncontrollably at the thought that they could bring bananas and pineapples home to their grandchildren.

After a generation, the Berliners had forced the Wall to yield. All the feelings pent up for almost thirty years burst forth. And everybody, from the highest world leaders to the East German workers holding their nieces and nephews for the first time, knew that things in Germany and Europe had changed forever.

The Wall Falls

President Kennedy had let the Wall go up in order to avoid a war and to keep Europe stable, if divided. He had then decided that the Germans themselves should deal with the German question and with unification. Germany remained divided, giving the United States and the Soviet Union the bases they wanted in Europe and giving France, Great Britain, and other European states no reason to worry about a German return to power.

The Germans increasingly began to act on their own during the 1970s and 1980s. West Germany embraced East Germany, appearing to support it but actually overwhelming it by giving its people a sense for the world beyond that of the SED. The GDR felt safe behind the Wall, but the separation that Ulbricht had achieved only reinforced the yearning for unity.

On November 9, 1989, the East Germans acted. Not the government, but the people. They burst through the Wall. Exasperated by forty-five years of Communism after twelve years of Nazism, they decided that they had known enough dictatorship. They seized control, taking charge in ways that the occupation powers had not expected or perhaps even wanted.

The popular yearning for freedom and for the West which had forced Ulbricht and Khrushchev to build the Wall in 1961 finally forced the Wall itself to collapse in 1989. Few thought this could or would happen. George Kennan wrote in early 1989 that he expected Germany to remain divided and the Wall to remain in place for quite some time yet.[7] Most experts agreed with that view. But Schabowski observed in retrospect that a system which would collapse as soon as its people could travel freely would deserve whatever fate it suffered.[8]

Even Gorbachev did not expect the system to fall. He, like other outsiders, did not foresee that the East Germans would ultimately revolt against the accumulation of hypocrisy and suppression that they faced every day. The East German people wanted the same democracy that the West Germans had. In anger and deep frustration, they chose revolt. Once they made that choice, the Wall had to go.

During the night of November 9, 1989, the East Berliners wrote as sure an end to the old order as the Parisian revolutionaries had done 200 years and four months before. And, like those Parisians, they did not know and did not really care what would come next.

What Kennedy, Nixon, Brandt, Bahr, and their successors had done was to permit Khrushchev and Ulbricht and their successors to preserve their system when it might have been disastrous to destroy it or to let it be destroyed. The Wall did that. But it could not survive any kind of opening between East and West.

Thus what Kennedy had said at the city hall in Berlin to the consternation of his advisers ultimately turned out to be true. The Berliners did not give up. They insisted on freedom and on unity. They got their wish, much later than they had hoped but at a time when others would accept it. In an age of détente and accommodation, the Wall could not survive.

Much to the surprise of everybody—except, perhaps, the Berliners—the Wall had to go. And so it did, to remain only in photographs and in museums, and in the often painful memories of the many who had been forced to live with it for almost a generation.

Notes

Chapter 1

1. Richard Reeves, *President Kennedy* (New York: Simon & Schuster, 1993), 535.

2. Vladislav Zubok, "Khrushchev and the Berlin Crisis," *Cold War International History Project Working Paper* 6 (Washington, D.C.: Woodrow Wilson International Center for Scholars, May 1993), 23.

3. John F. Kennedy Library, President's Office Files, Box 45, Speech Files, Germany, contains a number of drafts produced by Ted Sorensen and also shows Kennedy's notes, handwritten on the final text cards as he prepared to give his city hall speech.

4. Comments on the draft texts are in Andreas W. Daum, *Kennedy in Berlin* (Paderborn: Schöningh, 2003), 113–120.

5. Kennedy's principal speechwriter, Ted Sorensen, informed me in e-mail exchanges in June 2006 that Kennedy often changed texts just before he gave them and sometimes even as he was giving them. Sorensen always felt that Kennedy was really his own speechwriter.

6. Reeves, *Kennedy*, 536.

Chapter 2

1. Text of Khrushchev speech is in U.S. Department of State, *Documents on Germany, 1944–1985* (Washington, D.C.: U.S. Department of State, 1985), 542–546 (hereinafter cited as *Documents, 1944–1985*).

254 ⚌ Kennedy and the Berlin Wall

2. Douglas Selvage, "New Evidence on the Berlin Crisis, 1958–1962," *Cold War International History Project Bulletin 11* (Washington, D.C.: Woodrow Wilson International Center for Scholars, Winter, 1998), 200–202 (hereinafter cited as CWIHP and as WWICS); Hope M. Harrison, *Driving the Soviets up the Wall* (Princeton: Princeton University Press, 2003), 198–199.

3. Selvage, "New Evidence," 202.

4. Selvage, "New Evidence," 202.

5. *Documents, 1944–1985*, 545.

6. *Documents, 1944–1985*, 552–559, has text of Soviet note.

7. Harrison, "New Evidence on Khrushchev's 1958 Berlin Ultimatum," *CWIHP Bulletin 4*, WWICS, Fall 1994, 36.

8. Aleksandr Fursenko and Timothy Naftali, *Khrushchev's Cold War* (New York: Norton, 2006), 191–192.

9. Vladislav Zubok, "The Case of Divided Germany," in William Taubman, Sergei Khrushchev, and Abbott Gleason, eds., *Nikita Khrushchev* (New Haven: Yale University Press, 2000), 278.

10. Author's conversation with Sergo Mikoyan, March 14, 2008.

11. Henry A. Kissinger, *Diplomacy* (New York: Simon & Schuster, 1994), 569.

12. Report by Khrushchev's son Sergei Khrushchev, *New York Times*, September 25, 2007, D6.

13. For refugee statistics see Jörg Roesler, "Ende der Arbeitsknappheit in der DDR?," Daniel Küchenmeister, ed., *Der Mauerbau* (Berlin: Berliner Debatte, 2001), 75; Otto von der Gablentz, ed., *Documents on the Status of Berlin, 1944–1959* (Munich: Oldenbourg, 1959), 239.

14. Harrison, *Driving the Soviets*, 110.

15. Strobe Talbott, ed., *Khrushchev Remembers* (Boston: Little, Brown, 1970), 454–456.

16. Fursenko and Naftali, *Cold War*, 200.

17. Harrison, *Driving the Soviets*, 101.

18. Sergei Khrushchev, *Nikita Khrushchev and the Creation of a Superpower* (University Park: Pennsylvania State University Press, 2000), 407.

19. Gerhard Wettig, *Chruschtschows Berlin-Krise 1958 bis 1963* (Munich: Oldenbourg, 2006), 15.

20. *Foreign Relations of the United States, 1955–1957*, XXVI, 376–377 (hereinafter cited as FRUS).

21. William Burr, " The Eisenhower Administration and Berlin," *Diplomatic History*, 18, 2 (Spring, 1994), 181–182.

22. Text in FRUS, *1958–1960*, VIII, 491–492.

23. Harold Macmillan, *Pointing the Way* (London: Macmillan, 1972), 73.

24. Macmillan, *Riding the Storm* (London: Macmillan, 1971), 573–575.

25. Macmillan, *Riding*, 585.

26. Macmillan, *Riding*, 595–631 on Macmillan's visit to the Soviet Union and his meetings with Khrushchev; another report is John Gearson, *Macmillan and the Berlin Wall Crisis* (New York: St. Martin's, 1998), 57–78.

27. Gearson, *Macmillan*, 39.

28. Macmillan, *Riding*, 614.

29. Fursenko and Naftali, *Cold War*, 211.

30. *FRUS, 1958–1960*, VIII, 515.

31. *FRUS, 1958–1960*, VIII, 520–521.

32. Charles de Gaulle, *Memoirs of Hope, Renewal and Endeavor*, trans. Terence Kilmartin (New York: Simon & Schuster, 1971), 223.

33. *FRUS, 1958–1960*, VIII, 652–655.

34. *FRUS, 1958–1960*, VIII, 654.

35. De Gaulle, *Memoirs*, 215.

36. De Gaulle, *Memoirs*, 215.

37. De Gaulle, *Memoirs*, 229.

38. Gearson, *Macmillan*, 59, 64.

39. Burr, "Eisenhower," 199.

40. Fursenko and Naftali, *Cold War*, 206–211.

41. De Gaulle, *Mémoires* (Paris: Editions Gallimard, 2000), 1032.

42. De Gaulle, *Mémoires*, 1032–1035.

43. Author's conversation with Hans-Peter Schwarz, Adenauer's biographer, in Munich, February 2006.

44. *FRUS, 1958–1960*, VIII, 685.

45. *CWIHP Bulletin 11*, 207–211.

46. *CWIHP Bulletin 11*, 207–211.

47. *CWIHP Bulletin 11*, 210.

48. *CWIHP Bulletin 11*, 211.

49. Macmillan, *Pointing*, 74–75.

50. Sergei Khrushchev, *Superpower*, 330.

51. Harrison, *Driving the Soviets*, 117.

52. *FRUS, 1958–1960*, IX, 43–44.

53. Harrison, *Driving the Soviets*, 119.

54. Author's conversation with Sergo Mikoyan, March 14, 2008.

55. De Gaulle, *Memoirs*, 245–252, summarizes pre-summit discussions; *FRUS, 1958–1960*, IX, 159–526, reviews summit preparations and reports.

56. Michael Lemke, *Die Berlinkrise 1958–1963* (Berlin: Akademie Verlag, 1995), 148.

57. *Der Spiegel*, No. 41, 1989, 170.

Chapter 3

1. For preparation and text of Kennedy's inaugural address, see Theodore C. Sorensen, *Kennedy* (New York: Harper & Row, 1965), 270–278.

2. Richard Reeves, *President Kennedy* (New York: Simon & Schuster, 1993), 30–33.

3. William Taubman, *Khrushchev* (New York: Norton, 2003), 487.

4. Kai Bird, *The Color of Truth* (New York: Simon & Schuster, 1998), 203.

5. Richard C. Holbrooke, "The Doves Were Right," *New York Times Book Review*, November 30, 2008, 12–13. Author's conversation with Michael Maccoby, former editor of the *Harvard Crimson*, October 18, 2008.

6. Thomas L. Hughes, Oral History, U.S. Department of State, September 1, 1999.

7. Dean Rusk with Richard Rusk, *As I Saw It* (New York: Norton, 1990), 218.

8. Curtis Cate, *The Ides of August* (London: Weidenfeld & Nicolson, 1978), 322.

9. Hughes Oral History; author's conversation with Hughes, November 10, 2008.

10. Cate, *Ides*, 321–322.

11. Rusk, *As I Saw It*, 240.

12. Thomas J. Schoenbaum, *Waging Peace and War* (New York: Simon & Schuster, 1988), 358.

13. Eric Roll, "Harsh Realities of Postwar Britain," *Financial Times*, July 13, 1995, 10.

14. Author's conversation with Hughes, November 10, 2008.

15. Arthur M. Schlesinger, Jr., *A Thousand Days* (Greenwich, Conn.: Fawcett, 1965), 356.

16. Sorensen, *Kennedy*, 319–320.

17. Author's conversation with Schoenbaum, May 14, 2006.

18. Reeves, *Kennedy*, 137. For a detailed description of Bolshakov's background and his activities, see Aleksandr Fursenko and Timothy Naftali, *One Hell of a Gamble* (New York: Norton, 1997), 109–128.

19. Reeves, *Kennedy*, 196.

20. Honoré M. Catudal, *Kennedy and the Berlin Wall Crisis* (Berlin: Berlin Verlag, 1980), 255.

21. Author's conversation with Thomas Hughes, November 10, 2008.

22. Schlesinger, *A Thousand Days*, 350–352.

23. Schlesinger, *A Thousand Days*, 356.

24. Schlesinger, *A Thousand Days*, 355–357.

25. Bundy, *Danger and Survival* (New York: Random House, 1988), 362.

26. Bird, *Truth*, 203.

27. Taubman, *Khrushchev*, 488.

28. Vladislav Zubok and Constantine Pleshakov, *Inside the Kremlin's Cold War* (Cambridge, Mass.: Harvard University Press, 1996), 241

29. Sergei Khrushchev, *Nikita Khrushchev and the Creation of a Superpower* (University Park: Pennsylvania State University Press, 2000), 434–437.

30. Sergei Khrushchev, *Nikita Krushchev*, 434–437.

31. Taubman, *Khrushchev*, 485.

32. Zubok, "Khrushchev and the Berlin Crisis," *Cold War International History Project Working Paper* 6 (Washington, D.C.: The Woodrow Wilson International Center for Scholars, May, 1993), 23.

33. Reeves, *Kennedy*, 286.

34. Jeremi Suri, *Henry Kissinger and the American Century* (Cambridge, Mass.: Belknap Press, 2007), 173–174; Marvin Kalb and Bernard Kalb, *Kissinger* (Boston: Little, Brown, 1974), 61–64.

35. Henry Kissinger, "Memorandum for the President," March 29, 1961, John F. Kennedy Library, President's Office Files, Box 127A, United Kingdom (hereinafter cited as JFKL and POF).

36. Kissinger, "Memorandum for the President," May 5, 1961, JFKL, National Security Files, Box 81, Berlin (hereinafter cited as NSF). There is no indication on the document whether Kennedy ever saw it.

37. Kissinger memorandum, "Berlin: What About Negotiations?", June 26, 1961, JFKL, NSF, Box 81.

38. Kissinger, "Some Reflections on the Acheson Memorandum," August 16, 1961, JFKL, NSF, Box 81.

39. Author's conversation with Kissinger, June 2007.

40. Suri, *Kissinger*, 176.

41. Suri, *Kissinger*, 175; author's conversation with Kissinger, June 2007.

42. Willy Brandt, *Begegnungen mit Kennedy* (Munich: Kindler, 1964), 41; also author's conversations with Brandt and his staff, 1962–1963.

Chapter 4

1. Author's conversation with members of British Mission in Berlin, fall 1960.

2. *Foreign Relations of the United States, 1957–1959*, V, 515 (hereinafter cited as FRUS).

3. *FRUS, 1961–1963*, XIV, 36–44.

4. Henning Hoff, *Grossbritannien und die DDR, 1955–1973* (Munich: Oldenbourg, 2003), 236.

5. John Gearson, *Harold Macmillan and the Berlin Wall Crisis* (London: Macmillan, 1998), 39.

6. Gearson, 32.

7. Memorandum of conversation, Dean Rusk and Charles de Gaulle, August 8, 1961, File "Rusk Memcons," National Security Archive, quoted in Frank Mayer, *Adenauer and Kennedy* (New York: St. Martin's, 1996), 39.

8. Charles de Gaulle, *Memoirs of Hope, Renewal and Endeavor*, trans. Terence Kilmartin (London: Weidenfeld & Nicolson, 1971), 217, 223, 227.

9. *FRUS, 1958–1960*, VIII, 426.

10. Alistair Horne, *Macmillan* (London: Macmillan, 1989), 383.

11. Pierre Maillard, *De Gaulle et l'Allemagne* (Paris: Plon, 1990), 77–87, 173–179.

12. Don Cook, *Charles de Gaulle* (New York: Putnam's, 1983), 337.

13. John F. Kennedy, "A Democrat Looks at Foreign Policy," *Foreign Affairs*, October 1957, 49. Although Kennedy, like many political figures, probably did not write his *Foreign Affairs* article himself, he put his name to it and presumably read and endorsed it. He certainly continued to appear to believe what he had written about Adenauer.

14. Mayer, *Adenauer*, 7–8.

15. Mayer, *Adenauer*, 8.

16. Hans-Peter Schwarz, *Konrad Adenauer*, trans. Geoffrey Penny (Oxford: Berghahn Books, 1997), 515.

17. Schwarz, *Konrad Adenauer*, 519.

18. Schwarz, *Konrad Adenauer*, 516.

19. Mayer, *Adenauer*, 23.

20. Michael Beschloss, *The Crisis Years* (New York: HarperCollins, 1991), 240–242.

21. Willy Brandt, *People and Politics*, trans. J. Maxwell Brownjohn (London: Collins, 1978), 80.

22. Schwarz, *Konrad Adenauer*, 517.

23. *Der Spiegel*, No. 41, 1989, 157.

24. Mayer, *Adenauer*, 24.

25. Beschloss, *The Crisis Years*, 241.

26. Mayer, *Adenauer*, 46–48.

27. Mayer, *Adenauer*, 25.

28. *FRUS, 1961–1963*, XIV, 644–647.

29. For a full discussion of Adenauer's foreign policy and its impact on Adenauer's attitudes regarding allied policies toward Berlin, see Hans-Peter Schwarz, "*Aussenpolitik*," in *Anmerkungen zu Adenauer*, Schwarz, ed. (Munich: Deutsche Verlags-Anstalt, 2004), 73–116.

30. Letter from Khrushchev to Ulbricht, October 24, 1960, cited in Hope Harrison, *Driving the Soviets up the Wall* (Princeton: Princeton University Press, 2003), 148. The most detailed account of consultations among Khrushchev, Ulbricht, and their allies between the time of Kennedy's election and August 13, 1961, is provided by Harrison, *Driving the Soviets*, 30–56. Another source, more recent and based on further documents, is Gerhard Wettig, *Chruschtschows Berlin-Krise 1958 bis 1963* (Munich: Oldenbourg, 2006).

31. Matthias Uhl and Armin Wagner, eds., *Ulbricht, Khruschtschow und die Mauer* (Munich: Oldenbourg, 2003), 16–17; Harrison, *Driving the Soviets*, 149–151.

32. Harrison, *Driving the Soviets*, 151.

33. Harrison, *Driving the Soviets*, 152.

34. Harrison, *Driving the Soviets*, 157–159.

35. Harrison, *Driving the Soviets*, 36.

36. Pervukhin's report of December 15, 1960, cited in Harrison, *Driving the Soviets*, 159.

37. Text of Ulbricht's letter in "*Stichwort-Protokoll der Beratung des Politbüros am 4. Januar, 1961,*" cited in Harrison, *Driving the Soviets*, 161–163.

38. Harrison, *Driving the Soviets*, 166.

39. In Georgi Bolshakov's record of Kennedy-Khrushchev messages as cited in Wettig, *Berlin-Krise,* 143.

40. William Taubman, *Khrushchev* (New York: Norton, 2003), 483.

41. Honoré Catudal, *Kennedy and the Berlin Wall Crisis* (Berlin: Berlin Verlag, 1980), 48–51.

Chapter 5

1. *Foreign Relations of the United States, 1961–1963,* V, 163–164 (hereinafter cited as *FRUS, 1961–1963).*

2. *FRUS, 1961–1963,* 161–163.

3. *FRUS, 1961–1963,* 161.

4. Edwin O. Guthman and Jeffrey Schulman, *Robert Kennedy* (Toronto: Bantam, 1988), 276–277.

5. Guthman and Schulman, *Robert Kennedy,* 276–277.

6. Richard Reeves, *President Kennedy* (New York: Simon & Schuster, 1993), 153.

7. This account of the Presidium meeting is drawn from Aleksandr Fursenko and Timothy Naftali, *Khrushchev's Cold War* (New York: Norton, 2006), 355–358. It is supported by Anatoly Dobrynin, *In Confidence* (New York: Times Books, 1995), 43–44, and by my conversation with Sergo Mikoyan, March 14, 2008.

8. Robert Slusser, *The Berlin Crisis of 1961* (Baltimore: Johns Hopkins University Press, 1973), 8.

9. Taubman, *Khrushchev* (New York: Norton, 2003), 490.

10. Text of Thompson cable is in *FRUS, 1961–1963*, XIV, 78; for Khrushchev's remarks, see Fursenko and Naftali, *Cold War*, 352–355.

11. Peter Lusak, "Khrushchev and the Berlin Crisis" *Cold War History*, III, 2, January 2003, 53–62.

12. Gerhard Wettig, *Chruschtschows Berlin-Krise 1958 bis 1963* (Munich: Oldenbourg, 2006), 147–148.

13. Alistair Horne, *Macmillan* (London: Macmillan, 1989), 300.

14. Letter from Sir Harold Caccia to McGeorge Bundy, April 24, 1961, John F. Kennedy Library, President's Office Files, Box 127a, United Kingdom (hereinafter cited as JFKL, POF).

15. Author's conversation with Thomas L. Hughes, U.S. State Department Director for Intelligence in 1962, on November 10, 2008.

16. Charles de Gaulle, *Mémoires d'Espoir: Le Renouveau* (Paris: Plon, 1970), 269–273; for other reports on de Gaulle's exchanges with Kennedy, see Michael Beschloss, *The Crisis Years* (New York: HarperCollins, 1991), 184, and Taubman, *Khrushchev*, 494.

17. Reeves, *Kennedy*, 148.

18. Reeves, *Kennedy*, 148.

19. Taubman, *Khrushchev*, 495.

20. The full edited transcript of the Kennedy-Khrushchev summit of June 3 and 4 is in JFKL, POF, Box 233, Trips and Conferences; a copy is in *FRUS, 1961–1963*, V, 173–230. Both had several excisions, as discussed in the text. Two summaries, largely based on that transcript, are in Beschloss, *The Crisis Years*, 193–231, and in Taubman, *Khrushchev*, 491–500.

21. Kenneth O'Donnell, *Johnny, We Hardly Knew Ye* (Boston: Little, Brown, 1970), 295–296. The JFKL and *FRUS* transcripts, while reflecting Khrushchev's aversion to the word *miscalculation*, do not give the full text or flavor of Khrushchev's most aggressive comments nor of his often crude language.

22. One of the main reasons for the Kennedy Library's and the Kennedy family's refusal for decades to release the record of the summit meeting may have been the fear that Kennedy would be seen as having consigned Poland, Hungary, and other satellite nations to the Soviet sphere of control and influence. The Kennedy Library and the Kennedy family did not release the transcript until after the 1980s, when the clamor from historians and scholars grew too insistent to ignore and when the Soviets had already lost their East European empire. Kennedy biographies written by his former staffers paint a more favorable picture of

Kennedy's discussion about Eastern Europe during the summit, although none of the authors were in the private meetings.

23. Taubman, *Khrushchev*, 499.
24. O'Donnell, *Johnny*, 297.
25. Thomas J. Schoenbaum, in the authorized biography on Dean Rusk entitled *Waging Peace and War* (New York: Simon & Schuster, 1988), wrote on page 336 that Kennedy said: "Then, Mr. Chairman, there will be war. It will be a cold winter." Schoenbaum got that information from Dean Rusk, who was not in the final private meeting but claimed to have learned of that remark later. A similar report is in *As I Saw It*, by Dean Rusk as told to Richard Rusk (New York: Norton, 1990), 221, although with a different word sequence.

The record in the Kennedy Library and in all other official versions and earlier Kennedy biographies does not include the phrase "there will be war." But it is in several books published after Schoenbaum's, presumably because of his information. Earlier records, such as Beschloss, *The Crisis Years*, 224, or the various biographies by Kennedy's White House aides, record that Kennedy said only: "It will be a cold winter."

On two separate occasions in 2007, I asked Alexander Akalovsky, the American interpreter during the entire summit and the only American other than Kennedy in the brief and private final session, whether he recalled Kennedy predicting that there would be war. Akalovsky said that he definitely did not, and he added that he would certainly have remembered anything like that. He did not give the impression that he had been muzzled.

The remark "there will be war" is not recorded in the Russian version cited by Khrushchev's various biographers, by Khrushchev himself, or by Khrushchev's son Sergei. Sergei informed me in March 2008 that he did not believe Kennedy had said it. Khrushchev himself never spoke of it to anybody. A meticulous German scholar, Gerhard Wettig, who reviewed the Soviet record of the meeting as well as the East German record, reported in his footnotes for pages 151–153 of his *Chruschtschows Berlin-Krise* that he did not find it in either version. Any such remark would certainly not have been in keeping with Kennedy's general demeanor during the summit.

I met several times with Schoenbaum, who is a reliable scholar and who told me that Rusk told him about that Kennedy remark. But Rusk biographies include some other instances in which the former secretary of state recalls himself or Kennedy using tougher language than appears on the established and accepted record. That may be what happened here, with Rusk in retrospect recalling (or imagining) a firmer Kennedy remark than the record shows. Thus it seems clear, at least to me, that Kennedy did not say "there will be war."

26. Author's conversation with William Stearman, U. S. Embassy Bonn 1961 official, March 23, 2009.

27. Frederick Taylor, The Berlin Wall (New York: HarperCollins, 2007), 128.

28. Taubman, Khrushchev, xvii–xx.

29. Sergei Khrushchev, Nikita Khrushchev and the Creation of a Superpower (University Park: Pennsylvania State University Press, 2006), 442.

30. Author's conversations with Alexander Akalovsky, in July and December 2007.

31. Author's conversation with Sergo Mikoyan, March 14, 2008.

32. Arkady Shevchenko, Breaking with Moscow (New York: Knopf, 1985), 117–118.

33. Taubman, Khrushchev, 495.

34. Kai Bird, The Color of Truth (New York: Simon & Schuster, 1998), 206.

35. Thomas L. Hughes, Oral History, September 1, 1999.

36. Guthman, Robert Kennedy, 28.

37. O'Donnell, Johnny, 299.

38. O'Donnell, Johnny, 300.

39. Macmillan, Pointing the Way, 1959–1961 (London: Macmillan, 1972), 356–358.

40. Theodore Sorensen, Kennedy (New York: Harper & Row, 1965), 629.

41. Horne, Macmillan, 302.

42. Horne, Macmillan, 310.

43. Caccia message to the prime minister, July 7, 1961, in Macmillan, Pointing, 365.

44. De Gaulle, Mémoires, 259.

45. Text in New York Times, June 7, 1961, 1.

46. O'Donnell, Johnny, 310.

47. Taubman, Khrushchev, 496.

48. Robert Dallek, An Unfinished Life (Boston: Little, Brown, 2003), 417.

49. Quoted by Taubman, Khrushchev, 766.

50. Sergei Khrushchev, Superpower, 444.

51. Slusser, Berlin Crisis, 1–20; full text in The Soviet Stand on Germany (Moscow: Crosscurrents Press, 1961), 17–43.

52. The Soviet Stand, 22–43.

53. Taubman, Khrushchev, 766.

Chapter 6

1. Kenneth O'Donnell, Johnny, We Hardly Knew Ye (Boston: Little, Brown, 1970), 306.

2. Michael Lemke, *Die Berlinkrise 1958 bis 1963* (Berlin: Akademie Verlag, 1995), 161–162.

3. Egon Bahr, "*Entspannt Berlin!*" *Die Woche*, June 15, 2001, 6.

4. Honoré Catudal, *Kennedy and the Berlin Wall Crisis* (Berlin: Berlin Verlag, 1980), 125; for German text, see Matthias Uhl and Armin Wagner, eds., *Ulbricht, Khruschtschow und die Mauer* (Munich: Oldenbourg, 2003), 25.

5. Uhl and Wagner, *Ulbricht*, 28.

6. Uhl and Wagner, *Ulbricht*, 28–29.

7. Robert Slusser, *The Berlin Crisis of 1961* (Baltimore: Johns Hopkins University Press, 1973), 10.

8. Julij Kwizinskij, *Vor dem Sturm* (Berlin: Siedler, 1993), 181–183.

9. Lemke, *Berlinkrise*, 164.

10. Lemke, *Berlinkrise*, 163–164.

11. Lemke, *Berlinkrise*, 164.

12. Lemke, *Berlinkrise*, 165.

13. John Ausland (U.S. State Department Berlin desk) comment to the author, July 1961.

14. Ausland, comment.

15. Ausland, comment.

16. For the text of Acheson's report and summaries of pertinent NSC meetings and decisions as well as some basic points of Kennedy's later speech, see John F. Kennedy Library, National Security Files, Boxes 82 and 313.

17. The Acheson report is summarized in Catudal, *Wall Crisis*, 143–147.

18. Catudal, *Wall Crisis*, 144–145.

19. Howard Jones, *Crucible of Power* (Wilmington, Del.: Scholarly Resources, 2001), 235.

20. William Taubman, *Khrushchev* (New York: Norton, 2003), 490.

21. Catudal, *Wall Crisis*, 260.

22. Robert Dallek, *An Unfinished Life* (Boston: Little, Brown, 2003), 423.

23. Text of Kennedy's speech is in *Public Papers of the Presidents of the United States: John F. Kennedy, 1961*, 533–540.

24. Aleksandr Fursenko and Timothy Naftali, *Khrushchev's Cold War* (New York: Norton, 2006), 376.

25. Richard Reeves, *President Kennedy* (New York: Simon & Schuster, 1993), 195.

26. Michael Beschloss, *The Crisis Years* (New York: HarperCollins, 1991), 243n.

27. Willy Brandt, *People and Politics*, trans. J. Maxwell Brownjohn (Boston: Little, Brown, 1978), 21.

28. Beschloss, *Crisis Years*, 265.

29. Wjatscheslaw Keworkow, *Der Geheime Kanal* (Berlin: Rowohlt, 1995), 29.

30. Reeves, *Kennedy*, 204.

31. Beschloss, *Crisis Years*, 264.

32. Alexei Filitov, "Soviet Policy and the Early Years of Two German States, 1949–1961," paper prepared for the Cold War International History Project of the Woodrow Wilson International Center for Scholars, 1994, 12 (hereinafter cited as CWIHP and WWICS).

33. Dean Rusk with Richard Rusk, *As I Saw It* (New York: Norton, 1990), 224.

34. Fursenko and Naftali, *Cold War*, 364.

35. Fursenko and Naftali, *Cold War*, 364.

36. Sergei Khrushchev, *Nikita Khrushchev and the Creation of a Superpower* (University Park: Pennsylvania State University Press, 2006), 440–446, has Khrushchev's full comments to his son on the Vienna summit.

37. Vladislav Zubok, *A Failed Empire* (Chapel Hill: University of North Carolina Press, 2007), 143.

38. Fursenko and Naftali, *Cold War*, 338.

39. Fursenko and Naftali, *Cold War*, 444.

40. Fursenko and Naftali, *Cold War*, 445.

41. Fursenko and Naftali, *Cold War*, 445.

42. Fursenko and Naftali, *Cold War*, 482.

43. Taubman, *Khrushchev*, 503–504.

44. Filitov, "Soviet Policy," throughout.

45. Zubok, *Empire*, 141.

46. Uhl and Wagner, *Ulbricht*, 31.

47. Taubman, *Khrushchev*, 482.

48. Strobe Talbott, ed. and trans., *Khrushchev Remembers* (Boston: Little, Brown, 1970), 455.

49. Talbott, *Khrushchev Remembers*, 506.

50. Vladislav Zubok, *Khrushchev and the Berlin Crisis*, CWIHP, WWICS, May, 1993, 26–27.

51. Fursenko and Naftali, *Cold War*, 380.

52. For a record of much of the published part of the Warsaw Pact meeting, see Bernd Bowetsch and Alexei Filitov, "Chruschtschow und der Mauerbau," *Vierteljahrshefte für Zeitgeschichte*, 48 (2000), 155–198; for summary reports on the meeting, see Catudal, *Wall Crisis*, 207–212; Hope Harrison, *Driving the Soviets up the Wall* (Princeton: Princeton University Press, 2003), 192–205; and Wettig, *Berlin-Krise*, 175–183.

53. Wettig, *Berlin-Krise*, 181–183; Sergei Khrushchev, *Superpower*, 454.

54. Lemke, *Berlinkrise*, 167.

55. Lemke, *Berlinkrise*, 171.

56. *Cold War International History Project Bulletin Number 4* (Washington, D.C.: WWICS, 1994), 28.

57. Slusser, *Berlin Crisis*, 124; for the threatening tone of Khrushchev's speeches before August 13, see texts in *The Soviet Stand on Germany* (Moscow: Crosscurrents Press, 1961), throughout.

58. *Financial Times*, August 25, 1991, IX.

59. Uhl and Wagner, *Ulbricht*, 36–39.

60. Fursenko and Naftali, *Cold War*, 377.

61. Ann Tusa, *The Last Division* (Reading, Mass.: Addison-Wesley, 1997), 268–269.

62. Marc Trachtenberg, *A Constructed Peace* (Princeton: Princeton University Press, 1999), 323.

63. Wettig, *Berlin-Krise*, 181–183; Taubman, *Khrushchev*, 506.

64. Kwizinskij, *Sturm*, 186.

65. Kwizinskij, *Sturm*, 184.

66. Wettig, *Berlin-Krise*, 184; Kwizinskij, *Sturm*, 187.

Chapter 7

1. Unless otherwise specified, the descriptions in this chapter of the sealing of East Berlin are based on the personal recollections of the author and on Curtis Cate, *The Ides of August* (London: Weidenfeld & Nicolson, 1978).

2. Egon Bahr, *Zu Meiner Zeit* (Munich: Blessing, 1996), 133; author's conversation with Bahr, June 2007.

3. John C. Ausland and Col. Hugh F. Richardson, "Crisis Management: Berlin, Cyprus, Laos" *Foreign Affairs*, 44, 2, January 1966, 301.

4. Howard Trivers, *Three Crises in American Foreign Policy and a Continuing Revolution* (Carbondale: Southern Illinois University Press, 1970), 25–29.

5. Hope Harrison, *Driving the Soviets up the Wall* (Princeton: Princeton University Press, 2003), 207.

6. Honoré Catudal, *Kennedy and the Berlin Wall Crisis* (Berlin: Berlin Verlag, 1980), 38.

7. Trivers, *Three Crises*, 25.

8. State Department Telegram 858 from London, August 28, 1961, John F. Kennedy Library, National Security Files, Box 90, Berlin, reviews Macmillan's later efforts to play down his initial comment (hereinafter cited as JFKL, NSF).

9. Author's conversation with French official in Berlin, August 15, 1961.

10. Cate, *Ides*, 289.

11. Cate, *Ides*, 304.

12. Egon Bahr, speech at the Goethe Institute, Washington, May 8, 2002; later conversation with the author.

13. Julij Kwizinskij, Vor dem Sturm (Berlin: Siedler, 1993), 185.

14. Matthias Uhl and Armin Wagner, Ulbricht, Khruschtschow und die Mauer (Munich: Oldenbourg, 2003), 48.

15. Brandt's letter and Kennedy's reply are in Foreign Relations of the United States, 1961–1963, XIV, 345–346 and 352–353 (hereinafter cited as FRUS, 1961–1963). Kennedy's reaction to Brandt's letter is in Der Spiegel, No. 48, 1989, 156. Brandt's comments on his letter are in Willy Brandt, People and Politics, trans. J. Maxwell Brownjohn (London: Collins, 1978), 31.

16. Der Spiegel, No. 48, 1989, 156.

17. Ann Tusa, The Last Division (Reading, Mass.: Addison-Wesley, 1997), 299.

18. Peter Wyden, "Wir machen Berlin dicht," Der Spiegel, No. 42, 1989, 192; author's conversations with Bahr.

19. Willy Brandt, People and Politics, 20.

20. John C. Ausland, Kennedy, Khrushchev, and the Berlin-Cuba Crisis (Oslo: Scandinavian University Press, 1996), 124–125.

21. Trivers, Three Crises, 40.

22. This information is based on several talks by author with James O'Donnell in Berlin in the fall of 1961 when both were working for General Clay; also, Cate, Ides, 349–352.

23. Jean Edward Smith, Lucius D. Clay (New York: Holt, 1990), 651.

24. Peter Wyden, Wall (New York: Simon & Schuster, 1989), 166.

25. Richard Reeves, President Kennedy (New York: Simon & Schuster, 1993), 213. For text of Murrow letter, see FRUS, 1961–1963, XIV, 339–341.

26. Wyden, Wall, 274.

27. Cate, Ides, 405; author's conversations with Clay in Berlin, October 1961.

28. Smith, Clay, 642; Cate, Ides, 402–404; author's conversations with Clay, October 1961.

29. Smith, Clay, 642; Clay later told me that he thought it had been a courageous decision for Kennedy, especially because many of his advisers had opposed it.

30. Edwin O. Guthman and Jeffrey Shulman, Robert Kennedy (New York: Bantam Books, 1988), 276.

31. Sergei Khrushchev, Nikita Khrushchev and the Creation of a Superpower (University Park: Pennsylvania State University Press, 2006), 458.

32. Ausland, Berlin-Cuba Crisis, 133–134.

33. Jerrold L. Schecter with Vyacheslav Luchkov, eds. and trans., Khrushchev Remembers: The Glasnost Tapes (Boston: Little, Brown, 1990), 169–170.

34. Bruce Menning, "The Berlin Crisis of 1961 from the Perspective of the Soviet General Staff." Paper presented at the conference "The Soviet Union, Germany, and the Cold War, 1945–1962," Potsdam, Germany, June 28–July 3, 1994, 9–10.

35. Wyden, *Wall*, 279.

36. Charles De Gaulle, *Memoirs*, trans. by Alan Sheridan (London: Weidenfeld & Nicolson, 1971), 260.

37. Smith, *Clay*, 644.

38. William Taubman, *Khrushchev* (New York: Norton, 2003), 506.

39. Harrison, *Driving the Soviets*, 186.

40. Taubman, *Khrushchev*, 506.

41. Harrison, *Driving the Soviets*, 186.

42. Brandt, *People and Politics*, 40.

43. *Frankfurter Allgemeine Zeitung*, December 4, 1992, 3.

Chapter 8

1. Letter from President Kennedy to General Clay, August 30, 1961, John F. Kennedy Library, National Security Files, Box 86, Berlin (hereinafter cited as JFKL, NSF).

2. Jean Edward Smith, *Lucius D. Clay* (New York: Holt, 1990), 652.

3. Smith, *Clay*, 651–652.

4. Ann Tusa, *The Last Division* (Reading, Mass.: Addison-Wesley, 1997), 264.

5. Memo from Bundy to the president, August 28, 1961, JFKL, NSF, Box 86, Berlin.

6. Comments on Berlin opinion are based on the author's frequent meetings and talks with Berliners during his assignment to the city.

7. Information on General Clay's policies and attitudes during his nine months in Berlin as President Kennedy's personal representative is drawn from four principal sources: (1) my own frequent talks with Clay, whom I saw every day in the office and accompanied on most of his appointments and trips in and around Berlin; (2) the John F. Kennedy Library folders on Clay's service in Berlin, which also show that most of Clay's telegrams and letters were sent to Kennedy's office at the president's explicit instruction; (3) Jean Edward Smith, his biographer, in *Clay*, 629–665, and from talks with the author; and (4) Curtis Cate, *The Ides of August* (New York: Evans, 1978), 325–390. Other sources will be cited as appropriate.

8. William Taubman, *Khrushchev* (New York: Norton, 2003), 506.

9. Howard Trivers, *Three Crises in American Foreign Policy and a Continuing Revolution* (Carbondale: Southern Illinois University Press, 1970), 4.

10. Michael Lemke, *Die Berlinkrise 1958 bis 1963* (Berlin: Akademie Verlag, 1995), 173.

11. Berlin telegram 884 to Department of State, October 30, 1961, JFKL, NSF, Box 86, Berlin.

12. Bruce W. Menning, "The Berlin Crisis of 1961 from the Perspective of the Soviet General Staff," paper presented at the conference "The Soviet Union, Germany, and the Cold War, 1945–1962: New Evidence from Eastern Archives," Essen and Potsdam, Germany, June 28 to July 1, 1994, 15–19.

13. Honoré Catudal, *Kennedy and the Berlin Wall Crisis* (Berlin: Berlin Verlag, 1980), 131–135. For more on Clay's visit to Steinstücken, see Catudal, *Steinstücken* (New York: Vantage Press, 1971), 15–16, 104–109.

14. Clay showed me the text of what he was sending to Kennedy.

15. John C. Ausland, *Kennedy, Khrushchev, and the Berlin-Cuba Crisis, 1961–1964* (Oslo: Scandinavian University Press, 1996), 37.

16. JFKL, NSF, Box 86, Berlin, has full text of the letter. So does *Foreign Relations of the United States, 1961–1963*, XIV, 509–513 (hereinafter cited as *FRUS, 1961–1963*).

17. Berlin telegram 624 to State Department, September 28, 1961, JFKL, NSF, Box 86, Berlin.

18. Information we received from Washington journalists visiting Berlin.

19. Menning, "Berlin Crisis of 1961," 13–20.

20. Tusa, *Division*, 333.

21. Matthias Uhl and Armin Wagner, eds., *Ulbricht, Chruschtschow und die Mauer* (Munich: Oldenbourg, 2003), 94.

22. Cate, *Ides*, 476.

23. Trivers, *Three Crises*, 40–56, recalls the incident as the U.S. official on the scene; Cate, *Ides*, 457–495, also gives a detailed report on the Checkpoint Charlie crisis.

24. *FRUS, 1961–1963*, XIV, 524.

25. JFKL, NSF, Box 86, Berlin.

26. Trivers, *Three Crises*, 48; Smith, *Clay*, 661; my own talks with Clay and others in Berlin.

27. Smith, *Clay*, 661; author's notes on the call.

28. *Der Spiegel*, No. 43, 1989, 160; Strobe Talbott, ed. and trans., *Khrushchev Remembers* (Boston: Little, Brown, 1970), 470.

29. Uhl and Wagner, *Ulbricht*, 55–57.

30. Menning, "Berlin Crisis," 10–13.

31. Hope Harrison, *Driving the Soviets up the Wall* (Princeton: Princeton University Press, 2003), 211.

32. Berlin telegram 884 to Department of State, October 30, 2001, JFKL, NSF, Box 86, Berlin.

33. Evan Thomas, *Robert Kennedy* (New York: Simon & Schuster, 2000), 139.

34. For more on Robert Kennedy and Khrushchev regarding the tank withdrawal, see Edwin O. Guthman and Jeffrey Schulman, *Robert Kennedy* (New York: Bantam Books, 1988), 258–264; Aleksandr Fursenko and Timothy Naftali, *Khrushchev's Cold War* (New York: Norton, 2006), 402–405; *Der Spiegel*, 43, 1989, 160; Talbott, *Khrushchev Remembers*, 470.

35. Author's conversations with Clay on the Checkpoint Charlie incident, October and November 1961.

36. There was no record of any such call at the U.S. Operations Center in Berlin.

37. Clay reported Kennedy's thanks to the author after Clay returned from Washington. Clay's assistant James P. O'Donnell also heard about it from his Washington friends.

38. Uhl and Wagner, *Ulbricht*, 50; Harrison, *Driving the Soviets*, 221.

39. Lemke, *Berlinkrise*, 175.

40. Lemke, *Berlinkrise*, 175–176.

41. Harrison, *Driving the Soviets*, 212; Uhl and Wagner, *Ulbricht*, 55–57.

42. Menning, "Berlin Crisis," 17–18.

43. Fursenko and Naftali, *Cold War*, 404–407.

44. Berlin telegram 883 to State Department, October 30, 1961, JFKL, NSF, Box 86, Berlin.

45. Berlin telegram 696 to State Department, October 7, 1961, JFKL, NSF, Box 86, Berlin.

46. Harold Macmillan, *Pointing the Way, 1959–1961* (London: Macmillan, 1972), 405–408; Cate, *Ides*, 491; Wyden, *Wall*, 264.

Chapter 9

1. Memorandum from Bundy to Kennedy, January 6, 1962, John F. Kennedy Library, National Security Files, Box 86, Berlin (hereinafter cited as JFKL and NSF).

2. Letter from Clay to Rusk, January 30, 1962, JFKL, NSF, Box 86, Berlin.

3. Hope Harrison, *Driving the Soviets up the Wall* (Princeton: Princeton University Press, 2003), 215.

4. Harrison, *Driving the Soviets*, 216–217.

5. Harrison, *Driving the Soviets*, 218.

6. John C. Ausland, *Kennedy, Khrushchev and the Berlin-Cuba Crisis, 1961–1964* (Oslo: Scandinavian University Press, 1996), 49–62, summarizes the 1962 dispute over the air corridor reservations. For sample State Department and White House messages on the topic, see *Foreign Relations of the United States, 1961–1963, Berlin Crisis,* XIV, 782–867, and XV, 17–94 (hereinafter cited as *FRUS, 1961–1963*).

7. Some of Clay's cables on this topic were Berlin telegrams to Department of State 1531, February 17, 1962; and 1733, March 19, 1962, JFKL, NSF, Box 86, Berlin.

8. Douglas Selvage, "The End of the Berlin Crisis, 1961–62," *Cold War International History Project Bulletin 11,* Winter 1998, 218–224.

9. Sergei Khrushchev, *Nikita Khrushchev and the Creation of a Superpower* (University Park: Pennsylvania Sate University Press, 2006), 420–425, 475–478.

10. Jerrold Schecter and Peter Deriabin, *The Spy Who Saved the World* (New York: Scribner's, 1992), 271–275.

11. William Taubman, *Khrushchev* (New York: Norton, 2003), 541.

12. Berlin cable 1531, February 15, 1962, JFKL, NSF, Box 86, Berlin.

13. John Gearson, *Harold Macmillan and the Berlin Wall Crisis* (London: Macmillan, 1998), 192–193.

14. Memorandum from Home to Macmillan, Prime Minister's files, cited in Henning Hoff, *Grossbritannien und die DDR, 1955–1973,* 239.

15. David Brandon Shields, *Kennedy and Macmillan* (Lanham, Md.: University Press of America, 1984), 63.

16. Telegram from Clay, January 11, 1962, JFKL, NSF, Box 86, Berlin.

17. Telegram from Clay to Rusk, January 13, 1962, JFKL, NSF, Box 86, Berlin.

18. Memorandum to General Taylor, December 12, 1961, JFKL, NSF, Box 86, Berlin.

19. Arthur Schlesinger, Jr., *A Thousand Days* (Greenwich, Conn.: Fawcett, 1965), 373; author's recollection of the speech.

20. Author's talk with Clay after Robert Kennedy's visit, February 25, 1962.

21. Ann Tusa, *The Last Division* (Reading, Mass.: Addison-Wesley, 1997), 269.

22. Letter from Clay to Taylor, September 7, 1962, in George C. Marshall Research Library, Virginia Military Institute, Lexington, Va.

23. Letter from Kennedy to Clay, March 1, 1962, JFKL, President's Office Files, Box 127A, Germany (hereinafter cited as POF).

24. Kennedy letter to Clay, March 15, 1962, JFKL, POF, Box 127A, Germany.

25. Smith, *Clay,* 642.

26. Clay's remarks to author at various times during their work and meetings in Berlin, September 1961 to May 1962.

27. Berlin telegram 1891, April 6, 1962, JFKL, NSF, Box 86, Berlin.

28. Berlin telegram 1891, April 6, 1962, JFKL, NSF, Box 86, Berlin.

Chapter 10

1. Bundy memorandum, August 28, 1961; cited in Henry Kissinger, *Diplomacy* (New York: Simon & Schuster, 1994), 586.

2. Kissinger, *Diplomacy*, 587.

3. Rusk's records of these talks, held in New York September 22, 27, and 30, 1961, are in *Foreign Relations of the United States, 1961–1963*, XIV, 431–433, 439–441, and 456–460 (hereinafter cited as *FRUS, 1961–1963*).

4. *FRUS, 1961–1963*, XIV, 835.

5. Author's conversation with General Clay, October 1961.

6. Michael Lemke, *Die Berlinkrise 1958 bis 1963* (Berlin: Akademie Verlag, 1995), 185.

7. *FRUS, 1961–1963*, XIV, 460–461.

8. Ann Tusa, *The Last Division* (Reading, Mass.: Addison-Wesley, 1997), 318 and 322; *FRUS, 1961–1963*, XIV, 834.

9. *FRUS, 1961–1963*, XIV, 444–455.

10. *FRUS, 1961–1963*, XIV, 833.

11. Rudolf Morsey and Hans-Pater Schwarz, eds., with Hans Peter Mensing, *Adenauer: Briefe, 1961–1963* (Paderborn: Schöningh, 2006), 24–25.

12. Morsey and Scwarz, eds., *Adenauer*, 26–28.

13. Harold Macmillan, *Pointing the Way, 1959–1961* (London: Macmillan, 1972), 144.

14. John Gearson, *Harold Macmillan and the Berlin Wall Crisis, 1958–1962* (London: Macmillan, 1998), 196–197.

15. Henning Hoff, *Grossbritannien und die DDR, 1955–1973* (Munich: Oldenbourg, 2003), 236.

16. Macmillan, *Pointing*, 417–425.

17. Marc Trachtenberg, *A Constructed Peace* (Princeton: Princeton University Press, 1998), 334.

18. *FRUS, 1961–1963*, XIV, 377–378.

19. Author's conversation with Hans-Peter Schwarz, Adenauer's biographer, December 12, 2007.

20. Frank Mayer, *Adenauer and Kennedy* (New York: St. Martin's, 1996), 89.

21. *FRUS, 1961–1963*, XIV, 759–760.

22. *FRUS, 1961–1963*, XIV, 819–822.

23. Mayer, *Adenauer*, 77.

24. Author's conversation with Sergo Mikoyan, March 14, 2008.

25. Thompson-Gromyko talks December 1961–March 1962 are in *FRUS, 1961–1963*, XIV, 720–724, 751–755, 797–800, and 859–862.

26. *FRUS, 1961–1963*, 677.

27. *FRUS, 1961–1963*, XIV, 557–865, contains a lengthy record of Allied talks and meetings, letters and consultations at various levels, as well as the separately cited reports of talks between Thompson and Gromyko. Unless there is a specific quotation or situation, separate page numbers will not always be given.

28. *FRUS, 1961–1963*, 679–881.

29. *FRUS, 1961–1963*, 749.

30. *FRUS, 1961–1963*, 659.

31. *FRUS, 1961–1963*, 663.

32. *FRUS, 1961–1963*, 696.

33. *FRUS, 1961–1963*, 92–95.

34. *FRUS, 1961–1963*, 92–95.

35. Author conversation with Sergo Mikoyan, March 14, 2008.

36. *FRUS, 1961–1963*, XIV, 780–783.

37. Author's conversation with Egon Bahr, June 2007.

38. Author's conversation with Henry Kissinger, November 2007; Trachtenberg, *Constructed Peace*, 339.

39. This report on the early 1962 negotiations is based on Mayer, *Adenauer*, 111–120; Kissinger, *Diplomacy*, 585–590, and Michael Lemke, *Die Berlinkrise 1958–1963* (Berlin: Akademie Verlag, 1995), 174–186.

40. Trachtenberg, *A Constructed Peace*, reviews the matter of West German nuclear weapons in great detail.

41. Author's conversation with Henry Kissinger, November 2007.

42. *FRUS, 1961–1963*, XIV, 824–827.

43. John F. Kennedy Library, National Security Files, Box 84A, Germany and Berlin; text of underlined paper is in *FRUS, 1961–1963*, XV, 95–98; further information on the Principles Paper and Adenauer's reaction to it is in Mayer, *Adenauer*, 68–71.

44. JFKL, NSF, Box 84A, Germany and Berlin.

45. Mayer, *Adenauer*, 85.

46. State Department Memorandum of Conversation, April 13, 1962, JFKL, NSF, Box 84A, Berlin and Germany.

47. *FRUS, 1961–1963*, XV, 101–103.

48. JFKL, NSF, Box 78, Germany and Europe; the German original of the letter, even more curt and harsh in its tone and language, is in Morsey and Schwarz, eds., *Briefe, 1961–1963*, 111.

49. Adenauer Memorandum for the Record, April 24, 1962, Morsey and Schwarz, eds., *Briefe, 1961–1963*, 111–114

50. John C. Ausland, "Kennedy, Khrushchev and Berlin" (paper published by the U.S. Foreign Service Institute, n.d.), 17.

51. Author's conversation with Sergo Mikoyan, March 14, 2008.

52. John R. Mapother, "Berlin and the Cuban Crisis," *Foreign Intelligence Literary Scene*, 12, 1, January 1993, 1–3; Ray S. Cline, "Commentary: The Cuban Missile Crisis," *Foreign Affairs*, Fall, 1989, 190–196; author's many conversations with Mapother and others in Berlin, summer and fall 1962.

Chapter 11

1. *Foreign Relations of the United States, 1961–1963*, VI, 137–141 (hereinafter cited as *FRUS, 1961–1963*). This volume holds the full Khrushchev-Kennedy correspondence, or at least that portion which has been declassified in the United States.

2. *FRUS, 1961–1963*, VI, 142–147.

3. *FRUS, 1961–1963*, VI, 157.

4. Anatoly Dobrynin, *In Confidence* (New York: Times Books, 1995), 68.

5. William Taubman, *Khrushchev* (New York: Norton, 2003), 539.

6. Udall memorandum upon his return to Washington, cited in Aleksandr Fursenko and Timothy Naftali, *One Hell of a Gamble* (New York: Norton, 1997), 208–209.

7. Kroll memorandum of conversation, September 11, 1962, cited in Fursenko and Naftali, *Khrushchev's Cold War* (New York: Norton, 2006), 458–459.

8. Gerhard Wettig, *Chruschtschows Berlin-Krise 1958 bis 1963* (Munich: Oldenbourg, 2006), 246.

9. Wettig, *Berlin-Krise*, 246.

10. Taubman, *Khrushchev*, 555.

11. Ernest May and Philip Zelikow, *The Kennedy Tapes* (Cambridge, Mass.: Harvard University Press, 1997), 61.

12. I will not try to go into detail on the Cuban missile crisis but will concentrate on its relation to Berlin. Out of hundreds of books that have been written on the crisis, I will use mainly Fursenko and Naftali, *Gamble*; Robert Kennedy, *Thirteen Days* (New York: Norton, 1969); and May and Zelikow, *Tapes*. Short but excellent summaries are in Michael Beschloss, *The Crisis Years* (New York: HarperCollins, 1991); and Richard Reeves, *President Kennedy* (New York: Simon & Schuster, 1997).

13. Fursenko and Naftali, *Gamble*, 241

14. Kennedy, *Thirteen Days*, 64.

15. Dobrynin, In Confidence, 81–95.

16. Kennedy, Thirteen Days, 87.

17. Dobrynin, In Confidence, 90.

18. Robert Kennedy never acknowledged the Khrushchev letter on the missiles in Turkey. The letter does not appear in documents at the Kennedy Library, but it appeared in an unofficial translation prepared by the Soviet Embassy for publication in Problems of Communism, Special Edition, Spring 1992, 60–62.

19. Raymond Garthoff, "Cuban Missile Crisis: The Soviet Story," Foreign Policy, Fall 1988, 75.

20. Vladislav Zubok, "Khrushchev and the Berlin Crisis," Cold War International History Project Working Paper No. 6 (Washington, D.C.: Woodrow Wilson International Center for Scholars, May 1993), 16.

21. Wettig, Berlin-Krise, 244.

22. John R. Mapother, "Berlin and the Cuban Crisis," Foreign Intelligence Literary Scene, 12, 1, January 1993, 1–3; Ray S. Cline, "Commentary: The Cuban Missile Crisis," Foreign Affairs, Fall 1989, 190–196.

23. Fursenko and Naftali, Gamble, 171.

24. Sergei Khrushchev, Nikita Khruschev and the Creation of a Superpower (University Park: Pennsylvania State University Press), 536; Arkady Shevchenko, Breaking with Moscow (New York: Knopf, 1985), 117–118.

25. Arnold L. Horelick, "The Cuban Missile Crisis," World Politics, XVI, 3, April 1964, 369.

26. Author's conversations and exchanges with Sergo Mikoyan and Sergei Khrushchev, March–April 2008.

27. Pravda, January 17, 1963, cited in Horelick, "The Cuban Missile Crisis," 369.

28. Fursenko and Naftali, Gamble, 170–180; Dobrynin, In Confidence, 71–73.

29. May and Zelikow, Tapes, 175.

30. May and Zelikow, Tapes, 176.

31. May and Zelikow, Tapes, 283.

32. May and Zelikow, Tapes, 309.

33. May and Zelikow, Tapes, 144, 183.

34. Harold Macmillan, At the End of the Day (London: Macmillan, 1973), 199.

35. May and Zelikow, Tapes, 148.

36. May and Zelikow, Tapes, 341.

37. Kennedy, Thirteen Days, throughout.

38. May and Zelikow, Tapes, 280.

39. Jerrold L. Schecter with Vyacheslav Luchkov, eds. and trans., Khrushchev Remembers: The Glasnost Tapes (Boston: Little, Brown, 1990), 182.

40. Strobe Talbott, ed. and trans., *Khrushchev Remembers* (Boston: Little, Brown, 1970), 500.

41. Garthoff, "Cuban Missile Crisis," 80.

42. Sergei Khrushchev, *Superpower*, 560.

43. Macmillan, *At End*, 182.

44. Macmillan, *At End*, 187.

45. May and Zelikow, *Tapes*, 256, 284–285, 483.

46. Beschloss, *The Crisis Years*, 478.

47. Hans-Peter Schwarz, *Adenauer: Der Staatsmann: 1952–1967* (Stuttgart: Deutsche Verlags-Anstalt, 1991), 770.

48. Schwarz, *Adenauer*, 772–773.

49. Horelick, "Missile Crisis," 388.

50. Willy Brandt, *People and Politics*, trans. J. Maxwell Brownjohn (London: Collins, 1978), 89–90.

51. Bahr, Goethe Institute briefing, Washington, D.C., May 8, 2002.

52. "Memorandum from David Klein," U.S. Mission, Berlin, August 3, 1963, in private files of John Mapother, Washington, D.C.

53. Schwarz, *Adenauer*, 773.

54. *FRUS, 1961–1963*, VI, 189–249.

55. *FRUS, 1961–1963*, VI, 230–233.

56. *FRUS, 1961–1963*, XV, 469.

57. *FRUS, 1961–1963*, XV, 486.

58. Sergei Khrushchev, *Superpower*, 656–657.

59. Author's conversation with General Clay, Links Club, New York City, November 1962.

Chapter 12

1. Charles De Gaulle, *Mémoires* (Paris: Editions Gallimard, 2000), 1032.

2. For a detailed report on Adenauer's move toward France and Kennedy's reaction, see Frank Mayer, *Adenauer and Kennedy* (New York: St. Martin's, 1996), 77–94.

3. Rudolf Morsey and Hans-Peter Schwarz, eds., with Hans Peter Mensing, *Adenauer: Briefe, 1961–1963* (Paderborn: Schöningh, 2006), 115.

4. Quoted in Pierre Maillard, *De Gaulle et l'Allemagne* (Paris: Plon, 1990), 85–86; De Gaulle, *Mémoires*, 1037–1039.

5. John F. Kennedy Library, National Security Files, Box 79, Germany (hereinafter cited as JFKL, NSF).

6. These comments on Adenauer's relations with Macmillan and de Gaulle are based on the author's conversations with Hans-Peter Schwarz, Adenauer's biographer, during February 6 and 7, 2006.

7. Hans-Peter Schwarz, Adenauer: Der Staatsmann: 1952–1967 ((Stuttgart: Deutsche Verlags-Anstalt, 1991) 739–750.

8. Schwarz, Adenauer, 739–750.

9. Telegram from Paris to Department of State, January 16, 1963, JFKL, NSF, Box 73A, France.

10. Mayer, Adenauer, 87.

11. Schwarz, Adenauer, 770.

12. Schwarz, Adenauer, 113.

13. Morsey and Schwarz, eds., with Mensing, Briefe, 150–151.

14. John Gearson, Harold Macmillan and the Berlin Wall Crisis (London: Macmillan, 1998), 199–201.

15. For the sequence of events regarding the Franco-German link and Kennedy's growing concern, see Mayer, Adenauer, 80–87.

16. Author's conversation with Hans-Peter Schwarz, April 25, 2008.

17. Author's conversation with Hans-Peter Schwarz, April 25, 2008.

18. Mayer, "Adenauer and Kennedy," German Studies Review, XVII, 1, February 1994, 95.

19. Mayer, "Adenauer and Kennedy," 95.

20. Memorandum of conversation, March 21, 1963, JFKL, NSF, Box 82, Germany.

21. Morsey and Schwarz, eds., Briefe, 1961–1963, 227–228.

22. Erin Mahan, Kennedy, de Gaulle, and Western Europe (New York: Palgrave Macmillan, 2002), 58.

23. Rudolf Morsey and Hans-Peter Schwarz, eds., with Hans Peter Mensing, Adenauer: Teegespraeche, 1961–1963, 336–343.

24. Kurt Birrenbach, Meine Sondermissionen (Düsseldorf: Econ Verlag, 1984), 173–174.

25. Birrenbach, Meine Sondermissionen, 173–174.

26. W. W. Kulski, De Gaulle and the World (Syracuse, N.Y.: Syracuse University Press, 1996), 278.

27. On the entire controversy surrounding the Elysée Treaty, see Kulski, De Gaulle, 271–279.

28. Numerous messages from U.S. embassies and the U.S. Mission in Berlin about Kennedy's prospective visits to Germany and Berlin, as well as White House opinions and proposals for the president's activities in Germany, are in JFKL, NSF, Trips and Conferences (hereinafter cited as T&C), Box 241, Germany and Berlin.

29. "Reasons Why President Should Visit Berlin," undated, JFKL, NSF, T&C, Box 241.

30. Memorandum for McGeorge Bundy, March 14, 1963, JFKL, NSF, T&C, Box 241.

31. Memorandum for McGeorge Bundy, March 14, 1963, JFKL, NSF, T&C, Box 241.

32. Excerpts from the State Department's scope paper for Kennedy's visit are in *FRUS, 1961–1963*, XV, 525–526. Full text in JFKL, NSF, T&C, Box 241.

33. "Suggestions for President Kennedy's Public Statements in Germany," May 3, 1963, JFKL, NSF, T&C, Box 239, Germany and Berlin.

34. JFKL, NSF, T&C, Boxes 239 and 241, Germany and Berlin.

35. Mahan, *Kennedy*, 138.

Chapter 13

1. Author's conversation with Lochner, July 1963.

2. Marc Trachtenberg, *A Constructed Peace* (Princeton: Princeton University Press, 1999), 395. The document has no explanation for the grammatical mistake in the German text.

3. Richard Reeves, *President Kennedy* (New York: Simon & Schuster, 1993), 535; Andreas Daum, *Kennedy in Berlin* (Paderborn: Schöningh, 2003), 132–136.

4. John F. Kennedy Library, National Security Files, Trips and Conferences, Box 241, "President's Trip to Europe and Germany," contains numerous cables and memoranda about the threat from de Gaulle (hereinafter cited as JFKL, NSF, T&C).

5. JFKL, President's Office Files (hereinafter cited as POF), Box 45, "Speech Files, Germany," contains a number of drafts that emerged from Ted Sorensen. Further comments on the texts and on the changes that Kennedy later made are in Daum, *Kennedy*, 113–120. Sorensen himself made clear to the author in e-mail exchanges in June 2006 that Kennedy often changed texts just before or even as he gave them.

6. This description of Kennedy's tour of West Berlin is based on the author's recollections from being in the motorcade and also from Daum, *Kennedy*, 111–131.

7. Daum, *Kennedy*, 134–136, makes the Rome-Berlin connection. After extensive research, Daum concluded that *"Ich bin ein Berliner"* had been Kennedy's own idea, although many persons claimed and still claim to have inspired the phrase. Daum also studied and wrote about Kennedy's thoughts and actions en route. So did Ted Sorensen in *Counselor* (New York: Harper, 2008), 323.

8. Daum, *Kennedy*, 133–135, reviews this part of Kennedy's preparation. I also discussed it with Kennedy's speech interpreter, Heinz Weber, on July 10, 2006.

9. The phrase "I am a jelly doughnut" has become a common canard in any discussion of Kennedy's Berlin speech, especially among Americans who want to show that they know something of colloquial German. One rarely hears it in Berlin. In his conversation with me, Weber denounced it categorically. He said that nobody who was in the crowd that day, and nobody whom he saw after the speech, ever understood Kennedy to have said anything different from what he had meant to say. The word *Berliner* as a slang term for a jelly doughnut is much less used in Berlin than in other parts of Germany. Moreover, I remember that during the days after Kennedy's speech I met with a number of Berlin friends who had been in the crowd and not a single one of them laughed at the phrase that Kennedy had used. Quite the contrary, they were exhilarated by it and by the recognition it implied of their unique role in the world.

10. Robert H. Lochner, *Ein Berliner unter dem Sternenbanner* (Berlin: Edition Goldbeck-Löwe, 2002), 138–139. A copy of the document on which Kennedy wrote the phonetic version of the remarks he was to make in German is now in the Kennedy Library archives: JFKL, POF, Box 45, Germany. The original is kept among the special handwritten documents of the JFK Library and is not available to scholars, but the staff of the library assured the author that the words were written in Kennedy's own handwriting, which is what Weber also recalls because he saw Kennedy write the words.

11. Text, as Kennedy finally gave it, is in *Public Papers of the Presidents, John F. Kennedy, 1963*, 268–269. Also in JFKL, POF, Box 45, Germany.

12. JFKL, POF, Box 241, contains a number of draft texts as well as some recommendations for amendment of the speech that Kennedy was to give. None resemble what Kennedy finally said.

13. Author's conversation with Weber, July 10, 2006.

14. Daum, *Kennedy*, 124.

15. Author's conversation with Teltschik, February 20, 2006.

16. Author's conversation with Scharioth, September 25, 2007.

17. Author's conversations with Teltschik, Scharioth, Egon Bahr, and others between 2006 and 2008.

18. Report to the author from a former Central Intelligence Agency official who had been in Berlin at the time and who had seen a monitored report of the conversation.

19. Reeves, *Kennedy*, 536.

20. Reeves, *Kennedy*, 536; Daum, *Kennedy*, 138–143.

21. Text in *Public Papers of the Presidents, John F. Kennedy*, 270–272.

22. Author's talks with Berliners after Kennedy's visit.

23. Author's conversations with Brandt and Bahr from the 1960s and with Bahr through the 1990s.

24. Author's conversation with Bahr, June 27, 2006.

25. Reeves, *Kennedy*, 537.

Chapter 14

1. Bonn telegram 43 to Department of State, July 3, 1963, John F. Kennedy Library, National Security Files, Trips and Conferences, Box 241A, Germany (hereinafter cited as JFKL, NSF, T&C).

2. Text of speech in JFKL, NSF, T&C, Box 241A, Germany.

3. *Berliner Zeitung*, June 29, 1963, 1.

4. CIA Office of National Estimates, Staff Memorandum, "Khrushchev and Berlin," January 22, 1963, JFKL, NSF, Box 85A1, Berlin, throughout.

5. Telegram 71 from Bonn to Department of State, July 7, 1963, JFKL, NSF, Box 79, Germany.

6. Airgram 78 from Bonn to Department of State, July 10, 1963, JFKL, NSF, Box 79, Germany.

7. Telegram 148 from Paris to Department of State, July 9, 1963, JFKL, NSF, Box 79, Germany.

8. W. W. Kulski, *De Gaulle and the World* (Syracuse, N.Y.: Syracuse University Press, 1996), 278.

9. Rudolf Morsey and Hans-Peter Schwarz, eds., with Hans Peter Mensing, *Adenauer: Briefe, 1961–1963* (Paderborn, Schöningh, 2006), 318.

10. Willy Brandt, *People and Politics*, trans. J. Maxwell Brownjohn (Boston: Little, Brown, 1976), 91–92. Other views of Berlin and German officials about the Wall crisis and about later moves toward détente are covered in Egon Bahr, *Zu Meiner Zeit* (Munich: Blessing, 1996), Willy Brandt, *Erinnerungen* (Berlin: Ullstein, 1989), and later sections of Brandt's *People and Politics*.

11. Brandt, *People and Politics*, 41; Egon Bahr briefing at the Goethe Institute in Washington, D.C., May 8, 2002, and his conversation with author, June 27, 2006.

12. Brandt, *People and Politics*, 75–76.

13. Bahr, *Zu Meiner Zeit*, 152–161; text in Manfred Uschner, *Die Ostpolitik der SPD* (Berlin: Dietz, 1991), 182–202; 203–210.

14. Author's conversation with Karl Kaiser, former adviser to Brandt, October 14, 2008.

15. Bahr, *Zu Meiner Zeit*, 167–169.

16. Brandt, *My Life in Politics*, trans. Anthea Bell (New York: Viking, 1992), 55–70.

17. Text in U.S. State Department, *Documents on Germany, 1944–1985* (Washington, D.C.: U.S. Department of State, 1985), 860.

18. Jochen Staadt, *Die geheime Westpolitik der SED 1960–1970* (Berlin: Akademie Verlag, 1993), 82–87.

19. J. A. Kwizinskij, *Vor dem Sturm* (Cologne: Siedler Verlag, 1992), 221.

20. Staadt, *Geheime Westpolitik*, 274–276.

21. For excerpts, see *Deutsche Aussenpolitik* (Bonn: Bonn Aktuell, 1989), 217–221 (hereinafter cited as *Aussenpolitik*).

22. Wjetcheslaw Keworkow, *Der Geheime Kanal* (Berlin: Rowohlt, 1995), 29 and 47.

23. Arnulf Baring, *Machtwechsel* (Stuttgart: Deutsche Verlags-Anstalt, 1982), 82.

24. Henry A. Kissinger, *White House Years* (Boston: Little, Brown, 1979), 147–150.

25. Kissinger, *White House Years*, 147–150.

26. Kwizinskij, *Vor dem Sturm*, 218–225.

27. William E. Griffith, *The Ostpolitik of the Federal Republic of Germany* (Cambridge, Mass.: MIT Press, 1973), 206–209.

28. For the official German texts of these agreements, see *Verträge, Abkommen und Vereinbarungen zwischen der Bundesrepublik Deutschland und der Deutschen Demokratischen Republik* (Bonn: Presse und Informationsamt der Bundesregierung, 1973).

29. Jean Edward Smith, *Lucius D. Clay* (New York: Holt, 1990), 686.

Chapter 15

1. Elizabeth Pond, *Beyond the Wall* (Washington, D.C.: Brookings Institution Press, 1991), 88.

2. Material for this chapter, unless otherwise cited, comes from the author's travels to Berlin and East Germany during the fall of 1989 and from Hannes Bahrmann and Christoph Links, *Chronik der Wende* (Berlin: Links Verlag, 1994), throughout; Robert Darnton, *Berlin Journal* (New York: Norton, 1991), throughout; Volker Gransow and Konrad Jarausch, eds., *Die Deutsche Vereinigung: Dokumente* (Cologne: Verlag Wissenschaft und Politik, 1991), 52–110; Cornelia Heins, *The Wall Falls* (London: Grey Seal, 1994), 181–249; Links and Bahrmann, *Wir Sind das Volk* (Wuppertal: Peter Hammer Verlag, 1990), throughout; Elizabeth Pond, *After the Wall* (New York: Priority Press, 1990), 1–153; Ralf George Reuth and Andreas Bönte, *Das Komplott* (Munich: Piper, 1993), throughout. The wider views of German and U.S. officials about the breakdown of the Wall and German unification are covered in Egon Bahr, *Zu Meiner Zeit*

(Munich: Blessing, 1996); Willy Brandt, *Erinnerungen* (Berlin: Ullstein, 1989), *People and Politics*, trans. J. Maxwell Brownjohn (Boston: Little, Brown, 1976), and ". . . *was zusammengehört*" (Bonn: Dietz, 1993); Horst Teltschik, *329 Tage* (Berlin: Siedler, 1991); and Philip Zelikow and Condoleezza Rice, *Germany Unified and Europe Transformed* (Cambridge, Mass.: Harvard University Press, 1995).

3. Günter Schabowski, *Der Absturz* (Berlin: Rowohlt, 1992), 249–252.

4. The most detailed review of events in East Berlin and along the Wall on November 9, 1989, is in Hans-Hermann Hertle, *Chronik des Mauerfalls* (Berlin: Ch. Links, 1997), 118–212. For text of GDR travel regulations, see Gransow and Jarausch, eds., *Deutsche Vereinigung*, 93–94.

5. Author's conversation with J. D. Bindenagel, former minister at U.S. Embassy in East Berlin, August 20, 1998.

6. Günter Schabowski, "Wie ich die Mauer öffnete," (*Die Zeit*, March 18, 2009), 3

7. George Kennan, *The German Problem: A Personal View* (Washington, D.C.: American Institute for Contemporary German Studies, 1989), 6.

8. Schabowski, *Absturz*, 311.

Bibliographic Essay

To tell the story of President John F. Kennedy and the Berlin crisis that dominated his presidency, I wanted to combine recent and hitherto unexploited sources with standard Kennedy biographies in order to bring fresh insights into Kennedy's own development as well as to flesh out some hitherto unknown or ignored aspects of the crisis. For new materials, I drew heavily on freshly declassified documents in the John F. Kennedy Library in Boston, on recently available American, Soviet, West German, and East German documents, and on unpublished materials as well as on my own recollections from service in Berlin during the crisis. When I was not able to read recently published documents myself, I relied on others whom I know and whose research I respect. For background information, I used widely available books that recount what has generally become public knowledge. I have not cited those specifically except for quotes or other unique pieces of information because many facts about the crisis and about the Kennedy presidency are widely known and do not warrant specific citation.

Those readers who want further material on Kennedy can turn to the biographies produced by his assistants: Arthur Schlesinger, Jr., *A Thousand Days* (Boston: Houghton Mifflin, 1965); and Theodore C. Sorensen, *Kennedy* (New York: Harper, 1965). Another, more casual, is by Kenneth O'Donnell and David Powers with Joe McCarthy, *Johnny, We Hardly*

Knew Ye (Boston: Little, Brown, 1970). I used those as general sources but often went beyond their interpretations.

I also used more recent works, by Richard Reeves, *President Kennedy* (New York: Simon & Schuster, 1993) and Michael Beschloss, *The Crisis Years* (New York: HarperCollins, 1991).

Books that concentrate specifically on Kennedy and Berlin include: John C. Ausland, *Kennedy, Khrushchev, and the Berlin-Cuba Crisis* (Oslo: Scandinavian University Press, 1996); Honoré M. Catudal, *Kennedy and the Berlin Wall Crisis* (Berlin: Berlin Verlag, 1980); and Christof Munger, *Kennedy, die Berliner Mauer und die Kubakrise* (Paderborn: Schöningh, 2003).

Kennedy's differences with his allies regarding Berlin policy have not been widely cited in the general literature, but they remain important because they had more of an effect on his policy toward Berlin than is generally known. They are documented in the memoirs and biographies of his principal allies: Konrad Adenauer, *Errinerungen: 1958–1963* (Stuttgart: Deutsche Verlags-Anstalt, 1968); Charles de Gaulle, *Mémoires d'Espoir* (Paris: Gallimard, 2000); and Harold Macmillan, *Pointing the Way* and *At the End of the Day* (New York: Harper, 1972 and 1973). I have also used collections of Adenauer's letters and private conversations (often more revealing than other sources) as edited by Rudolf Morsey and Hans-Peter Schwarz with Hans Peter Mensing, *Adenauer: Briefe, 1961–1963* (Paderborn: Schöningh, 2006), and *Teegespräche, 1961–1963*, (Paderborn: Schöningh, 2007).

Scholarly assessments, authorized or otherwise, are, for Adenauer: Frank Mayer, *Adenauer and Kennedy* (New York: St. Martin's, 1996); Anneliese Poppinga, *Das Wichtigste ist der Mut* (Bergisch Gladbach: Gustav Lübbe, 1994); and Hans-Peter Schwarz, *Adenauer* (Stuttgart: Deutsche Verlags-Anstalt, 1991). For Macmillan: John Gearson, *Harold Macmillan and the Berlin Wall Crisis* (London: Macmillan, 1998); Henning Hoff, *Grossbritannien und die DDR, 1955–1973* (Munich: Oldenbourg, 2003); and Alistair Horne, *Macmillan* (London: Macmillan, 1989). For de Gaulle: Jean Lacouture, *De Gaulle: The Ruler*, translated by Alan Sheridan (New York: Norton, 1992); Eric Mahan, *Kennedy, de Gaulle, and Western Europe* (New York: Palgrave Macmillan, 1996); and Pierre Maillard, *De Gaulle et L'Allemagne* (Paris: Plon, 1990).

The recollections of Kennedy's secretary of state, Dean Rusk, are covered in his autobiography with Richard Rusk, *As I Saw It* (New York:

Norton, 1990), and in his authorized biography by Thomas J. Schoenbaum, *Waging Peace and War* (New York: Simon & Schuster, 1988). Both leave unanswered questions, like other materials about Rusk, but I have tried to answer at least some.

Soviet Premier Nikita Khrushchev's decision to build the Berlin Wall is documented in his memoirs. They have similar titles and overlapping editors and translators. In chronological sequence, they are: Strobe Talbott, editor and translator, *Khrushchev Remembers* (Boston: Little, Brown, 1970); Strobe Talbott, editor and translator, *Khrushchev Remembers: The Last Testament* (Boston: Little, Brown, 1974); and Jerrold J. Schecter and Vyacheslav V. Luchkov, editors and translators, *Khrushchev Remembers: The Glasnost Tapes* (Boston: Little, Brown, 1990). The biography written by his son Sergei Khrushchev, *Nikita Khrushchev and the Creation of a Superpower* (University Park: Pennsylvania State University Press, 2006), adds important new insights and comments by Khrushchev about Kennedy as well as about Berlin. Other biographies, useful for information and context, are Aleksandr Fursenko and Timothy Naftali, *Khrushchev's Cold War* (New York: Norton, 2006); and William Taubman, *Khrushchev* (New York: Norton, 2003).

Khrushchev's discussions and arguments about Berlin with East Germany's Walter Ulbricht get their most thorough survey in Hope M. Harrison, *Driving the Soviets up the Wall* (Princeton: Princeton University Press, 2003). Some basic documents can be found in Matthias Uhl and Armin Wagner, eds., *Ulbricht, Khruschtschow und die Mauer* (Munich: Oldenbourg, 2003).

Anatoly Dobrynin, *In Confidence* (New York: Times Books, 1995), covers the range of Soviet-American relations into which the Berlin crisis and the related Cuban crisis fitted. Julij A. Kwizinskij, *Vor dem Sturm* (Berlin: Siedler, 1993), offers revealing insights from the Soviet diplomatic service.

The Berlin Wall has produced countless books that report not only on the Wall itself but on its effects. The main works used for this book include Curtis Cate, *The Ides of August* (London: Weidenfeld & Nicolson, 1978); Norman Gelb, *The Berlin Wall* (London: Michael Joseph, 1986); Robert Slusser, *The Berlin Crisis of 1961* (Baltimore: Johns Hopkins University Press, 1973); Frederick Taylor, *The Berlin Wall* (New York: HarperCollins, 2006); Howard Trivers, *Three Crises in American Foreign Affairs and* a *Continuing Revolution* (Carbondale: Southern Illinois University Press, 1970); Anne Tusa, *The Last Division* (Reading, Mass.: Addison-Wesley, 1997); and Peter Wyden, *Wall* (New York: Simon & Schuster, 1989). Some German reports on the Wall, often covering similar events, are Daniel Küchenmeister, *Der Mauerbau* (Berlin: Bugrim, 2001); Michael Lemke, *Die Berlinkrise, 1958 bis 1963* (Berlin: Akademie Verlag, 1995); Hans-Peter Schwarz, ed., *Berlinkrise und Mauerbau* (Bonn: Bouvier, 1985); Rolf Steininger, *Der Mauerbau* (Munich: Olzog, 2001); Gerhard Wettig, *Chruschtschows Berlin-Krise 1958 bis 1963* (Munich: Oldenbourg, 2006); and *Der Bau der Mauer durch Berlin* (Bonn: Ministerium für Gesamtdeutsche Fragen, 1968).

The Berlin connection to the 1962 crisis over Soviet missiles in Cuba is reported in Graham T. Allison, *Essence of Decision* (Boston: Little, Brown, 1971); Aleksandr Fursenko and Timothy Naftali, *One Hell of a Gamble* (New York: Norton, 1997); and Ernest R. May and Philip D. Zelikow, *The Kennedy Tapes* (Cambridge, Mass.: Harvard University Press, 1997). Robert F. Kennedy, *Thirteen Days* (New York: Norton, 1971), also cites U.S. worries about risks to Berlin in the Cuban crisis. The Berlin connection to Cold War arms control efforts is covered in Marc Trachtenberg, *A Constructed Peace* (Princeton: Princeton University Press, 1999).

Kennedy's triumphal 1963 visit to Berlin is mentioned in every biography of Kennedy but has received its most detailed treatment in two German books: Andreas W. Daum, *Kennedy in Berlin* (Paderborn: Schöningh, 2003), translated by Dona Geyer as *Kennedy in Berlin* (Cambridge and New York: Cambridge University Press, 2008); and Andreas Etges, ed., *John F. Kennedy* (Wolfratshausen: Minerva, 2003). Kennedy's interpreter, Robert Lochner, also reported his thoughts on the president's Berlin visit in *Ein Berliner unter dem Sternenbanner* (Berlin: Goldbeck-Löwe, 2003).

The views of Berlin and German officials about the Wall crisis, later German moves toward détente and, finally, the breakdown of the Wall and German unification are covered in Egon Bahr, *Zu Meiner Zeit* (Munich: Blessing, 1996); Willy Brandt, *Erinnerungen* (Berlin: Ullstein, 1989), *People and Politics*, trans. J. Maxwell Brownjohn (Boston: Little, Brown, 1976), and *". . . was zusammengehört"* (Bonn: Dietz, 1993); Horst Teltschik, *329 Tage* (Berlin: Siedler, 1991); and Philip Zelikow and

Condoleezza Rice, *Germany Unified and Europe Transformed* (Cambridge, Mass.: Harvard University Press, 1995).

Material on the actual fall of the Wall in November 1989 comes from the author's own travels to Berlin and East Germany during the fall of 1989 and from Hannes Bahrmann and Christoph Links, *Chronik der Wende* (Berlin: Links Verlag, 1994); Robert Darnton, *Berlin Journal* (New York: Norton, 1991); Volker Gransow and Konrad Jarausch, eds., *Die Deutsche Vereinigung: Dokumente* (Cologne: Verlag Wissenschaft und Politik, 1991); Cornelia Heins, *The Wall Falls* (London: Grey Seal, 1994); Links and Bahrmann, *Wir Sind das Volk* (Wuppertal: Peter Hammer Verlag, 1990); Elizabeth Pond, *After the Wall* (New York: Priority Press, 1990); and Ralf George Reuth and Andreas Bönte, *Das Komplott* (Munich: Piper, 1993).

As indicated above, I supplemented these published sources with unpublished materials on the topics listed above from various libraries and document collections as noted. I also tried to combine them all with my own recollections to give the full picture of what happened during the Berlin Wall crisis during and after the Kennedy presidency.

Index

About the Author

W. R. Smyser served at the U. S. Mission in Berlin from 1960 to 1964 and was Special Assistant to General Lucius Clay during the Berlin Wall crisis. He later served in the White House at Henry Kissinger's request. He rose to the ranks of Assistant Secretary of State and Assistant Secretary-General of the U.N. He has written numerous books and articles on Germany, on U.S. foreign policy, and on diplomacy. He teaches at Georgetown University.